Eastern Orthodoxy
through Western Eyes

Eastern Orthodoxy through Western Eyes

Donald Fairbairn

Westminster John Knox Press
LOUISVILLE • LONDON

Scripture quotations from the New Revised Standard Version of the Bible are copyright © 1989 by the Division of Christian Education of the National Council of the Churches of Christ in the U.S.A. and are used by permission.

Excerpts from Ouspensky, Leonid, and Vladimir Lossky, *The Meaning of Icons,* rev. ed., trans. G. E. H. Palmer and E. Kadloubovsky (Crestwood, N.Y.: St. Vladimir's Seminary Press, 1982), 15, 26, 31–32, 34, 36, 43–44, 60, 67–68, 76, 213. Used by permission of St. Vladimir's Seminary Press, 575 Scarsdale Road, Crestwood, NY 10707.

Excerpts from Lossky, Vladimir, *The Mystical Theology of the Eastern Church* (Crestwood, N.Y.: St. Vladimir's Seminary Press, 1976), 28, 58, 80, 87, 97, 99, 126, 133, 135–36, 156–57, 162–63, 172, 180. Used by permission of St. Vladimir's Seminary Press, 575 Scarscale Road, Crestwood, NY 10707.

Book design by Sharon Adams
Cover design by Design Point, Inc.

First edition
Published by Westminster John Knox Press
Louisville, Kentucky

This book is printed on acid-free paper that meets the American National Standards Institute Z39.48 standard. ♾

PRINTED IN THE UNITED STATES OF AMERICA

02 03 04 05 06 07 08 09 10 11 — 10 9 8 7 6 5 4 3 2 1

Library of Congress Cataloging-in-Publication Data is on file at the Library of Congress, Washington, D.C.

ISBN 0-664-22497-0

In memory of Nelson C. ("Bud") Hinkson,
because of whose vision I first set foot
in what was then the Soviet Union
and came into contact with the world of
Eastern Christianity

Contents

Preface

*E*arly in 1991, I wrote the initial version of the essay that evolved into the present book, after a year of Christian ministry in Soviet Georgia had piqued my interest in Orthodoxy and had given me a desire to understand the phenomenon I had encountered. At that time, Eastern Orthodoxy was still relatively unknown to Western Christians. The monumental increase in contact between Eastern Europe and the West had only just begun. The Soviet Union was more or less intact, and the August 1991 coup attempt was still some months away. Orthodoxy in the West at that time was certainly not limited to Eastern European immigrants, but it had not yet protruded noticeably into the mainstream religious consciousness in Britain or North America. As a result, Eastern Orthodoxy Christianity was of interest primarily to the relatively small number of Western Christians working in Eastern Europe and the Soviet Union, a number that would multiply astonishingly over the next few years. Accordingly, I intended the first version of this essay (as well as the major revision that followed in 1995) for Western Christians working in predominantly Orthodox countries.

Now, eleven years later, the situation in both East and West is dramatically different. The Soviet Union is no more, and in the economic and political chaos of Russia and (perhaps to a lesser degree) other Eastern European states, the Orthodox Church stands virtually alone as an emblem of stability and trustworthiness, commanding more respect from the people than any other social entity. Because of this position, Orthodoxy frequently finds its way into the Western news, and Patriarch Alexis II is well known to many people. At the same time, in the West (especially in the English-speaking world), Orthodoxy has seen substantial growth and has become a major part of the religious landscape. Orthodoxy is now both in our news and on our doorstep. More and more Westerners are hearing of, learning about, and even experiencing the world of Eastern Christianity, and throughout the 1990s a steady stream of people left Protestant or Roman Catholic churches to join Eastern Orthodox communions.

In addition to these changes, my own understanding of and appreciation for Orthodoxy have grown considerably since 1991, as I have continued to live and work in the former Soviet Union and to study both the early Church and modern Eastern theology. Some of the things that I saw then as absolute differences between Eastern and Western Christianity I now recognize to be differences of emphasis, and I am well aware of how much Western Christians have to learn from the East. But on the other hand, even as I learn from Orthodoxy, I am continually reminded that its vision of Christian life differs significantly from Western Christianity's. To a great degree, Eastern and Western Christians see the faith through other eyes.

These changes—in the degree of contact that Westerners have with Orthodoxy and in my own grasp of Eastern Christianity—have prompted me to undertake another major revision to this introductory study of Orthodox theology and to offer it for the first time in published form. I am trying now to serve the interests of more general readers: Western Protestants and Roman Catholics who have come into contact with Eastern Orthodoxy and are curious about this unfamiliar and seemingly alien vision of Christianity. Of course, I believe that the work still holds value for Westerners doing Christian ministry in Eastern Europe or among ethnic Easterners in the West, and I call the attention of those readers to appendix B, in which I offer specific suggestions for ministry among Eastern Europeans.

I am a Reformed Protestant, and readers will see that the book as a whole reflects Protestant concerns. However, my hope is that this work will also help Roman Catholic and Eastern Orthodox readers. Accordingly, I would like to address a few words to readers from each of these three major Christian groups.

First, to Protestant readers: Perhaps you have become acquainted with Orthodox people and have found yourself puzzled by the strangeness of their faith and by your inability to connect with each other when you try to explain your respective ways of following Christ. Maybe you know people who have become Orthodox and who now speak of having returned to the one true Church. You might wonder whether Orthodoxy could be the answer to the problem of a fractured Protestantism. Whatever the source of your interest in Eastern Orthodoxy, I hope this book will help you establish a point of contact, begin to understand the mysterious vision of Eastern Orthodoxy, and see and evaluate the major differences between Orthodoxy and Western Christianity. Perhaps more important, I hope your reading of this book will enable you to see more clearly our own perspective on Scripture and Christian life.

As we look at the lenses through which Orthodoxy sees the Christian faith, we will perhaps become more aware of our own lenses, our own vision.

Second, to Roman Catholic readers: You may often find that you fall outside the bounds of my discussion, that you agree neither with my own Western Protestant perspective, nor with the Orthodox perspective I attempt to describe. However, as you read you may be surprised that your own view of the Christian faith is less different from the Protestant perspective than you might have thought. In spite of disagreements between Roman Catholics and Protestants on such issues as papal authority, the authority of Scripture alone, and justification by faith, a similarity of perspective unites both groups and distinguishes both of us from the Orthodox. To a certain degree, both Protestants and Roman Catholics look at the faith through the same lenses, the same Western perspective inherited from the ancient Roman world. Perhaps this book will help you understand better not only the perspective of Eastern Orthodoxy, but also the common perspective that (to some degree) unites all of Western Christendom.

Finally, a word to Orthodox readers: No doubt you will sometimes wince at the insufficiency of my understanding of Orthodoxy or at the lack of subtlety with which I explain it. You will be quick to correct me in some places—and I welcome such criticism—but these very places where I make you wince might be the most instructive, because they will show you, the Orthodox, something of the way we Westerners see you. Moreover, this book may give you a better sense of our Western concerns. While these concerns are not your own, they may still deserve your attention. As you read this book, you will see that I point out places where we need to pay attention to you, and my hope is that you will return the favor by listening carefully to us as well.

Donald Fairbairn
Erskine Theological Seminary
Due West, South Carolina
fairbairn@erskine.edu
April 2002

Acknowledgments

I would like to offer my thanks to some of the many people who offered encouragement as I began to study and write about the world of Eastern Orthodoxy.

First, the students and teachers of Tbilisi State University and Tbilisi Foreign Language Institute (Republic of Georgia) and of Donetsk Christian University (Ukraine), from whom in the early 1990s I received my first exposure to the world of Eastern Christendom. In particular, I would like to thank Malkhaz Songulashvili for his wisdom, friendship, and patience.

Second, Dr. Mark Elliott of the Institute for East-West Christian Studies (Samford University, Birmingham, Alabama), who for a decade has tirelessly encouraged my study of Orthodoxy and helped place my writing on the subject into the hands of people who might find it useful.

Third, Father John Jillions of the Institute for Orthodox Christian Studies (Cambridge, England), whose suggestions in the mid-1990s helped me to begin filling in the many gaps in my understanding of Orthodoxy.

Fourth, Father Alexander Golitzin of Marquette University (Milwaukee, Wisconsin) and Dr. Bradley Nassif of the Antiochian House of Studies (a U.S. extension of Balamand University, Lebanon), who reviewed the manuscript of this book and offered helpful criticisms prior to its final approval for publication. Perhaps they will excuse me for failing to follow their suggestions in the final version as closely as they would have liked.

Finally, Dr. Donald McKim and the staff at Westminster John Knox Press, for being willing to move into waters that are (for a Reformed publisher) very uncharted, by agreeing to publish a book on Eastern Orthodoxy.

Introduction

Double Vision

Western Christians who walk into an Eastern Orthodox church building for the first time recognize the dramatic difference between the visible forms by which Eastern and Western Christianity express themselves. Protestants are immediately struck by the dark sanctuary filled with icons, candles, and mosaics, which contrast with the well-lighted, sometimes undecorated auditoriums Protestants are accustomed to call churches. Roman Catholics, much more used to visual symbolism, nevertheless find the style of the icons unfamiliar and perhaps incomprehensible. In fact, even the shape of the building might baffle people who are used to the cross-shaped design of most Roman Catholic cathedrals and even of many Protestant church buildings.

If Western Christians attend the celebration of the liturgy, their confusion is likely to increase further. Unaccompanied choir music takes the place of congregational singing with musical accompaniment. The prominence of preaching in Western worship (both Roman Catholic and Protestant) is seemingly absent, even though the liturgy consists substantially of reading and chanting passages from Scripture. Much of the worship service takes place behind a partition (called the iconostasis), somewhat out of the worshipers' sight. Perhaps most stunning is the splendor of the worship, from the elaborate rituals to the finery of the clerical dress to the liberal display of gold throughout the service. The mood is grandiose, extravagant, and quite alien even to Roman Catholics and high-church Protestants such as some Episcopals and Anglicans. Protestants from low-church traditions may think they have entered another world altogether.

Confusion and Questions

In the midst of this bewilderment, Western Christians may find themselves asking, What is Eastern Orthodoxy? How can worship that proclaims itself to be

1

Christian differ so drastically from anything we have experienced? Of course, the short answer is that Eastern Orthodoxy looks and feels so different because of its different history. In the process of fighting different historical battles, Orthodoxy has developed a different vision of Christian life. To try to summarize the history of Eastern Christianity would be beyond the scope of this book, but from time to time I will refer to specific historical events that have been instrumental in shaping the Eastern vision of Christian life.[1]

Even if one understands that different histories produce different visions and forms of worship, more fundamental questions may also come to mind. Many Protestants might wonder, Does the attention the Orthodox give to saints and icons amount to idolatry? Why does teaching the Bible receive so little apparent attention in Orthodox worship and life? How is the message of salvation proclaimed, or is it proclaimed at all? At the same time, Roman Catholics might wonder whether some of the recognizable similarities between the Orthodox and themselves are real or simply apparent. What, they might also ask, is Orthodoxy's attitude toward authority, toward Rome?

As quickly as such questions may spring into the minds of Western Christians, these questions cannot be an appropriate starting point from which to explore the world of Eastern Christianity. Nor may one simply look at Orthodoxy in light of questions that have dominated Protestant/Roman Catholic debates since the Reformation.[2] While Orthodoxy has some parallels with Roman Catholicism, the categories in which ideas are expressed and many of the theological distinctives are quite different. In fact, the deepest division within Christendom is between East and West, not between Protestants and non-Protestants or Roman Catholics and non-Catholics. In terms of dominant theological emphases, Protestantism and Roman Catholicism are much closer to each other than either Western group is to Eastern Orthodoxy. As a result, an attempt to understand Orthodoxy in terms of issues borrowed from Protestant/Roman Catholic debates would constitute a failure to recognize the true distinctiveness of the Orthodox way of viewing the faith, as well as a failure to engage Eastern Christianity on its own terms.

Accordingly, simply identifying aspects of Orthodox thought and practice that seem foreign to Westerners and comparing these to our own practices is not sufficient. We must first understand before we can evaluate, and in order to understand Orthodoxy, we must look past its most obvious elements (darkened sanctuaries, icons and candles, chanting, and so on) to the underlying vision of the world, of life, and of Christianity that produces those elements. Only then can we see how the mysterious and foreign atmosphere of Orthodox worship functions within Eastern Christianity as a whole, and only then can we even begin to ask whether such a vision is appropriate.

From Questions toward Understanding

In order to help us gain a glimpse of the Orthodox vision, I would like this book to accomplish three major tasks. First, I attempt to acquaint Western readers with the milieu that provides the source for the Orthodox vision, a milieu that is subsumed under the broad term "tradition." In contrast to the Western insistence that truth rests with a particular source of authority (either the Bible alone or the Bible as interpreted by the Church hierarchy), Eastern Christianity sees truth as a possession of the Church in its entirety, as the expression of the life that the Church has through the Holy Spirit. This truth manifests itself in various ways, such as the writings of the Bible, the works of the church fathers, the decrees of the ecumenical councils, the liturgy, and even the architecture and arrangement of icons within church buildings. All of these manifestations constitute the means by which the Church preserves and communicates the truth that the Holy Spirit has entrusted to it, and all grow out of the tradition that is the basis for Orthodox theology. As foreign, and even suspicious, as this idea sounds to Westerners (especially to Protestants), we must grasp it if we are to begin understanding Orthodoxy as a whole. Thus, in part 1 of this book I attempt to explain the Orthodox idea of tradition as the source for the Eastern Christian vision.

My second task is to explain what could be called the renaissance strand of Eastern Orthodox theology.[3] The term "renaissance" refers to a rebirth, or more particularly, to a return of a culture or religion to the vibrancy of its historical roots. Of course, the fifteenth-century Renaissance in Western Europe brought about (among other things) a desire to return to the world of early Christianity, and this Renaissance helped to make possible sweeping changes in the Western Church in the sixteenth century, through both the Protestant and the Roman Catholic Reformations. While the Eastern Christian world did not take part in the fifteenth-century Renaissance, it underwent a renaissance of its own in the nineteenth and twentieth centuries. This Eastern renaissance rejected Western patterns for doing theology (which had been adopted in the East during the previous centuries) and strove to return to Eastern patristic sources.[4] In the early twentieth century, the Bolshevik Revolution in Russia forced many members of the Russian intelligentsia into exile in the West and effectively shifted the locus of the Eastern renaissance. While the process of reexamining the sources of Orthodox thought was somewhat stifled in Russia and the East, this process flourished among expatriate Russian Orthodox thinkers living in Western Europe (and later, North America). This renaissance has given contemporary Orthodoxy a vitality and vibrancy seldom before experienced, but as a result the most vital thinking in the Eastern

Orthodox world has taken place in the West, rather than in the East itself. This so-called renaissance strand of Eastern Orthodox theology constitutes the main focus of my work, partly because this approach represents Orthodoxy at its best, and partly because this form of Orthodoxy is the one that Western Christians are most likely to encounter.

Some of the key figures in this renaissance movement have been expatriate Russians, such as Vladimir Lossky, Georges Florovsky, Alexander Schmemann, and John Meyendorff, as well as Greeks such as John Zizioulas and ethnic Westerners such as Englishman Kallistos Ware. I rely most heavily on these writers. As a result, readers who are already familiar with Orthodoxy should notice three striking omissions in this book. First, I generally omit direct quotations of Eastern patristic writings because the book would become too cumbersome for a general readership if I included a great deal of patristic literature. In a number of places I briefly discuss patristic debates, and in these cases I indicate in notes where interested readers may turn to examine the sources themselves. However, the bulk of my exposition focuses on modern Orthodox writers. Second, I omit many Western Orthodox theologians. Third, I avoid secondary literature almost completely. The reason for these last two omissions is certainly not that such sources would be irrelevant, but again, the primary considerations are the purposes and intended audience of this work. I have not sought to be comprehensive in my use of sources, but rather I have tried to be representative, to listen to a number of Orthodox voices that truly illustrate Eastern Orthodoxy at its best.

As I examine Orthodox thought in part 2 of this work, I organize my presentation around what I believe to be the heart of Eastern Christianity's vision: the vocation of humanity to acquire the divine likeness, to become united to God.[5] Orthodox teaching asserts that humanity's major purpose is to become divine, in the sense of being transformed so as to see God, partaking of God's immortality and incorruption, sharing in communion with him, and acquiring qualities (such as love, justice, and mercy) that characterize him. This concept, which I explain in some detail in chapter 5, is perhaps the major unifying idea around which Orthodox theologians organize various other aspects of theology and practice. By discussing Eastern theology in this fashion, I hope to enable Westerners to understand, to some degree, how Orthodoxy fits together as a whole, how various aspects of Orthodox practice relate to each other and to the overall vision of Christian life from which they spring.

The third task of this book is to discuss some of the problems within Orthodoxy. In spite of the comprehensiveness of the Orthodox renaissance in the last two centuries, popular piety and practice still deviate substantially from the official vision of Christian life in a number of ways. These popular practices often lead Westerners to charge that the Orthodox are idolaters or even pagans. Any honest treatment of Orthodoxy must deal with such distortions, but we need to remember that popular Western Christianity (Protestant and Catholic) often deviates significantly from the best expression of our own theology as well. To compare Orthodoxy at its worst with Western Christianity at its best is simply not fair. We must first hear the best expression of Orthodox theology, and only then may we consider the dangers inherent in some of its more popular expressions. In addition, a significant strand of Orthodox thought is very closely tied to nationalism, which argues that to be Greek (or Russian, or Romanian, and so on) is necessarily to be Orthodox. This strand is becoming increasingly apparent in Russia today, as some Orthodox leaders work with the political apparatus to grant an almost exclusive status to the Russian Orthodox Church and to curtail the activities of other Christian groups. In part 3 of this work, I discuss these popular and nationalistic elements within Orthodoxy.

In keeping with my assertion that we must first seek to understand as thoroughly as we can before we evaluate, I offer my own thoughts about Orthodoxy only toward the end of this work, at the end of part 2 and during part 3. During the bulk of the book, I seek to point out differences of perspective between Eastern and Western Christianity without unduly judging between the competing views. The reader should find that I do not assume the Orthodox are wrong simply because they disagree with Western Christians. Instead, I suggest that in several important ways we would do well to learn from them, just as they need to learn from us in certain ways as well. I believe that both Eastern and Western Christians need to learn to see our faith through the other's eyes.

Two Ways of Viewing the World

Throughout this book, I return to several fundamental ways in which Eastern and Western Christianity view reality differently, in order to show how these differences lead Orthodoxy and Western theology to different visions of Christian life. Obviously, all of Christian theology seeks to be faithful to the scriptural teaching about God, humanity, and salvation, but no one's mind is a blank slate when reading the Bible. Everyone brings certain assumptions to Scripture, and these assumptions influence (without necessarily determining) the way that person reads the Bible. Many of these assumptions are shaped by a person's culture, which is in turn influenced by the history of thought (especially religious thought) in one's home region. The Latin mind and Roman culture have profoundly shaped all of Western Christianity, whether Roman Catholic or Protestant. Similarly, Eastern Orthodoxy reflects the influence of the Greek mind and culture. The differences between these mindsets show up in three ways that are significant for the study at hand, and I would now like to mention these three ways briefly.

First, Western Christianity (especially Protestantism) tends to emphasize the individual, whereas Eastern Orthodoxy focuses on the whole, the group. In the West the notion of individual rights holds highest priority; the East is more concerned with corporate responsibility. The West tends to make distinctions between individual people and ideas and feels a need to evaluate these, to set one over another. Western Christians are thus suspicious of anything that might seem to detract from, for example, the uniqueness of the Bible as God's revelation or Christ as the one mediator between God and human beings. In contrast, the Christian East is able to see an individual person or doctrine only in connection with the whole. The East is thus able to honor other sources of truth along with Scripture and other saints along with Christ, without thereby detracting from the worship of Christ. The contrast between an individual outlook and a strong corporate consciousness emerges repeatedly throughout this study.

Second, Western Christianity tends to view Scripture through a legal lens, whereas Eastern Christendom's orientation is more personal and mystical, more concerned with participation in divine life. The ancient Romans were among history's greatest lawyers, and the Latin legal expertise bequeathed to the Western Church a mindset that understands biblical words such as "justification" in terms of legal status, guilt and innocence, punishment and mercy. In contrast, the Greek mind has long been fascinated with the quest of the soul to gain union with God, and this mystical bent has helped to shape Orthodoxy's view of Christian life as a pilgrimage leading from death to life, from alienation to reconciliation, from this world to the eternal sphere of divine life. In both East and West, the mindsets that Christians have inherited from their Greek or Latin heritages have influenced those aspects of the biblical picture of salvation they emphasize most strongly, and these mindsets have also colored the way Christians interpret key biblical concepts. Westerners and Eastern Orthodox are heirs of two substantially different heritages, and as I hope to show, we look at Scripture through different lenses.

Third, in the West the approach to meaning is oriented (or at least, until the latter part of the twentieth century, has been oriented) around a text, whereas the East is more pictorial and image-oriented in its approach to reality. Western Europeans and North Americans are (or at least have been) people of a book, people who have wrestled meaning for their lives out of documents and texts. In contrast, the East has long found meaning in pictures, in the relation between images and in the glimpses those images give us into the character of God and the nature of eternity. If one asks a typical Western Christian what the expression "Word of God" refers to, that person will probably answer, "Scripture." When asked the same question, an Orthodox person is much more likely to answer, "Christ." The incarnate Christ, the visible representation of God, the image of the invisible Father, is the one whom the Orthodox celebrate in their churches full of icons and other visual images. On the other hand, in most of Western Protestantism (and to a lesser degree, in Roman Catholicism), the preaching of the Word, the exposition of a biblical text, holds a central place in worship.

I should stress here that these three divergences are differences in emphasis, not absolute differences. Neither Eastern nor Western Christendom is at all monolithic, and Protestantism in particular shows great variety. The differences in emphasis between the Orthodox and those Protestants who are the heirs of the moderate or radical branches of the Reformation (that is, Presbyterians/ Reformed, Baptists, Mennonites, and so on) are especially pronounced. Roman Catholics and Protestants from the more conservative branches of the Reformation (that is, Anglicans/Episcopals, Lutherans, and Wesleyans/ Methodists) will find that the lines between the Orthodox and themselves on the issues I have just discussed are less sharply drawn.[6] To some degree, the distinctions I mention are oversimplifications. Nevertheless, I believe they can be helpful in enabling us to understand more fully how and where Orthodoxy diverges most sharply from Western Christianity.

Two Visions of Christian Life

From these divergent ways of looking at reality come two significantly different visions of salvation. (Again, I should emphasize that the differences are of emphasis and are not absolute contradictions.) One may say in general that in Western Christianity, especially in Protestantism, salvation is understood as a condition in which God places a person. God takes people who are sinners (and thus guilty before him and separated from him), and he places them in a condition of forgiveness and fellowship with him. Western Christians disagree on how God's action and human action interact in the process of moving from one state to another and on how great a role the Church plays in that process. We also disagree on how secure the saved condition is, whether or not a true Christian can depart from that state. In spite of these differences, we tend to emphasize that salvation is something God does for and to us, and Christian life flows from the new condition that God has already given the believer.

In contrast, Eastern Orthodoxy is prone to view salvation not as a condition, but as a journey. Perhaps the most widely read book on Orthodoxy in the Western world is entitled simply *The Orthodox Way*. Christian life is not primarily a state, but a way, a journey, a path leading to perfect union and perfect fellowship with God. Orthodoxy places more emphasis than the West does on the human task of walking this pathway with God's help, and in fact many Orthodox writers are uncomfortable with the word "salvation" itself. They see it as being too negative and therefore too incomplete, and their preferred term is "vocation." Human beings are called to begin, to continue in, and to complete a journey leading to God. We do not walk this journey alone; countless people have followed it. Our calling is not to blaze a trail, for Christ has done that for us. Rather, our task is to join the many who have walked and are walking the path, to follow the footprints leading to eternity and to God.

The spirituality of the West is largely (although not exclusively) a backward-looking spirituality: we motivate ourselves for Christian life by remembering what God has already done in saving us. In contrast, the Orthodox see the journey not so much as stemming *from* something that has already happened, but as moving *toward* God, toward perfect union with him. Orthodox spirituality is largely forward-looking: *anticipation* more than *memory* provides the motivation. Thus, Westerners (especially Western Protestants) are more likely to say that they are already saved, whereas the Orthodox emphasize that they are on the pathway to salvation.

Some of my readers have likely already become uncomfortable with the way I describe these different visions of the world and Christian life. Perhaps yellow flags are already emerging in your minds. On the other hand, some readers may already sense that Orthodoxy is speaking of concepts that we Westerners have forgotten, approaches that are important to Christian life and which we would do well to emulate. Whether I have piqued your interest, aroused your suspicions, or perhaps simply bewildered you, I ask you to suspend judgment for now. We need first to understand, then to evaluate. If we are to understand, we need for a moment to step away from a Western way of looking at reality and attempt to see the world, the Scriptures, and Christian life through other eyes. Only with such double vision can we be in a position to begin evaluating Eastern Orthodoxy. This task of understanding is the one to which I now turn in parts 1 and 2 of this book.

PART I   The Source of the
Orthodox Vision: Tradition

Chapter 1

Authority versus Life

*F*rom a Western point of view, the first issue which one must consider in formulating theology is that of authority. To us, the question of who or what has the right to determine truth logically precedes the question of what actually is true. To phrase the question a different way, Who speaks for God? Are the ancient prophets and apostles (the biblical writers) the only ones who speak for God? If so, which writings are genuinely prophetic or apostolic? How do we know which of the many ancient writings carry divine authority? Does the Church speak for God? If so, which of the Church's many voices is the authoritative one? For that matter, which (if any) of the many churches has divine authority? While Western Christians may not agree on the answers to these questions, virtually all of us concur that the questions themselves are of first importance. If we want to discover what is true, we must first ask where the authority to determine truth lies.

As soon as we ask about authority, however, we discover that this question is inappropriate (and perhaps even incomprehensible) in an Eastern Orthodox context. Because of the differences in its view of reality (which I discussed in the introduction to this book), Eastern Christianity generally does not raise the issue of authority, at least not in the same way that Western theology does.[1] Instead, Orthodoxy understands Scripture and other aspects of the Church's life as expressions of one whole, the tradition of the Church. In this chapter, I attempt to examine the reasons for this lack of emphasis on authority and to explain what the Orthodox mean by the word "tradition."

The Deemphasis of Authority in Eastern Thought

A Westerner who has some familiarity with Orthodoxy may have heard it described as the "Church of the Seven Councils." One might be prone to think

11

that whereas Protestantism locates authority with the Bible alone and Roman Catholicism with the Church hierarchy (principally the pope himself), Orthodoxy locates the authority for determining doctrine with the ecumenical councils.[2] However, contrary to this perception, the Orthodox do not ascribe to any council an inherent authority to determine truth. Greek theologian John Zizioulas points out that no conciliar decision carries binding force until the communities of faith which have sent their bishops as delegates to the council receive that decision. He concludes, "It is for this reason that a true council becomes such only *a posteriori*; it is not an institution but an *event* in which the entire community participates and which shows whether or not its bishop has acted according to his *charisma veritatis* [his gift of truth]."[3] Similarly, English Orthodox writer Kallistos Ware states, "At a true Ecumenical Council the bishops recognize what the truth is and proclaim it; this proclamation is then verified by the assent of the whole Christian people, an assent which is not, as a rule, expressed formally and explicitly, but *lived*."[4] Russian scholar and theologian Georges Florovsky is even more direct when he states that no council was accepted as valid in advance, and those councils which were accepted were recognized "because of their *charismatic* character: under the guidance of the Holy Spirit they have witnessed to the Truth, in conformity with the Scripture as handed down in the Apostolic Tradition."[5]

These citations clearly demonstrate that in the Orthodox understanding, groups of bishops do not gather in a council in order to determine what is true; they gather to listen to the truth and to proclaim it. No council's decision is valid simply because a gathered group of bishops made that decision. Rather, the community of faith, the Church as a whole, accepts or rejects a decision of its bishops. As a result, Orthodoxy's view of the Church hierarchy and the councils is quite different from that of Roman Catholicism: Orthodox bishops and councils do not possess any inherent authority in themselves. They are not raised up above the rest of the Church as sources of authoritative teaching. Rather, their function is to recognize the truth within the Church, within the community.

Such a concept of the relation between the Church leaders and the communities is immediately puzzling to Westerners. We might want to ask: Where does authority lie, if the emphasis falls on bishops and councils, and yet the communities have the right to reject the decisions of the bishops and councils? Here we encounter two of the three major differences in the ways Eastern and Western Christians tend to view reality. Recognizing these differences can help us to understand the apparent lack of emphasis on authority in Orthodoxy.

The first of the differences is that Western Christianity (especially Protestantism) emphasizes the individual to a substantial degree, whereas the Eastern Orthodox are more corporate in their outlook. As one Orthodox theological student commented in a conversation with me, "The difference between your faith and ours is that yours is a personal faith, but ours is an idea of the Church." With an emphasis on the individual comes a recognition of distinctions between different ideas, people, and so on, and a corresponding sense of the need to define which of these ideas, people, and so on, is most in possession of the truth. Western Christianity is thus led to set an individual person, organization, or book over others, resulting in a strong idea of authority. Because Protestants distinguish between the Bible and its various interpretations, we say the Bible alone is authoritative. Because Roman Catholicism sees a difference between various groups and people within the Church, it insists that the pope has authority over the rest of the Church. In both cases, our well-defined ideas of authority relate to our emphasis on the individual.

In contrast, Eastern Orthodoxy's "idea of the Church," its emphasis on the Church as a whole, results in a much less defined understanding of authority. The prophets and apostles, the early church fathers, the bishops, and the laypeople are all understood as being intimately connected with each other. Placing one of these groups over the others as the locus of authority is not necessary. All of them are witnesses to the truth that the entire Church possesses, and Eastern Christianity generally does not attempt to distinguish between them. In fact, many Orthodox regard Protestantism's fracturing into thousands of different denominations and theological perspectives as being a result of the individualistic mindset of the West.[6] They argue that once a group loses its sense of connection with the whole Church and the entire body of truth that the Church possesses, nothing can prevent competing ideas from multiplying until one group becomes many different groups. According to many Orthodox, the question of authority becomes important only when such fracturing has already taken place and different groups claim allegiance to different sources of authority.

The second major difference is between the juridical or legal perspective in the West and the personal and mystical orientation in the East. The question of authority is much more prominent within a legal framework than in a relational framework. An approach to Christian life that emphasizes the legal status of the Christian before God also tends to be concerned with the status of various people and writings with respect to each other. In contrast, when the concern is to bear witness to the common life of the Church and to aid people in the quest for union with God, there is much less need to consider the position of various "authorities" relative to one another.

Eastern Orthodoxy's corporate understanding of reality and its comprehension of Christianity in terms of participation in divine life (rather than in juridical categories) have helped to create a climate in which there is very little developed understanding of theological authority at all. Early nineteenth-century Russian statesman Alexey Khomiakov charges both Protestantism and Roman Catholicism with an excessively individualistic approach to Christianity and contends that only the Orthodox Church has preserved the original corporate understanding of the faith. He concludes, "Infallibility resides solely in the ecumenical fellowship of the Church united by mutual love; the guardianship of dogmas and the purity of rites is entrusted, not to the hierarchy alone but to all members of the Church who are the body of Christ."[7] Similarly, Russian historian Nicolas Zernov writes, "The East has never fully grasped the implications of this essentially Western dispute [over the authority of the Bible versus that of the pope], for it has adhered to a conception of authority in which there is no place for special sources of infallibility."[8] Russian theologian Nicolas Arseniev asserts,

> The Eastern Church recognises no formal, juridical authority. For her, Christ, the apostles, the Church councils are not "authority." There is no question here of authority, but of an infinite stream of the life of grace, which has its source in Christ and with which each individual is borne along as a drop or as a ripple.[9]

These three statements clearly illustrate not only that the question of authority holds less prominence in Orthodoxy than in the West, but also that this fact is tied to the differences in Eastern and Western mindsets. Khomiakov directly asserts that the issue is one of Western individualism versus Eastern corporate understanding. Zernov refers to "special sources of infallibility," while Arseniev cites a "juridical authority." These writers have in mind the Western idea that one source of knowledge is set above others, given a higher legal position so that in a juridical sense, that source has authority over the rest. Orthodoxy, Arseniev insists, has no such juridical authority because it thinks in terms of "the life of grace" rather than in terms of position or legal status. Furthermore, Arseniev's assertion that each individual is "borne along" in this "stream of the life of grace" indicates that the entire stream receives the emphasis, not individuals.

In short, then, the Orthodox response to a typical Western question about the locus of authority is that the question is misstated. What should be emphasized, according to Eastern Christianity, is the entire life of the Church, the whole truth that Christ has entrusted to his body. Placing one aspect of that life above others as a special source of authority is not necessary, because the life of grace in its entirety is more important. One should not conclude that there is no concept of authority in Orthodox thought; in fact, we shall see that Orthodox writers do discuss authority to some degree. Their emphasis lies not on authority, however, but on the truth that comes through the Church's life. Of course, this preliminary answer will hardly satisfy a typical Westerner. Let us look further at the Orthodox understanding of the relation between various aspects of the life of grace God has given the Church.

The Relation between Scripture and Other Aspects of Church Life

Orthodox theologians have two basic approaches to the issue of relating Scripture and church life. The majority of writers believe that no qualitative distinction exists between the books of the Bible and other facets of Orthodox tradition. However, a few theologians argue for the supremacy of Scripture but point out that only the Church can interpret Scripture properly.

In an introduction to traditional Orthodox thought, Greek theologian Archimandrite Chrysostomos writes,

> Scripture is a body of knowledge passed down in the Church in many forms. The holy ecumenical synods, the Fathers of the Church, their inspired writings, and the corpus of tradition that constitutes Orthodoxy are, in many ways, Scripture itself, completing and witnessing, yet never supplanting or contradicting, the written biblical canon.[10]

Chrysostomos makes clear that these pronouncements of the Church do not replace the Bible, but his reference to them as "Scripture" and his mention of the fathers' writings as "inspired" indicate that he sees these declarations along with Scripture as valid expressions of divine truth. Similarly, Maximos Aghiorgoussis (a Greek-American Orthodox bishop) declares,

> The Holy Bible, and more specifically the New Testament, does not contain all the doctrine and teachings of Christ. The Church, which has produced the Bible, does not completely submit itself to only one of the *epiphenomena* of its life, even if it is the most authoritative one, the Holy Scriptures. An important part of the teachings and doctrine of Christ continues to be present and handed down to the generation of Saints through other means and ways that are also part of the life of the Church, a life in the Holy Spirit.[11]

Russian Orthodox theologian Vladimir Lossky makes an even stronger statement by asserting that Scripture and the Church's tradition are not separate but are "one and the same fulness of Revelation communicated to the Church." He continues by writing that the Church possesses the truth as passed down from the apostles' preaching, and the Church could just as well have communicated this truth orally without ever fixing it in writing as Scripture.[12] Thus, the Church's ability to proclaim truth is not limited to statements taken from the Bible, nor would this truth be absent if there were no Bible at all.

To justify this belief that the Church's repository of truth is not limited to Scripture, Orthodox theologians point to the fact that the Church existed and flourished before the New Testament books were written. Early twentieth-century Russian priest Sergei Bulgakov comments that modern study of the New Testament has revealed the sources behind the books. He concludes, "Holy Scripture thus becomes a sort of written tradition, and the place for those individual writers who were once thought to have written, so to say, under the dictation of the Holy Spirit becomes less and less."[13] Lest it appear that Bulgakov's statement relegates the Bible to an insignificant position, one should note that he gives Scripture greater priority than other aspects of Church life: "Tradition is recognized," he writes, "when founded on Scrip-ture."[14] Nevertheless, Bulgakov clearly indicates that the Church as a whole has priority over Scripture. The fact that the Church has not always had the Bible "shows that it is the Holy Spirit, living in the Church, which is essen-tial, and not one or another of its manifestations."[15] These arguments demon-strate that for Bulgakov, as for other Orthodox writers, the books of the Bible are one portion of the Church's life, one of the ways in which the Holy Spirit is manifested in the Church. Although Scripture is held in special esteem, the Bible does not constitute a separate authority over the Church. Rather, to the Orthodox, the Bible is one of the products (indeed, the major product) of the Church's life. Ware aptly summarizes this concept by declaring,

> It [the Bible] must not be regarded as something set up *over* the Church, but as something that lives and is understood *within* the Church (that is why one should not separate Scripture and Tradition). It is from the Church that the Bible ultimately derives its authority, for it was the Church which originally decided which books form a part of Holy Scripture; and it is the Church alone which can interpret Holy Scripture with authority.[16]

This conception of the relation between the Church and Scripture appears to be dominant among Orthodox writers, but it is not the only understanding. In his study of the Bible, the Church, and tradition, Florovsky asserts that the reason for the Orthodox insistence on other sources of truth besides the Bible is that different people interpret Scripture differently. Thus, Church tradition is true precisely because it is the authentic interpretation of the Bible.[17] Unlike the other writers I cited above, Florovsky sees Scripture as prior to Church tradition. John Meyendorff also envisions a distinction between Scripture and tradition when he affirms, "The writings [of the New Testament] owed their authority to the fact that they had been composed by the eye witnesses of Christ. The Church could only confirm this authenticity through the guidance of the Holy Spirit promised by Jesus Himself, not create it."[18] This statement seems to reflect a concept of the New Testament's authority similar to that which Protestants espouse: the authority of the Bible is not conferred on it by the Church, but lies in the writings themselves. The Church has simply recognized which writings bear this divine authority and thus which writings belong in the Old and New Testaments. In fact, Russian theologian Alexander Schmemann makes precisely this assertion when he writes that the New Testament writings "were received by the Church—that is, were recognized—because their content coincided with the image of Christ and the content of His teachings that the Church already knew. The Church did not 'sanction' the New Testament writings; it recognized them as the Word of God, the source of its existence from the start."[19]

Despite the apparent similarities between Florovsky's, Meyendorff's, and Schmemann's views and those of Protestants, none of these scholars proceeds to locate authority in Scripture alone. Meyendorff writes, "Scripture, while complete in itself, presupposes Tradition, not as an addition, but as a *milieu* in which it becomes understandable and meaningful."[20] Tradition, as he understands it, is the Church's interpretation and use of the Bible, and therefore, to assert that only in the midst of tradition can Scripture become meaningful is virtually the same as asserting that the Church's interpretation of Scripture is true. One could argue, as many Westerners do, that the proper milieu for understanding the Bible is not the Church's interpretation of Scripture, but the historical context in which the books were originally written. Accordingly, focusing on the recovery of this context enables one to interpret Scripture correctly. Florovsky responds to this challenge as follows:

> Western thought always dwells in the past, with such intensity of historical recollection that it seems to be compensating for unhealthy defects in its mystical memory. The Orthodox theologian must also offer his own testimony to this world—a testimony arising from the inner memory of the Church—and resolve the question with his historical findings. Only the inner memory of the Church fully brings to life the silent testimony of the texts.[21]

Here Florovsky indicates that only in conjunction with tradition, with "the inner memory of the Church," can one truly grasp the meaning inherent in the Scriptures. Historical study of the Bible alone cannot compensate for the failure to follow the Church's use of Scripture in its teaching and worship.

Near the conclusion of his study on Scripture and the Church, Florovsky writes, "The ultimate 'authority' is vested in the Church which is for ever the Pillar and Foundation of Truth."[22] The fact that he places the word "authority" in quotation marks may indicate that Florovsky (like other Orthodox writers) has qualms about using this word, since the main issue is not one of authority as Westerners understand it, but of truth and life. Nevertheless, if one does insist on speaking in terms of authority, Florovsky locates this authority in the Church itself, not in Scripture alone. As a result, Florovsky's conception of the relationship between Scripture and Church does not lead to a different idea of authority from that of other Orthodox writers. Whether one views Scripture as one manifestation of the Church's life or believes that the Bible possesses authority of its own (but only if interpreted and used according to Church tradition), the end result is the same. In either case, the mystical memory of the Church, embodied in Church tradition, stands alongside Scripture as the proclaimer of truth and life.

The Orthodox Idea of Tradition

Thus far, we have seen that Eastern Orthodoxy holds neither a strong notion of authority nor a sharp distinction between Scripture and other forms of Church life. The emphasis lies on the stream of grace, the truth and life embodied in the Church as a whole. In the process, we have seen that Orthodox writers frequently refer to "tradition" in their discussions of the Church's life and truth. We need to understand as well as possible what Eastern Christianity means by "tradition."

From Meyendorff's discussion of the relation between Scripture and tradition cited above, one might think that Orthodox tradition is simply a group of writings (works by the church fathers, decrees of the ecumenical councils, and so forth) that comprise the true interpretation of Scripture. In actuality, tradition is much more, and not primarily a matter of writings at all. Schmemann asserts that Orthodox theology rests largely on patristic tradition and reflects on the danger that theology will succumb to the temptation of historical reduction of that tradition. He explains,

> By "historical" reduction I mean here the limitation of theology—or rather of its sources—to *texts,* to "conceptual" evidence to the exclusion of the living *experience* of the Church, from which the theology of the Fathers stems, to which it refers and bears testimony, without which it cannot be understood in its total and precisely "existential" meaning and significance.[23]

Later, Schmemann elaborates on this idea,

> It is not enough simply to quote the Fathers, to make them into "authorities" certifying our every theological proposition, for it is not quotations, be they scriptural or patristic, that constitute the ground of theology, but the

experience of the Church. And since, in the ultimate analysis, she has no other experience but that of the Kingdom, since her whole life is rooted in that unique experience, there can be no other source, no other ground and no other criterion for theology, if it is truly to be the expression of the Church's faith and the reflection on that faith.[24]

In these quotations, we again see the distinction between authority and life. Orthodox theology does not simply rely on additional texts, additional authorities, besides the Bible. Instead of being concerned with interpreting authoritative texts, Orthodoxy sees its task as testifying to the life (the experience) of the Church. (In fact, Schmemann calls the restriction of theology to explaining the meaning of texts a danger, something to be avoided, whereas many Western Christians would say that interpretation is the major part of theology's task.) This life or experience of the Church, to which Orthodox theology testifies, is tradition.

In his introduction to a work on the meaning of icons, Lossky offers an excellent explanation of tradition:

If the Scriptures and all that the Church can produce in words written or pronounced, in images or in symbols liturgical or otherwise, represent the different modes of expression of the Truth, Tradition is the unique mode of receiving it. We say specifically *unique mode,* and not *uniform mode,* for to Tradition in its pure notion there belongs nothing formal. It does not impose on human consciousness by formal guarantees of the truths of faith, but gives access to the discovery of their inner evidence. It is not the word, but the living breath which makes the word heard at the same time as the silence from which it came; it is not the Truth, but a communication of the Spirit of Truth, outside which the Truth cannot be received.[25]

For Lossky, tradition is not so much an actual entity as a milieu, a context. Tradition is the life (what Schmemann calls the "experience") that the Church has by virtue of possessing the Holy Spirit. This life enables the Church to recognize the truth as God reveals it and to express that truth through the various forms (scriptural and otherwise) that Lossky mentions.

John Zizioulas brings together various strands of thought about tradition and authority when he explains the divergent views of apostolic succession in East and West. He argues that the New Testament presents two pictures of this succession: historical and eschatological.[26] In the historical picture, God the Father sends Christ, Christ sends the apostles, and the apostles transmit the message of Christ by establishing churches and ministers. In the eschatological picture, the apostles surround Christ and form an invisible college representing the entire Church, the gathering of the dispersed people of God to Christ in one place.[27] Zizioulas concludes,

In this historical approach the apostles are the *creators* of history whereas in the eschatological approach they are the *judges* of history. Correspondingly, in the first case the Church is apostolic when she faithfully *transmits* the apostolic kerygma; in the second case she is apostolic when she *applies* it to a particular historical context and then *judges* this context in a prophetic way through the vision of the eschata which she is supposed to maintain.[28]

Here one should remember that (as I mentioned in the introduction and as we shall see more clearly later) Orthodoxy views Christian life primarily as a journey to communion with God and with one another. The spirituality is forward looking. In light of this approach, one should see the life that the Church possesses and expresses as the life of the future age, what Zizioulas calls "the vision of the eschata" and Schmemann calls "the experience of the Kingdom." The eschatological understanding of apostolic succession does not simply look back to an authoritative deposit of truth that the Church has received and must preserve; this understanding looks ahead to the life of the divine kingdom, a life to which the Church bears witness in this age.

The first of these models is the picture that dominates in the Western Church. While Western Christians disagree about whether the authoritative transmission of the message ceased with the apostles themselves (the New Testament writers) or continued with their successors, we all see apostolic succession in connection with the transmission of previously given truth. The second picture is the one that dominates in Orthodoxy. The Church's life is a communal one, in which believers gather to celebrate the life of the coming age and to progress toward the fullness of that life, that union with God. For this reason, the community is the ultimate judge of the decisions of the councils and the ultimate interpreter of the Scriptures. In Orthodoxy, tradition is not primarily a deposit of writings given in the past that must be faithfully preserved and proclaimed. Tradition is rather a future life, a future union and fellowship with God, on the basis of which the Church judges present teaching and experience now. When we understand tradition in this way, we are better able to fathom Orthodoxy's vision, in which the source of theology is neither Scripture *per se,* nor any other writing, person, or council. Rather, the source of theology is the entire community's experience of the life of the future kingdom, an experience that goes by the name of tradition.

From this chapter, it should be apparent that the perspectives from which Orthodoxy and Western Christianity view the starting point for theology are strikingly different. In the West, theology generally begins with the question of authority. Having established where the authority for determining truth lies, the task for Westerners is to understand and systematize the truth contained in that authoritative source, and to apply that truth to Christian life. In contrast, the East sees the source of theology as the life or experience of the Church, a life that is called tradition. The task of theology is to give expression to that life in its unity and beauty. As a result, the Bible becomes one of several forms by which tradition is expressed, rather than the source of theology and Christian life itself. This does not mean that the Bible is unimportant. It is clearly the major form for expressing tradition, and Eastern writers sometimes use the word "authoritative" to refer to Scripture. The dominant emphasis, though, falls not on the authority of the Bible, the writings of the fathers, or any other sources, but on the Church's inner life in the Holy Spirit, a life that will be realized fully in the age to come.

To a Western Christian, this idea of tradition might seem to be an unmanageably ambiguous starting point for understanding Christian faith and practice. In order to understand more concretely that life on which the Orthodox base their faith, we need to examine the Eastern understanding of the Church in relation to tradition and to look at the various forms by which tradition expresses itself. These issues are the subjects of chapters 2 and 3.

Chapter 2

Tradition and the Church

Some Protestants view the Church as a community of people who have responded through faith in Christ to what God has revealed in his Word, while others prefer a concept of the Church as the place where the Word is truly preached and the sacraments are correctly administered. On the other hand, the traditional Roman Catholic understanding of the Church focuses on the hierarchy, the visible structure of bishops (the successors of the apostles), under the headship of the pope (the successor to Peter).

In contrast to these views, Eastern Orthodoxy sees the Church as a mystical entity that comprises God's direct activity. At the beginning of a book on the Orthodox Church, Bulgakov writes, "We ought to understand the Church as a sort of divine fixed quantity living in itself and comparable only with itself, as the will of God manifesting itself in the world."[1] Meyendorff begins his study of the Church with a similar assertion: "She [the Church] is what Christ and the Spirit make her to be. In her being she is not man-made. Human beings and human communities can rebel against her, but they cannot change her being."[2] One should not take these statements to mean that the Orthodox exclude all human elements from their definition of the Church. Eastern theologians insist that just as Christ, the head of the Church, was a union of divine and human, so also the Church, his body, includes a human element.[3] But in spite of this insistence, the Orthodox place more emphasis on the divine character of the Church than Western Christians do.

Vladimir Lossky explains the nature of the Church in Orthodox thought by noting that in Ephesians 1:23 Paul refers to the Church as both the body of Christ (cf. Rom. 12:5, 1 Cor. 12:12–13) and the fullness of the one who fills all things, the Holy Spirit (cf. Col. 2:10). Lossky concludes,

> Thus, the two definitions of the Church which St. Paul gives show two different poles within her which correspond to the two divine persons [that is, the two who were sent into the world, the Son and the Holy Spirit]. The

Church is *body* in so far as Christ is her head; she is *fullness* in so far as the Holy Spirit quickens her and fills her with divinity, for the Godhead dwells within her bodily as it dwelt in the deified humanity of Christ.[4]

In this chapter, I examine first the idea of the Church as fullness or wholeness of life in the Holy Spirit, and then the concept of the church as the body of Christ. In this way, I hope to clarify the relation between the Church and tradition in Orthodox thought.

The Church as *Sobornost*

Intimately linked with the idea of the Church as God's direct action in the world is the Orthodox concept that the Church consists of the unity, fullness, and wholeness of God made manifest. Orthodox writers argue that the Church is the answer to Jesus' prayer in John 17:20–22, "I ask not only on behalf of these [the apostles], but also on behalf of those who will believe in me through their word, that they may all be one. . . . The glory that you have given me I have given them, so that they may be one, as we are one." Aghiorgoussis explains this relation between the unity within the Trinity and the Church's unity:

> Called by God the Father as his holy people, being in Christ and the body of Christ justified by him, sanctified by God's Holy Spirit whose temple it is, the church of Christ is founded on the life of the three divine hypostases, the life of the all blessed and Holy Trinity. As a sacred society of members, constituted as such by this communion with the three divine persons, the church is a reflection of the life of the Holy Trinity.[5]

Just as God's own life is one of completeness and unity, his Church also possesses a life that reflects perfect wholeness. Eastern theologians express this unity by using the Greek adjective *katholikos* (from which we derive our English words "catholic" and "catholicity"), and by the Russian noun *sobornost* (derived from the verb root *sobirat,* meaning "to collect"). The Church's catholicity or *sobornost* consists of its reuniting people (who had been separated by the fall) to one another and its manifesting the fullness or wholeness of life in Christ.

Florovsky offers the most succinct explanation of this concept. He writes that the Church "is a unity, first of all, because its very being consists in reuniting separated and divided mankind. *It is this unity which is the 'sobornost' or catholicity of the Church.*"[6] Florovsky writes that catholicity refers not to the extent of the Church (which obviously does not include all people), but to the fullness and wholeness of life that comes from oneness, unity in Christ. He continues, "The growth of the Church is in the perfecting of its inner wholeness, its inner catholicity, in the 'perfection of wholeness'; 'that they may be made perfect in one.'"[7] As a result, catholicity is primarily an eschatologically oriented concept: the Church exhibits the fullness of divine life and the unity and fellowship that the persons of the Trinity share now and in which people will fully participate in the kingdom of God, in the age to come.

Schmemann explains this eschatological aspect of *sobornost* (without using the word itself) by describing the Church as both preparation and fulfillment. He writes, "The liturgy of the Church is always and primarily a preparation: it always points and tends beyond itself, beyond the present, and its function is to make us enter into that preparation and thus to transform our life by referring it to its fulfillment in the Kingdom of God." On the Church as fulfillment, he asserts, "The Holy Spirit has come and His coming has inaugurated the Kingdom of God. Grace has been given and the Church truly is 'heaven on earth,' for in her we have access to Christ's table in His Kingdom. We have received the Holy Spirit and can partake, here and now, of the new life and be in communion with God."[8]

The idea that the Church reflects the wholeness of life in the future kingdom of God and prepares people to enter that life through the Holy Spirit figures prominently in the examination of Orthodox theology in part 2 of this book. For now, I simply note that this concept of catholicity is closely related to the Eastern understanding of tradition discussed in the previous chapter. Since the Church is the wholeness or fullness of life in Christ, and since tradition is the experience or life of the Church, one could say that the Church *is* tradition. In fact, some writers (such as John Meyendorff) use the expression "living tradition" to designate the Church. This fact helps to explain why the Orthodox see no need to define a specific source of authority within the Church. Since it is a divine entity that is fully unified as a reflection of the unity within the Trinity, the Church cannot fail to possess truth in all its fullness. One may thus find truth in its fullness in any expression of the Church's life, not merely in one or another authoritative source.

Fullness or *sobornost* is one of the two concepts that Lossky uses to describe the Church in the passage near the beginning of this chapter. Let us now address the other (closely related) idea, the concept of the Church as the body of Christ.

The Church as a Sacramental Community

Eastern Christianity sees the expression of Church unity not in the fellowship of local churches (as in much of Protestantism), nor in the presence of a single Church structure (as in Roman Catholicism and some branches of Protestantism), but primarily in the liturgy and the sacraments. Virtually all authors considered here emphasize the priority of worship and the sacraments in Orthodoxy. Nicolas Zernov states that the Orthodox see the Church primarily as a worshiping community.[9] Anthony Ugolnik (a Russian-American Orthodox lay theologian) writes that to the Orthodox, right worship, rather than right doctrine, is the central standard.[10] Meyendorff asserts that the East sees the Church as "a communion in which God is present *sacramentally*,"[11] and Bulgakov claims that the sign of the true Church is possession of true, active sacraments.[12]

In Eastern Orthodoxy, the sacraments are not defined and categorized the way they are in Western theology. They are not called "means of grace" or "outward signs of an inward grace," nor do the Orthodox limit their number to only two (as in most of Protestantism) or seven (as in Roman Catholicism),[13] since Orthodoxy sees all of Christian life as bearing a sacramental character. For the most part, Orthodox theologians have not taken part in classic Protestant/Roman Catholic debates over issues such as the exact way the elements of bread and wine become the body and blood of Christ. Instead, Orthodoxy sees the sacraments as mysteries (the Greek and Russian words for a sacrament both mean "mystery"), whose purpose is to bear witness to the life of the Church and the reality of the coming age. Schmemann encapsulates the Orthodox view when he writes that every sacrament is by its very nature a real passage into the kingdom. A sacrament bestows on the worshiper the power both to participate in and to progress toward the kingdom of God. He concludes that "the sacrament is a passage, a journey."[14]

Of the sacraments, easily the most prominent is the Eucharist (what Roman Catholics normally call "the Mass" and most Protestants call "communion" or "the Lord's Supper"). Zizioulas asserts that the Eucharist is the primary means by which the local church expresses the whole Church's *sobornost*. He writes, "Catholicity, therefore, in this context [the context of the local church], does not mean anything else but the *wholeness* and *fulness* and *totality* of the body of Christ, 'exactly as' (*hosper*) it is portrayed in the eucharistic assembly."[15] Similarly, in an introduction to liturgical theology, Schmemann asserts,

> The Eucharist is *the* Sacrament of the Church, i.e. her eternal actualization as the Body of Christ, united in Christ by the Holy Spirit. Therefore, the Eucharist is not only the "most important" of all the offices, it is also source and goal of the entire liturgical life of the Church. Any liturgical theology not having the Eucharist as the foundation of its whole structure is basically defective.[16]

Later in the same work, Schmemann elaborates further on the Eucharist's centrality,

The Eucharist is the Sacrament of the Church. It is the *parousia,* the presence of the Risen and Glorified Lord in the midst of "His own," those who in Him constitute the Church and are already "not of this world" but partakers of the new life of the New Aeon. The day of the Eucharist is the day of the "actualization" or manifestation in time of the day of the Lord as the Kingdom of Christ.[17]

Through these statements, we see that in Orthodoxy, the life (or tradition) that is the heart of Christianity expresses itself primarily through the Eucharist. According to Schmemann, Christ's presence, the new age to come, and the kingdom of God are all represented and actualized through the Eucharist.

Russian theologian Nicolas Afanasiev explains the basis for this link between the Eucharist and the Church's life and unity by pointing out that at the Last Supper, Christ calls the bread his body (e.g. Matt. 26:26), and that Paul later refers to the Church as the body of Christ (Rom. 12:5, 1 Cor. 12:12–13). Just as the bread becomes Christ's body during the Eucharist, so also the people who partake of it are transformed into Christ's body, the Church.[18] Zizioulas concurs by writing, "A careful study of 1 Cor. 11 reveals that the term *ekklesia* [Church] is used in a dynamic sense: 'when you come together into, i.e. when *you become, ekklesia.*'"[19] As a result, the Eucharist is the means by which the Church expresses its catholicity precisely because Christians become the Church through the Eucharist. When Christians gather in one place to celebrate the Eucharist, they *become* the fullness of the Holy Spirit; they *become* the body of Christ.The two poles of Lossky's description of the Church come together here, and for this reason the Eucharist is called the central aspect of the Church's life.

Because of this idea, Eastern Orthodoxy asserts that whenever the Eucharist is celebrated, the Church's wholeness is made manifest. Each local church is thus not simply a part of the Church, but is the Church's very catholicity itself. Afanasiev concludes his discussion of the Eucharist by writing, "Every local church manifests all the fullness of the Church of God, because it *is* the Church of God and not just one part of it."[20] Meyendorff concurs: "Wherever there is the fullness of this sacramental organism, there is Christ, there is the Church of God, established on Peter."[21] This Eastern emphasis on the mystery of the Eucharist rather than on individual people, combined with the idea of catholicity or *sobornost,* enables the Orthodox to assert that the whole Church is present in each local eucharistic assembly.

In addition to the Eucharist, the other sacraments that Orthodoxy emphasizes strongly are baptism and penance. The Orthodox understand baptism as the beginning of Christian life, the entrance into the wholeness of the Church, and they perform this sacrament in infancy on the children of Orthodox parents and later in life on converts to Christianity.[22] (Baptism is accompanied by chrismation or anointing with oil, a rite that signifies the reception of the Holy Spirit. This act corresponds roughly to confirmation in Roman Catholicism and in pedo-baptistic Protestant churches, although Orthodox chrismation immediately follows baptism even in the case of infants.) Like the Eucharist, baptism is understood in terms of life. In an essay on the Orthodox understanding of humanity, Meyendorff explains that baptism is not so much a remission of sins as the gift of new life. Through baptism, people are freed from determinism and the bondage to sin in which they were held as a result of the fall.[23] In a work on the sacraments, Schmemann explains this idea more completely by writing that baptism is the sacrament of forgiveness, "not because it operates a juridical removal of guilt, but because it is *baptism into Jesus Christ,* who is the Forgiveness."[24] Meyendorff's and Schmemann's statements show clearly the difference between the Eastern stress on life and the Western juridical emphasis. The life of the Church mirrors the Trinity's life, and baptism brings one into Christ and therefore into the life of the Church, which reflects him. This life is characterized by unity and wholeness, which includes forgiveness (understood not so much as the removal of guilt but as freedom from slavery to sin) because the life places one in communion with Christ, the source of that freedom.

Just as the Orthodox understand baptism as the entrance into life, so also they view penance as the continual return to that life. Orthodox faithful are encouraged to confess their sins to priests regularly, but in contrast to Roman Catholic priests, Orthodox priests are not entitled to grant absolution (forgiveness) of sins.[25] Schmemann explains,

> It [penance] is the power of baptism as it lives in the Church. From baptism it receives its sacramental character. In Christ all sins are forgiven once and for all, for He is Himself the forgiveness of sins, and there is no need for any "new" absolution. But there is indeed the need for us who constantly *leave* Christ and *excommunicate* ourselves from His life, to return to Him, to receive again and again the gift which in Him has been given once and for all.[26]

Here again, the emphasis falls not on guilt and absolution (as in Western theology), but on the life that the Church possesses in Christ. By our sinful actions, we continually separate ourselves from the wholeness of that life, and by penance, we return to the life of the Church, the life that Christ has given us.

It should be clear at this point that the sacraments constitute the primary means by which the Church expresses the life (the tradition) that is the source of Christian faith. Through baptism and penance, people enter and reenter that life. Through the Eucharist, individual Christians are made into the body of Christ through the presence of Christ in the sacrament. In fact, the sacramental life of the Church is so important to Orthodoxy that the role of apostolic succession is not so much to preserve true teaching or a duly ordained Church hierarchy as to preserve the genuine celebration of the sacraments.[27] Closely tied to this sacramental understanding of Church life is the Orthodox concept of the role the bishops play in the Church.

The Church as a Community Headed by a Bishop

The Orthodox Church preserves its unity of worship and sacraments through the headship of its bishops over the worshiping communities.[28] According to Eastern theology, the fact that Christ alone presided over the celebration of the Last Supper implies that each eucharistic assembly should have a single person as its head. After Christ's ascension, this person was Peter, and subsequently bishops, the successors of Peter, have led the eucharistic celebrations. Accordingly, only one bishop presides in any given city, and this bishop represents Christ at the Eucharist.[29] Florovsky argues that the local church is included in the *sobornost* of the Church through the bishop, and he emphasizes how crucial the bishops are to the Church by quoting from a letter written in 1723 from the Eastern patriarchs to the bishops of Great Britain: "We affirm that the order of bishops is so necessary for the Church that without it the Church is not a Church and a Christian is not a Christian, and that they cannot even be so called."[30]

This emphasis on the bishops may be surprising to some Western Protestants, but the Orthodox insist that from the beginning of the Church, bishops have played a prominent role. In a historical overview of Eastern Christianity, Schmemann describes the role that the bishop played in the early Church,

> He was the head and source of the Church's life. His special gift consisted in transforming the gathering of Christians through the Sacrament into the Body of Christ and in uniting them in an indivisible union of new life. The power to dispense the sacraments was indissolubly linked with the power to teach; he taught at the meeting, not by his own initiative but according to the Spirit; he was the guardian of the apostolic tradition, the witness of the universal unity of the Church. "One must look on the bishop as on the Lord himself," writes St. Ignatius of Antioch in the beginning of the second century. Therefore "nobody must do anything that has to do with the Church without the bishop's approval. . . . Where the bishop is present, there let the congregation gather, just as where Jesus Christ is, there is the Catholic Church."[31]

From this passage, one can see that the nature of the Church as *sobornost* or fullness on one hand, and as a sacramental community, the body of Christ, on the other hand, come together in the person of the bishop. Christ gives the life of tradition to the Church, and the bishop (Christ's representative) maintains that life and gives it to the people through his celebration of the Eucharist and his teaching.

At this point, however, two items are important to note. First, one should not think that the bishop possesses power in himself. Rather, his priority is charismatic (a gift given to him by the Holy Spirit) and communal. In the quotation just above, Schmemann emphasizes that the bishop teaches "not by his own initiative but according to the Spirit." One cannot say that the bishop himself makes the people into the Church or gives life. Rather, the Holy Spirit does this through the bishop, whom God has gifted for this purpose. Moreover, the bishop is a bishop precisely because of his role as the head of a eucharistic assembly, and thus his priority in the Church is communal, not personal. Bulgakov writes, "The Episcopate neither legislates for, nor commands the Church independently of that organization, but is its specially endowed representative."[32] Zizioulas further asserts that just as one cannot conceive of Christ (the head of the Church) apart from his body, so also one should not consider the bishop in isolation from his flock, for without the flock the bishop can do nothing.[33] Later Zizioulas argues, "The bishop succeeds the apostles not in himself, i.e. as an individual, but as the head of his community."[34] No bishop, considered as an individual person, has power to speak for the Church. According to the Orthodox, such power would place the bishops above the Church and would give them authority over the Church. Instead, the bishop represents the Church, the community of which he is the head. Here again, we see the Eastern corporate outlook at work, and we should not assume from the prominence given to bishops that they have personal authority over their dioceses in a Western sense of the word "authority."[35]

The second important item is that the priority of the bishop is related not merely to the preservation of truth, but to the entire life of the Church as a eucharistic community. Zizioulas writes that the succession of catholic churches "should be viewed neither as a chain of individual acts of ordination nor as a transmission of truths, but as a sign and expression of the *continuity of the Church's historical life in its entirety,* as it was realized in each community."[36] The bishop is the head of his community not because he has the right to teach that community authoritatively (in Orthodoxy, teaching is primarily the role of the presbyters rather than the bishop), but because he embodies the fullness of the worshiping community at whose head he stands.

Of course, bishops play a major role in several branches of Western Christianity as well, but Orthodoxy views the succession of bishops from Peter to the present quite differently than the Roman Catholic Church. Western Catholicism, with its stress on individuals and thus on authority, insists that the Church was founded on the person of Peter and that a direct line of bishops of Rome (popes) extends from the time of Peter to the present. Each of these men has held a position of authority over the entire Church. In contrast, Eastern Christianity asserts that the Church was founded not on the person of Peter and his successors, but on the faith encompassed by Peter's confession in Matthew 16:16, "You are the Messiah [the Christ], the Son of the living God." Therefore, any bishop who adheres to Peter's faith is the successor to Peter for his diocese.[37]

The implication of this discussion for Orthodoxy is that no bishop (such as the pope) or group of bishops (such as a council) exercises authority over other bishops' spheres of influence.[38] Each bishop is the representative of Christ who manifests the catholicity of the Church within his own community, his own diocese. While the Orthodox do accord some bishops (such as the patriarch of Moscow and the ecumenical patriarch of Constantinople) primacy of honor, no power or authority over other bishops accompanies such positions. For this reason, the Orthodox insist (as discussed at the beginning of chapter 1) that when groups of bishops convene a council, their purpose is not to exert power over other bishops or their churches, nor to determine the truth that the Church must believe, but to bear witness to the Church's unity by recognizing and proclaiming what the whole Church does believe.

Florovsky summarizes this understanding of the succession of bishops: "The Apostolic Succession is a living and mysterious thread binding the whole historical fulness of Church life into one catholic whole." There are, he writes, two sides to this succession. The objective side is "the uninterrupted sacramental succession, the continuity of the hierarchy," and the subjective side is loyalty to the apostolic tradition, the fundamental dogmas of Orthodoxy.[39] As a result, wherever a duly ordained bishop stands at the head of his community in the succession of Peter, representing Christ at the Eucharist, and adhering to Orthodox belief (the faith of Peter), the fullness of the Church is present.

Because *sobornost* is realized through the bishops, these men stand in a unique position to give expression to the Church's life, its tradition. As a result, when groups of bishops meet at councils, they are able to bear witness to the living tradition of the Church. Nevertheless, the writings of bishops or councils are not accepted as truth simply because of the bishops' position. No bishop is entitled, purely by virtue of his office, to speak for the Church. Instead, if the bishops or councils are genuinely part of the Church's life, they will bear witness accurately to that life, and the rest of the Church will recognize their witness. If it is so recognized, then that witness becomes part of the expression of the Church's living tradition. If the Church recognizes that the witness is not accurate (which has sometimes happened in the case of would-be ecumenical councils,[40] as well as in the case of the writings of individuals), then the Church rejects the witness in order to safeguard the expression of tradition.[41]

If the Orthodox emphasis on life rather than authority (described in chapter 1) seems ambiguous to a Westerner, that ambiguity should be removed to some degree in the recognition that the Church expresses its life and unity through the bishops who stand in the place of Christ at the celebrations of the Eucharist. Through their sacramental leadership, these men bear concrete witness to the tradition that guides (and even constitutes) the Church. Admittedly, this situation still leaves many questions in the mind of a typical Westerner. How do we know whether the Church has approved a statement by the bishops, if not even the bishops necessarily speak for the Church? When disagreements occur, which bishops are accurately bearing witness to tradition? Is there no standard outside the life of the Church by which to judge the witness of the bishops?

While the Orthodox understanding of the relation between Church and tradition does not answer these questions to our satisfaction, we need again to remember that in the Eastern corporate mindset, such questions do not arise frequently. The Church is *sobornost*; it is united. The Orthodox believe that this unity or catholicity shines clearly in spite of any mistakes on the part of councils and disagreements among bishops, because the Church is ultimately a divine organism, not merely a human organization.

In addition to the sacraments and the bishops, Orthodoxy expresses its tradition in various other forms. The following chapter considers these forms briefly in an attempt to make this discussion of the source of Orthodox theology more complete.

Chapter 3

Tradition and Its Expressions

*I*n Orthodoxy, tradition is not a set of authoritative texts, but a life that sustains and guides the sacramental organism called the Church. Of course, this life expresses itself in concrete ways, primarily through the Eucharist, which is the supreme sacrament of the Church. In addition, tradition also expresses itself through the written and spoken Word and through images and symbols. Aghiorgoussis states that the dominant forms for bearing witness to tradition are Scripture, the doctrine of the fathers, the decrees of the ecumenical and local councils, the divine liturgy, and the architecture and iconography of the Church.[1] This chapter briefly considers each of these forms.

Scripture

From the emphasis that Orthodoxy places on tradition and its various forms, one could easily gain the impression that Scripture is minimized in Eastern Christianity, but such a conclusion would be wrong. Rather, the books of the Bible constitute the primary expression of Church tradition, and Orthodox public worship is filled with readings from Scripture. The liturgy contains more than two hundred biblical quotations and also includes daily readings from the Gospels and the New Testament letters. In addition, in the services for different parts of the Christian year, large portions of both the Old and New Testaments are read, including a number of books (Genesis, Exodus, Job, Psalms, Isaiah, the four Gospels, and Acts) in their entirety. In fact, Ware comments, "The Orthodox service books as a whole are in the last analysis little else than one vast and extended meditation upon Holy Scripture."[2]

In the case of the New Testament, the text that the Orthodox use is not greatly different from that which forms the basis for standard translations Western Christians use. The Orthodox Church does not use the critical text compiled from manuscripts discovered in the past 150 years (translations such as the NRSV, NEB, NASB, and NIV do follow this text for the most part), but instead uses a traditional Byzantine form of the text. In almost all cases, this text is the same as that which was used to translate the KJV. Of course, the number of passages that differ significantly between this text and the one standing behind most modern translations is small. A few of the more famous examples are Mark 16:9–20, John 7:53–8:11, Acts 8:37, and part of 1 John 5:8. All of these passages are present in the Bible of the Orthodox Church, as they are in the KJV. In most modern translations of the Bible, they are included with notations indicating that they are not present in the oldest manuscripts. Christians who are familiar with modern Western translations of the New Testament should not encounter any great surprises if they come into contact with Orthodox translations.

In the case of the Old Testament, the situation is more complicated. In addition to the Hebrew text, the Orthodox Church also considers the Septuagint (the translation of the Old Testament from Hebrew into Greek, begun about 250 B.C. and completed sometime before the birth of Christ), the Vulgate (the Latin translation completed about A.D. 400), and other early versions to be Scripture. Orthodox translations of the Old Testament have been made from the Hebrew text in the case of all books except Psalms, which was usually translated from the Septuagint. However, the Septuagint is the basis for the Old Testament readings in the Orthodox liturgical texts and thus plays an important role in Orthodox life and worship. Orthodox writers are quick to point out that the Septuagint was the version of the Old Testament most frequently quoted by the New Testament writers and most widely used by the early Church. Some Orthodox theologians argue that the Septuagint is the true text of the Old Testament and that the changes which took place from the older Hebrew text to the Septuagint were divinely inspired and constitute continued divine revelation.[3] On the other hand, most of the Orthodox are content to regard both the Hebrew Old Testament and the Septuagint as the true text and to live with greater ambiguity about the exact wording of Scripture than many Westerners would like. This attitude toward the text of Scripture derives from the lack of Orthodox emphasis on juridical authority. The Spirit dwelling in the community holds priority, not one or another variant of the written text of the Bible.

The Septuagint contains ten books not found in the Hebrew Old Testament (1 and 2 Esdras, Tobit, Judith, Wisdom of Solomon, Ecclesiasticus, Baruch, the Prayer of Manasseh, and 1 and 2 Maccabees), as well as four passages that were added to existing Hebrew books ("Song of the Three Hebrew Children," "Susanna," and "Bel and the Dragon," all added to Daniel, and additions to the book of Esther). Like Roman Catholics, the Orthodox consider these books and additions (which Protestants call the Apocrypha) to be inspired Scripture, although most people do not place them on the same level as the thirty-nine books that Protestants consider to constitute the Old Testament.[4]

Although the Greek Bible is the primary Scripture of the Orthodox Church, Eastern Christianity has never insisted on reading the Bible only in Greek. In contrast to the Western Church's use of the Latin Bible alone until the time of the Reformation, the East began very early to translate the Scriptures into local dialects. Versions in Georgian, Armenian, Syriac, and Coptic appeared as early as the third through fifth centuries, and translation of the Bible into Slavonic languages began in the ninth century. Orthodoxy has historically emphasized giving people the Bible (and also the liturgy, which was translated along with the Bible) in their own languages.

However, because of the antiquity of these translations, modern Orthodox regard them with a great deal of respect and are often reluctant to render Scripture into more contemporary language. In fact, even relatively recent translations such as the nineteenth-century Russian Synodical Version were deliberately written in archaic language in order to preserve the style of the older translations. Therefore, in many parts of the Orthodox world, Scripture is read and the liturgy conducted in archaic language (most notably the Old Slavonic of the Russian Church's liturgy) that few Orthodox laypeople can understand easily. This tendency, of course, runs counter to Orthodoxy's historical emphasis on giving people the Bible and the liturgy in a dialect they could understand, and it limits the influence of Scripture on the lives of the Orthodox faithful. One is more likely to find Scripture read and the liturgy conducted in comprehensible language in Orthodox churches in the West than in Eastern Europe or the Middle East, although even there, many groups (for example, in Romania and Serbia) are moving toward the use of contemporary language.

The Doctrine of the Fathers

We have already seen that Orthodoxy regards itself as the heir of the patristic tradition, the faith and life given to the early Church and expressed through the writings of the church fathers. The Orthodox generally see the patristic period as extending until about A.D. 800, although later figures are also considered fathers. Many of the church fathers were bishops in the early Church, although the writings of laymen and laywomen have also been treasured as expressions of tradition. In particular, the monastic movement that has had such a deep influence on Orthodoxy has recognized laypeople of both sexes among its "fathers." Among the many people whom the Eastern Church regards as fathers are the early theologians who laid the groundwork for the development of doctrine, the great patristic theologians who articulated the Church's faith concerning the Trinity and the person of Christ, and people who exemplified most fully the spiritual life that lies at the heart of Orthodoxy.

Perhaps the most revered of the earliest fathers is Irenaeus of Lyons (France) (ca. 130–ca. 200), who was the leader in the second-century Church's battle against gnosticism (a heresy that denigrated the physical world and saw salvation as the soul's escape from the prison of the body). In the process of combating this heresy, Irenaeus laid the foundation for an emphasis on human freedom that remains with Orthodoxy to this day, and he also began the long process of deliberation leading to the articulation of the trinitarian and christological dogmas. Also extremely influential was Origen of Alexandria (Egypt) (ca. 185–ca. 254). Origen was the first thinker to attempt a thoroughly systematic theology, and even though some elements of his thought were later condemned, his articulation of the eternality of the Son and his understanding of the soul's progress from its fallen state back to God would come to occupy major places in Orthodox thought.

The great heroes of the fourth-century trinitarian controversy were Athanasius of Alexandria (ca. 296–373) and the Cappadocians (Cappadocia is present-day central Turkey), Basil the Great (ca. 330–379), his brother Gregory of Nyssa (ca. 330–ca. 395), and their friend Gregory of Nazianzus (ca. 329–ca. 389). Athanasius was the most prominent defender of the truth that the Son is fully eternal and fully God and suffered five different exiles for insisting on this truth at a time when the emperors were hostile to it. The Cappadocians' major contribution was to distinguish clearly between the three divine persons while still maintaining their essential unity in the one godhead. Basil was also one of the influential figures in the development of early monasticism, and his monastic rule is still used in Orthodox monasteries. The two Gregories both played major roles in the Council of Constantinople, and Gregory of Nazianzus is dubbed "Gregory the Theologian" for his exposition of the doctrine of the Trinity. In addition to these fourth-century fathers, the Orthodox Church celebrates Photius of Constantinople (modern Istanbul, Turkey) (ca. 810–ca. 895) for his role in defending the Orthodox view that the Holy Spirit proceeds from the Father alone (not from the Father and the Son, as in Western theology).

The preeminent christological father of the Orthodox Church was Cyril of Alexandria (ca. 375–444), who followed in the footsteps of Athanasius and paved the way for the definition of the Council of Chalcedon. In opposition to Nestorius, Cyril insisted that God the Son took humanity into his own person at the incarnation in order to bring salvation to the human race. Later fathers who sharpened the Eastern understanding of Christ were Maximus the Confessor (who lived most of his life in North Africa) (ca. 580–662) and John of Damascus (Syria) (ca. 655–ca. 750). Maximus insisted that just as Christ had both divine and human natures, he also had both divine and human wills and energies. Christ's human will was not absorbed into his divine will, but in all cases submitted to that divine will. John provided the classic Orthodox defense of icons by insisting that images were emblems of the incarnation that proclaimed the fact that God the Son had assumed visible form. John also formulated the crucial distinction between worship (which is due to the Trinity alone) and veneration (which can be paid to saints and icons as well).

The Eastern Church reveres a great number of people for their contributions to the expression of Orthodox spirituality. Of these, perhaps the most celebrated is John Chrysostom (from Antioch in Syria and later bishop of Constantinople) (ca. 347–407), who was the most famous preacher of the early Church. (The name "Chrysostom" means "golden-mouthed.") The most frequently used form of the Orthodox liturgy bears the name of John Chrysostom, although there is little evidence for associating it with him directly. Also extremely influential were the Egyptian monks of the third through fifth centuries, whose reflections on the spiritual life were collected in a fifth-century work called *The Sayings of the Desert Fathers*. The foremost of the desert fathers was Antony (ca. 251–356), who for many years lived a solitary life but who later emerged from solitude to teach other monks and to organize them into a community, thus providing the pattern for both anchoritic (solitary) and cenobitic (communal) monasticism. Antony gave the Eastern Church one of its most famous ideals, that of the spiritual man who lives alone in pursuit of God, to whom pilgrims come for advice about their spiritual journeys.[5] Another extremely influential Eastern father was the anonymous writer known as Pseudo-Dionysius, whose writings appeared in Syria in the early sixth century. Pseudo-Dionysius played the major role in developing the Eastern concept of apophaticism (which is addressed in part 2). A much later monastic father who built on the work of Pseudo-Dionysius was Gregory Palamas (ca. 1296–1359), a monk of Mount Athos (the most celebrated monastery in Greece). Gregory helped to crystallize the concept of God as divine light and to formulate the distinction between the essence and energies of God, ideas that figure prominently in Orthodox salvation doctrine (also addressed later). Finally, another of the most significant sources of Orthodox spirituality is the *Philokalia* ("Love of the Beautiful"), an eighteenth-century collection of ascetic and mystical writings originally composed from the fourth through fifteenth centuries.

These fathers and others contributed greatly to the elucidation of the life and truth that lie at the heart of Orthodoxy. As a result, these ideas are explored further in part 2 of this book.[6] Because of this contribution, Eastern Christianity sees the writings of the fathers and the accounts of their holy lives as one of the dominant expressions of tradition—one of the primary sources of the Orthodox vision of Christian life.

The Ecumenical Councils

In addition to the witness of individuals to tradition, the united witness of bishops meeting at councils is also important. As we have seen, no council possessed the right, in advance, to determine truth, but rather councils were judged after their occurrence by the communities that the participating bishops represented. Of the councils held during the first eight hundred years of Christian history, the East recognizes seven as truly reflecting the life of the Church and designates these as ecumenical councils.

The first two ecumenical councils addressed the doctrine of the Trinity. The Council of Nicaea (on the northwest coast of what is now Turkey) was held in A.D. 325 to resolve the problem posed by Arianism, which argued for an extreme subordination of the Son to the Father and asserted that the Son was a created being. The bishops proclaimed that the Son is of the same substance (*homoousios*) as the Father, thus indicating the Son's full deity and eternality. This council did not fully resolve the issue, however, since the term *homoousios* was unclear and open to various interpretations. During the half-century of debate that followed Nicaea, the issue was expanded to include the question of the deity and personality of the Holy Spirit as well. The Second Ecumenical Council, convened at Constantinople in 381, attempted to clarify the decree given at Nicaea. This council saw the final rejection of Arianism and the clear assertion that both the Son and the Spirit are just as fully God as the Father. At Constantinople, the creed formulated at Nicaea in 325 was expanded to include a fuller section on the Son and a much more complete statement about the Holy Spirit. The result was the Nicene-Constantinopolitan Creed (generally referred to simply as the Nicene Creed), which to this day remains the dominant creedal statement for all of Christendom.[7]

The third through sixth ecumenical councils dealt with the person of Christ. The Council of Ephesus (in what is today western Turkey) in 431 saw the condemnation of the teachings of Nestorius (who so sharply distinguished between Christ's divine and human natures that Jesus seemed to be merely a man who was inspired and indwelt by the divine Son). The proceedings of that council were so confused (two rival councils were held simultaneously, arriving at opposite conclusions) that political tensions and rivalries between episcopal sees obscured the christological issues at stake. The confusion was reduced through a flurry of correspondence between Church leaders over the next twenty years, and the Council of Chalcedon (near Nicaea in northwestern Turkey) in 451 gave more definitive expression to the Church's faith in Christ. At Chalcedon, the bishops adopted a formula that preserved both the unity of Christ's person and the fact that he has two clearly distinguishable natures, divine and human.[8] The Fifth Ecumenical Council (also called the Second Council of Constantinople) met in 553 to provide further clarification of the Chalcedonian definition by insisting that in Christ, the two natures are genuinely united in the one person of the divine Son.[9] The sixth (called the Third Council of Constantinople) was the final chapter in the controversies that directly concerned the person of Christ. Meeting in 681, this council declared that Christ possessed two wills and two energies (divine and human) in his one person.[10]

The last of the ecumenical councils recognized by the Eastern Church took place in 787 in Nicaea (and thus is called the Second Council of Nicaea) and dealt with the controversy over icons.[11] At this council, the bishops repudiated a prior synod (which had met in 753) by insisting that the making of images was in accordance with tradition and was necessary in order to proclaim the incarnation. The council followed John of Damascus in distinguishing between worship and reverence, proclaiming that the former is due to the Trinity alone but that the latter can be offered to others besides God.[12]

After the period of the great ecumenical councils, other smaller councils have contributed to the expression of Orthodox tradition. The most important of these councils were two held in Constantinople in 1341 and 1351 to define the Orthodox doctrine of grace as God's divine energies. Like the writings of the fathers, the pronouncements of the councils are a major expression of Orthodoxy's life and a source of its theological vision, and are the subject of additional discussion later in this book.[13]

The Divine Liturgy

Because Orthodoxy sees the Church primarily as a sacramental, worshiping community, the liturgy (the pattern for worship and for the celebration of the Eucharist) is a crucial expression of the Church's life. Four basic variants of the Orthodox liturgy are in use. The first is the liturgy of St. Basil, which is the most ancient and the longest of the liturgies. At one time, the liturgy of St. Basil was the primary liturgy of the Eastern Church, but today this variant is used only ten days a year.[14] The second and most commonly used is the liturgy of St. John Chrysostom, which is a shorter form of the liturgy of St. Basil. The parts of the service that are spoken publicly before the people are essentially the same in both liturgies, but in the liturgy of St. John Chrysostom, the private prayers that the priest speaks within the sanctuary are much shorter than in the liturgy of St. Basil. The liturgy of St. John Chrysostom is used on Sundays and weekdays throughout the year. The third form is the liturgy of St. James (the brother of the Lord), which is used only on St. James' Day, October 23. The fourth form is called the liturgy of the presanctified gifts. Attributed to St. Gregory of Dialogus (a sixth-century bishop of Rome) and lacking the ritual for consecrating the bread and wine for the Eucharist, this liturgy is used on Wednesdays and Fridays during Lent and on Monday, Tuesday, and Wednesday during Holy Week (the week preceding Easter). On these days, the Eucharist is celebrated using bread and wine consecrated the previous Sunday, hence the absence of the ritual of consecration.[15]

The divine liturgy consists of three major sections: the *proskomede* or office of preparation, the liturgy of the catechumens, and the liturgy of the faithful. The office of preparation is conducted entirely within the sanctuary (behind the iconostasis) by the priest and his assistants. This section of the liturgy is essentially private, since normally only the clergy and other men and boys assisting in the service are allowed into the sanctuary. This office includes the preparation of the priest, the service of vesting (robing) the priest or bishop, the preparation of the eucharistic gifts of bread and wine, the blessing of the incense and covering the vessels used in the celebration of the Eucharist, and concluding prayers. This private office initiates the two great themes that will resound throughout the entire liturgy: the greatness and glory of God and the people's need for God's mercy. Glory is repeatedly ascribed to the Father, Son, and Holy Spirit, and the cry "Lord have mercy" (*Kyrie eleison*) is repeated throughout the office. Frequently the office of preparation concludes with the recitation in full of Psalm 51 as a way of beseeching God's mercy. This section also displays an emphasis on the unity and wholeness of the Church and on the role of all the saints in worship. Near the beginning, after the invocation of Christ's icon, Mary's and John the Baptist's icons are both invoked, and the names of other saints, clergy, and laypeople throughout history and throughout the world are included in the prayers as well. The office recalls the events surrounding the birth, death, and resurrection of

Christ and rejoices in the forgiveness, victory over death, and immortality that have come to us through him.

The second major section, the liturgy of the catechumens, is open to all (catechumens or "learners" are people who are not yet baptized and chrismated), and is thus conducted largely in the transept (the main part of the church building), although parts of the liturgy take place within the sanctuary. The major focus of this section is the public praise of God through liturgical prayers and songs of praise (usually sung by an unaccompanied choir) and the reading and celebration of two biblical passages, one from Acts or a New Testament letter and the other from one of the Gospels. God is praised for the greatness of his power, glory, mercy, and love for humanity, and Christ's saving acts of incarnation, death, and resurrection are remembered. Prayers are offered for the peace and safety of the world, for the leaders and laypeople of the Church, and for believers both living and departed. God is beseeched to be merciful to his people, and the refrain "Lord have mercy" is everywhere present. This section also calls attention to the unity of the entire Church (that is, the unity of believers on earth with the departed saints), and several of the prayers end with the refrain, "Remembering our most holy, pure, and glorious Lady, the Theotokos and ever-virgin Mary, with all the saints, let us commit ourselves and one another, and our whole life to Christ our God."[16] At the end of this section, the catechumens are dismissed, sometimes with prayers that they would receive mercy from God and remission of sins, and that they would be united to the Church and numbered among God's chosen flock.

The third section, the liturgy of the faithful, is for baptized Orthodox and is conducted mainly in the transept, with some events taking place in the sanctuary. This third section begins with prayers of thanksgiving that God has granted the people to come before him and to seek his compassion, followed by prayers that he would be merciful and would grant his people to grow in spiritual understanding and life. The bread and wine are ceremonially brought forth as the priest and people pray for mercy, and all recite the Nicene Creed. The central moment of the liturgy comes after Christ's death and resurrection are recalled. The priest recites Christ's words of institution, and as he raises the bread and wine aloft, he offers these gifts back to God. He asks that God would send his Holy Spirit upon them, making them the body and blood of Christ, so that those who partake of them would receive sobriety, remission of sins, communion with the Holy Spirit, and the fullness of the kingdom of God. Prayers are then offered in memory of the saints (especially Mary and John the Baptist), for the whole Orthodox Church, for rulers, and for others whom the worshipers name privately. The priest breaks the bread and places it in the chalice, mixing water with it as he does so. He distributes the

Eucharist to people who come forward to take it by feeding them the bread/wine/water mixture with a spoon. After the Eucharist, several prayers follow in which the worshipers express gratitude for being permitted to partake, and the priest dismisses the worshipers.

One can see that throughout the liturgy, the recurrent themes are the invocation of the triune God, the confession of the people's need for mercy, and the expression of gratitude for the incarnation and work of Christ. The daily celebration of the liturgy impresses these truths firmly into the consciousness of practicing Orthodox people, and this daily repetition of the liturgy, coupled with the regular cycle of accompanying Scripture readings, constitutes the primary means by which the Orthodox comprehend and participate in the life of the Church.

In addition to the daily liturgy, the Church's worship also encompasses a yearly cycle of feasts and fasts that not only bears witness to the major aspects of Christianity but also teaches the worshipers these truths and brings them into direct contact with the life of the Church. The calendar of feasts is headed, of course, by the feast of Easter (called "the feast of feasts"), the celebration of the resurrection of Christ. Besides Easter are twelve major feasts: the Nativity of the Mother of God, the Exaltation of the Cross, the Presentation of Mary in the Temple, Christmas, Theophany, the Meeting of Our Lord, the Annunciation, Palm Sunday, the Ascension, Pentecost, the Transfiguration, and the Dormition (death) of the Mother of God. These twelve feasts are divided into two groups, five feasts of the Mother of God and seven feasts of the Lord.

Of the feasts that celebrate Mary, the Nativity of the Mother of God (held on September 8/21)[17] initiates the Christian year and celebrates the beginning of God's action of salvation through the birth of the one who would bear the Messiah. The Presentation of Mary in the Temple (November 21/December 4) demonstrates her complete dedication to God, her readiness for her future vocation. The Meeting of Our Lord (February 2/15) celebrates the day Mary and Joseph brought Christ to the temple and presented him to his people, as represented by Simeon and Anna (see Luke 2:25–38). The Annunciation (March 25/April 7) commemorates God's initiative and Mary's response in the act of the incarnation. The Dormition of the Mother of God (August 15/28) proclaims that after Mary died, she was raised bodily from the dead as Christ was. According to Orthodoxy, she has already passed judgment and lives completely in the age to come, from which position she intercedes for us.

The first of the feasts of the Lord is the Exaltation of the Cross (September 14/27). This feast celebrates the place of the cross in important historical events. These events include Constantine's vision of the cross before his military victory in 312 (which led to the establishment of the Byzantine empire), the finding of the true cross by Constantine's mother Helena, and the dedication of the Church of the Resurrection on the site of Christ's tomb. The second feast of the Lord is Christmas (December 25/January 7), which celebrates the union of divinity and humanity in the person of Christ. After Christmas is the feast of Theophany, a word that means "the manifestation of God" (January 6/19), which commemorates the baptism of Christ. Palm Sunday (the Sunday before Easter) demonstrates the public presentation of Christ as king of the Jews. The feast of the Ascension of Christ (forty days after Easter) celebrates the completion of Christ's work with his restoration to the Father and the Spirit. Pentecost (fifty days after Easter) commemorates the birth of the Church through the gift of the Holy Spirit. Finally, the Feast of the Transfiguration (August 6/19) celebrates the revelation of Christ's divine glory to people.[18]

In addition to the major feasts, there are four primary periods of fasting in the Orthodox calendar. The Great Fast (Lent) begins on a Monday (not on a Wednesday, as in the Western Church) seven weeks before Easter and continues until midnight on Easter morning. The Fast of the Apostles begins on a Monday eight days after Pentecost and ends on June 28 (July 11). The Fast of the Dormition of the Mother of God lasts from August 1 to 14 (August 14–27). Finally, Christmas is preceded by a lengthy period of fasting and preparation, from November 15 to December 24 (November 28–January 6). In Orthodoxy, strict fasting (such as is prescribed for these periods) implies abstaining not from all food but from meat, fish, eggs, dairy products, olive oil, and wine. Various less strict regimens of fasting are prescribed for different times of the year. Absolute fasting is reserved for the days on which the Eucharist is taken, and no food or drink is to be consumed prior to the reception of the Eucharist (or in some cases, from the previous evening until one takes the Eucharist). In Orthodoxy, fasting is never seen as an end in itself, nor is it ever an individual matter. Fasting is always connected with the rhythms of corporate worship and the life of the Church.[19]

Of course, several of these holidays are familiar to all Christians, whereas others represent aspects of Orthodox life that are foreign to most Protestants and even to many Roman Catholics. I discuss the beliefs associated with the feasts of the Mother of God in chapter 7. At this point, however, it should be sufficient to note that repetition of these cycles of feasting and fasting is a major expression of Orthodox tradition. The saving truths of Christianity and the saving life of the Church are impressed on the minds and hearts of the faithful primarily through this repetition, rather than through discursive teaching.

Church Architecture and Iconography

Orthodoxy expresses its life not only through written and spoken proclamation, but also through visual symbols.[20] Many of these symbols exist, and in fact, all the ceremonies mentioned in the previous section are marked at least as much by visual representations as by verbal proclamation. Of these symbols, the dominant ones are the representations inherent in the structure of church buildings themselves and the arrangement of icons within the churches.

A typical Orthodox church building includes a small entry hall (the narthex) on the west side and a large open area with a very high domed ceiling (the transept or nave) in the center. On the east side of the building, a partition (the iconostasis) extends from wall to wall, dividing the transept from a smaller room, the sanctuary. The iconostasis does not extend to the ceiling, so the back wall of the sanctuary is visible above the top of the partition. The iconostasis has three doors, the royal door in the center, and north and south doors on either side. In the center of the sanctuary is the altar, which is visible through the royal doorway when that door is open. Orthodox churches in the East usually have no pews (although a few benches may be present on the side walls of the transept). Worshipers usually stand, and they may also bow, kneel, or prostrate themselves. (In the West, Orthodox churches typically have pews or seats, and this practice is now common in Greece as well.) Aghiorgoussis explains the symbolism of this arrangement as follows:

> The narthex is the preparation for the entrance into heaven; the transept of the church, with the dome above it, represents heaven itself; and the sanctuary, the "Holy of Holies," with the altar in its center, represents the "holy dwelling place" of God and God's throne. This symbolism is especially vivid in the celebration of the Divine Liturgy, during which "the Kingdom of God breaks through" to be present in the midst of the congregation.[21]

Clearly the architecture of Orthodox church buildings is a way of expressing the life of the kingdom of God, which characterizes the Church. The people enter the building in order to gain a taste of heavenly life and divine splendor, a taste that prepares them to receive the Eucharist, which makes them into the Church and gives them the life of the Holy Spirit. The eschatological perspective that we have already noted is obvious in this architectural arrangement: the life of the coming age, the kingdom of God, is present now in the eucharistic assembly.

Russian iconographer Leonid Ouspensky offers a slightly different, but complementary, explanation when he asserts that the transept represents the material world and the sanctuary the immaterial world, the dwelling place of God. The iconostasis divides these two. He writes,

> Although, on the one hand, it is a screen dividing the Divine world from the human world, the iconostasis at the same time unites the two worlds into one whole in an image which reflects a state of the universe where all separation is overcome, where there is achieved a reconciliation between God and the creature, and within the creature itself. Standing on the boundary line between the Divine and the human, it reveals by means of images as fully as possible the ways to this reconciliation.[22]

When Aghiorgoussis declares that the transept represents heaven, he is referring to the bringing of people to the sphere of the divine kingdom. Despite Ouspensky's different terminology, he is stressing the same thing: the architecture of the church building shows the way by which people can be lifted up to the immaterial realm of God's own being. The iconostasis, Ouspensky writes, plays the central role in demonstrating the way to reconciliation, and thus a detailed examination of the icons' arrangement on this partition may be helpful.

Although a great deal of variety exists from church to church, one typical arrangement divides the iconostasis into five levels or rows, each covered with icons. The lowest level (the largest one) contains the three doors, and usually four levels appear above the tops of the doors. The top row of icons on the iconostasis is that of the patriarchs and includes images of the major figures from the early part of Old Testament history. This row represents the Church of the Old Testament, whose task was to prefigure the New Testament Church through which union with God would become possible.

The second row also comes from the Old Testament period and is that of the prophets. This row contains images of the major prophets all holding scrolls on which are written prophecies of the incarnation. In the center of this row is an icon called "Our Lady of the Sign," in which Mary is depicted with her arms raised in prayer and with Christ in her womb. This icon (toward which the prophets all face) represents the fact that the incarnation is the fulfillment of the Old Testament prophecies.

The third row contains icons depicting events from the New Testament period that constitute the stages of God's major action in the world. These events are the ones celebrated in the major feasts; this row is called the "Holy Days."

The fourth row, which is the focal point of the entire iconostasis, is called *Tchin*[23] and depicts Christ seated on a throne. Surrounding this icon of Christ are images of Mary (on Jesus' right), John the Baptist (on his left), and other saints, apostles, and/or angels, all facing Christ in a posture of prayer.

The fifth row is on the level of the three doors. The central or "royal" door is the entrance to the Holy of Holies, and only the clergy can enter through it. On the royal door are icons of the four Gospel writers and, above them, an icon of the annunciation. Just above the door itself is an icon of the Last Supper. This door represents the entrance to the kingdom of God, and thus its icons announce that kingdom. On the iconostasis, to the left of the royal door (as one views it) is the icon of the Virgin and Child, and on the viewer's right is usually placed an icon of Christ the Savior (although an icon of the holy day or saint to whom that particular church is dedicated may be placed there instead). The north and south doors usually display icons of the angels Michael and Gabriel. Covering the rest of the lower level of the iconostasis are icons pertaining to different months or to events in the liturgical calendar. These icons are moved into a prominent position in front of the pulpit on the holidays they celebrate.

Ouspensky explains as follows the overall effect of this arrangement of icons on the iconostasis:

> In different storeys in a harmonious order and strict sequence are shown the stages of Divine Dispensation. From God to man, from above downwards there goes the ray of Divine revelation: gradually, through the preparation of the Old Testament, through things foreshadowed in the patriarchs and foretold by the prophets, towards the series of holy days, the fulfilment of what the Old Testament was preparing for, and through this storey towards the coming completion of the Dispensation, the image of the Kingdom of God—the Tchin. Below this there takes place the direct communion between God and man. These are the ways of the ascent of man. They proceed from below upwards. Through receiving the preaching of the Gospels and communion by prayer, through the union of the will of man with the will of God (in this aspect the icon of the Annunciation represents the iconography of the harmonious union of the two wills), and finally, through communion in the sacrament of the Eucharist man accomplishes his ascent to the Tchin, that is, enters the oecumenical union of the Church, becomes "of the same body" with Christ.[24]

The icons' depiction of God's descent to the level of humanity and the people's ascent to the sphere of God is directly related to the idea of Christian life as a journey toward union with God. The imagery of the church buildings clearly plays a major role in bearing witness to and teaching this vision of Church life. In Orthodoxy, the image is not something separate from verbal proclamation but is a part of that proclamation itself. Word and image are expressions of the same tradition, the same life, that forms the basis for Eastern faith and practice.

Readers should now understand the reason that Orthodoxy does not have a well-developed concept of theological authority, as well as the manner in which Eastern Christianity expresses the life of the age to come. Orthodox tradition is neither an authoritative entity nor a human response to an authoritative writing. Rather, tradition is the stream of grace in which the whole Church is carried along by the Holy Spirit; tradition is the life that the Church possesses in Christ. No external manifestation of the Church's life possesses a juridical authority over other manifestations, simply because no disharmony exists between them and thus adjudication between various "authorities" is not necessary. Scripture, the writings of the fathers and the councils, the liturgy, and visual representations of life such as icons and Church architecture, are all means of expressing the Church's tradition. Technically speaking, none of these expressions is the source of Orthodox theology; they are instead the windows through which we may view (and enter into) the life that is itself the source of theology.

As I have discussed these ideas in part 1, we have not only considered the source of the Orthodox vision itself, but we have also begun to peer through the windows, to gain glimpses of that understanding of Christian life. We have seen that the key ideas are the kingdom of God, a journey toward union with God, and a common life that all Christians share through the eucharistic assembly. In part 2 of this work, I examine these ideas more specifically and systematically by considering the substance of the Orthodox vision in its best expression, that which flowered in the twentieth century among expatriate Russians, Greeks, and others.

PART II   The Heart of the Orthodox
Vision: Union with God

Chapter 4

God as Darkness; God as Three

*I*n the areas of Trinitarian theology and Christology, all Christians owe a tremendous debt to the Eastern Church. When we are asked to explain the Trinity, we generally reply that God exists eternally as one essence in three distinct persons. We describe the person of Jesus Christ as being a mysterious union of two natures, one human, the other the divine nature of the Trinity's second person. We are so familiar with these expressions that we are prone to forget that they are not present in Scripture. The words "essence," "person," and "nature" are not used in the Bible in the specific senses we assign to them through these theological formulae, and the word "Trinity" does not occur at all in Scripture. Instead, these expressions are the result of several hundred years of intense discussion and study in the attempt to convey accurately and precisely the biblical teaching about God. Most of the people taking part in these debates (which were at their most intense during the fourth and fifth centuries) were the Eastern church fathers, the forerunners of today's Orthodox Church.

Despite our indebtedness to Eastern Christendom in these areas of theology, and in spite of the fact that Chalcedonian Orthodox, Roman Catholics, and Protestants all use the same Trinitarian and christological formulae,[1] the ways in which Eastern and Western Christians approach the doctrine of God are significantly different. We have already seen that Western Christianity adopts a juridical way of looking at Christianity, whereas the East has a more mystical and personal perspective. This chapter examines this difference of perspective more fully and explains its implications for Eastern and Western theology.

Apophatic Theology: The Darkness of God

At several points in the preceding chapters, I have used the word "mystical" to characterize the Eastern approach to reality, but I have not yet attempted to explain this idea. In general, one may say that mysticism stands in contrast to a knowledge-oriented perspective. English patristic scholar Andrew Louth writes,

> But it [mysticism] can be characterized as a search for and experience of immediacy with God. The mystic is not content to know *about* God, he longs for union with God. . . . The search for God, or the ultimate, for His own sake, and an unwillingness to be satisfied with anything less than Him; the search for immediacy with this object of the soul's longing: this would seem to be the heart of mysticism.[2]

Lossky explains this idea more fully when he asserts that in mystical theology, one is no longer aware of the distinction between the subject (the theologian) and the object (God). He continues, "God no longer presents Himself as object, for it is no more a question of knowledge but of union. Negative theology is thus a way towards mystical union with God, whose nature remains incomprehensible to us."[3] In the Eastern understanding, the task of theology, and indeed the calling of Christian life, is to be united to God, to gain such an intimacy with God that one is lost in divine life and divine communion.

The quotation from Lossky indicates that the path to such union is a negative one and that God remains incomprehensible as we seek intimacy with him. This idea that God is mysterious and beyond our knowledge is one of Orthodoxy's strongest emphases. Zernov writes that no matter how intimate one's communion with God, "the divine essence remains impenetrable to the human mind, since the Eastern emphasis on apophatic or negative theology insists that we can only say that God is beyond all our definitions and speculations."[4] Similarly, Greek monastic Hieromonk Auxentios emphasizes that God is ultimately unknowable and thus that the priority in theology should lie with negative methodology.[5] What these writers call negative or "apophatic" theology is a theological approach that declares what is not true of God, rather than affirming what is true of him (a method called "cataphatic theology"). Instead of listing and explaining the attributes of God (as Western theologians would probably do), Eastern theologians are more likely to consider aspects of our world that show imperfection or incompleteness and to declare that God does not have these qualities. God is not limited; he is not temporal; he is not sinful, and so on. Through such concentration on what is not true of God, people eventually reach the point at which they can no longer make negations. In the face of God's mysteriousness, they cannot declare whether some quality is true of him or not.

The apophatic approach of Eastern Christendom ultimately traces its roots back to the revelation of God to Moses on Mount Sinai. That revelation was characterized by darkness, by a thick cloud and smoke that shrouded the mountain (Exod. 19:16–18). The darkness continued in the form of the cloud that covered the tent of meeting (Exod. 40:34–38) and the blackness inside the Holy of Holies.[6] Building on this idea that God reveals himself to us in darkness and mystery, the fourth-century Cappadocians (Basil, Gregory of Nyssa, and Gregory of Nazianzus) emphasized that God is incomprehensible to us, and Pseudo-Dionysius (sixth century) and Maximus the Confessor (seventh century) brought apophaticism to the forefront of Eastern theology.[7] Zizioulas quotes Maximus the Confessor as asserting, "God has a simple, unknowable essence, inaccessible to all things and completely unexplainable, *for He is beyond affirmation and negation*."[8] Similarly, Lossky explains, "The apophaticism of Orthodox theology is . . . a prostration before the living God, radically ungraspable, unobjectifiable, and unknowable, because He is personal, because He is the free plenitude of personal existence."[9]

To a Western Christian, such statements seem close to agnosticism, as if the Orthodox did not believe we can actually know anything about God's character. This conclusion is not accurate, and Zizioulas defends the apophatic approach to theology from such a charge when he writes, "The principal object of this theology is to remove the question of truth and knowledge from the domain of Greek theories of ontology in order to situate it within that of *love* and communion."[10] According to the Orthodox, the cataphatic theological method brings one not to knowledge of the true God, but merely to a false knowledge of a philosophical idea of God as the highest being. (Zizioulas is referring to such an approach when he writes of "Greek theories of ontology.") Eastern Christendom makes a sharp distinction between rational or philosophical knowledge on one hand and personal, mystical communion on the other. This latter way of knowing God and being united to him is the goal of apophatic theology. Ware explains, "Our negations are in reality super-affirmations. Destructive in outward form, the apophatic approach is affirmative in its final effects: it helps us to reach out, beyond all statements positive or negative, beyond all language and thought, towards an immediate experience of the living God."[11]

Schmemann clarifies this contrast between philosophical and mystical approaches to God by linking divine incomprehensibility to God's holiness:

> "Holy" is the real name of God, of the God "not of scholars and philosophers," but of the living God of faith. The knowledge *about* God results in definitions and distinctions. The knowledge *of* God leads to this one, incomprehensible, yet obvious and inescapable word: holy. And in this word we express both that God is the Absolutely Other, the One *about* whom we can know nothing, and that He is the end of all our hunger, all our desires, the

inaccessible One who mobilizes our wills, the mysterious treasure that attracts us, and there is really nothing to know but Him.[12]

Clearly, Schmemann is using the word "holy" to refer to God's mysterious, unknowable nature, not to his intolerance of sin or separation from sinful people. Like Zizioulas, Schmemann contrasts the philosophical God from the true, living God of faith. This distinction between knowledge about God and knowledge of God is crucial. Rationally or philosophically, we can know nothing about God, since rational argument leads us only to an idea of the sort of God who is philosophically plausible, not to the true God. Personally and mystically, we can know the true God and be united to him. The apophaticism of Orthodox theology is a way of acknowledging that God is incomprehensible and beyond us, while still seeking to be united to him.

The Orthodox support this distinction between rational and personal knowledge by distinguishing between the essence of God, which they insist is unknowable, and what they call his energies, which are knowable. Like the apophatic emphasis, this distinction was also present in the Cappadocians, Pseudo-Dionysius, and Maximus the Confessor. The concept of knowledge of God's energies received its classic expression in the writings of the fourteenth-century monk Gregory Palamas, who focused his attention on Paul's ecstatic vision in 2 Corinthians 12. Palamas argued that in this vision, Paul saw not God's essence, but his energies. Similarly, the mystic can see and be united to God in his energies.[13] Meyendorff explains Palamas's thoughts as follows,

> The major point made by Palamas in his *Triads* is precisely that the darkness of the cloud surrounding God is not an empty darkness. While eliminating all perceptions of the senses, or of the mind, it nevertheless places man before a Presence, revealed to a transfigured mind and a purified body. Thus, divine "unknowability does not mean agnosticism, or refusal to know God," but is a preliminary step for a "change of heart and mind enabling us to attain to the contemplation of the reality which reveals itself to us as it raises us to God."[14]

Here again, we see that Orthodox apophaticism is not the same thing as agnosticism. One cannot know God's essence by the senses or the mind, but one can be raised up to God through his energies, through the Presence that one can "see" in the midst of the divine darkness.

Aghiorgoussis explains this distinction between essence and energies by noting that we recognize God as being both transcendent and immanent, as distant from us and yet close to us. He continues, "The theological explanation of the Orthodox tradition regarding both God's immanence and transcendence is simple: God is present to us through His *energies* (operations, activity) which 'descend toward us,' whereas He is completely transcendent, far away, unapproachable in His essence."[15] Ware insists that the energies of

God are not some sort of intermediary substance between God and the universe. "On the contrary," he writes, "the energies are God himself in his activity and self-manifestation. . . . The essence signifies the whole God as he is in himself; the energies signify the whole God as he is in action."[16]

From these statements, one might conclude that the Orthodox understanding of God's essence and energies corresponds to the typical Western distinction between the attributes and actions of God. While some degree of overlap may be present, this comparison is not actually fair. Lossky writes that one can call the energies God's "attributes" (not his actions, as the quotations from Aghiorgoussis and Ware seem to indicate), as long as "one remembers that these dynamic and concrete attributes have nothing in common with the concept-attributes with which God is credited in the abstract and sterile theology of the manuals [that is, systematic theology textbooks written by Westerners or influenced by Western theology]."[17] Here it is clear that the purpose of the essence/energies distinction, like the purpose of apophatic theology in general, is in part to protect the Orthodox understanding of God from reduction to a philosophical idea. Whether God's energies correspond to what we would call attributes or actions is not really a relevant question. The point is rather that God cannot be reduced to an idea that we can describe in philosophical language. At the same time, he is not a bare existence, a featureless "it." Rather, he is a personal being whose inner life is thoroughly unknown to us, but who makes himself known by showing us his outward life, his loving communion as directed toward his creation. Orthodoxy seeks not to peer into the mystery of God's inner life, but rather to rejoice that he has granted us to share in his outward life as we are united to him in his energies.

Chapter 6 addresses further this issue of God's energies, especially as they relate to the Eastern understanding of grace. For now, though, it is sufficient to recognize that Orthodoxy does not seek to know God by first learning about him, as much of Western theology does. God is never an object to be studied. Accordingly, the Orthodox insist that learning about God does not lead one to union with him, and in fact, such knowledge leads one *away* from the true God to an idea that is not God at all. Instead of seeking rational or philosophical knowledge, Orthodox theology seeks to bow before the mystery of God, to be filled with awe at the one who is so distant, so dark, and yet at once so close to us.

The Doctrine of the Trinity

The fact that Eastern Christianity emphasizes the mysteriousness of God to a greater degree than Western theology is closely connected to the different approaches to Trinitarian doctrine that have arisen in the East and West. Of course, all Christians regard God as both three and one. However, Eastern Orthodox theology focuses primarily on the threeness, the diversity of God, whereas Westerners tend to emphasize God's unity. Historically, this difference of emphasis emerged through varying concerns in East and West during the first Christian centuries. In the East, the major error against which early theologians sought to guard was called modalism, the belief that Father, Son, and Spirit are simply three different ways in which the one God has manifested himself. Modalists argued that God revealed himself as Father in the Old Testament, as Son during the time of the Gospels, and as Spirit during the Church age. These three manifestations (or modes of revelation, hence the name "modalism") do not imply any diversity within God himself; he is actually only one person. The Church correctly saw modalism as contrary to the biblical teaching about God, because of the implication that God the Father died on the cross. In order to combat this error, the Eastern church fathers (led principally by Basil, Gregory of Nyssa, and Gregory of Nazianzus, writing during the fourth century) carefully distinguished the three persons of the Trinity and defined the relationships between them. The Father is the sole unbegotten person, the Son is the person eternally begotten from the Father, and the Spirit is the person who proceeds from the Father.[18]

In contrast, the West was less concerned about the danger of modalism and instead saw pagan polytheism as its major threat. Because of this fear, early Western theology sought to explain the Trinity in a way which made clear that the three persons were not three separate gods. Led mainly by Augustine (354–430), Western theologians emphasized the unity of God and located this unity in his essence or substance (one could also call it his nature), which they usually defined as the totality of all God's characteristics or attributes. In this understanding of the Trinity, Father, Son, and Spirit are clearly all one God because they possess a single essence, an identical set of attributes.[19]

Because of Eastern theology's emphasis on the diversity of God, the Orthodox are wary of anything that blurs the distinctions between the three persons of the Trinity. Accordingly, when they do speak of God's unity, they seek to locate that unity not in an essence that the three persons share, but in the person of the Father. The Father is God, and the Son and Spirit are also God mainly by virtue of their relationship to the Father, not primarily because they have the same attributes as the Father (although Eastern theology affirms this similarity as well). God's unity does not depend on the abstract idea of his essence or on a list of attributes, but on a person, God the Father, who rules over the godhead. Auxentios writes, "The oneness of the Godhead is preserved by the monarchy of the Father, who is the sole source of divine nature."[20]

In keeping with this concept of the Father as the unifying principle and source of the godhead, Orthodox theologians assert that the other persons of the Trinity find their origin in him alone. The Son is generated or begotten from the Father alone, and the Spirit proceeds from the Father alone. Thus, the two are related directly to the Father, but they do not have as direct a relationship to each other. Lossky explains that the procession of the Holy Spirit from the Father alone is crucial to Orthodox Trinitarian doctrine because that procession preserves the diversity of the persons (by avoiding confusion of the Father and Son) and preserves the full monarchy of the Father.[21] Zizioulas concurs: "The one God is not the one substance but the Father who is the 'cause' both of the generation of the Son and of the procession of the Spirit."[22] In contrast, Western theology generally asserts that the Spirit proceeds from the Father and from the Son, since this formulation reveals clearly the commonality of the Father and Son: they are of one essence, from which the Holy Spirit (also of the same essence) proceeds.

This difference of opinion concerning the procession of the Holy Spirit was connected with one of the Church's bitterest disputes, the so-called *filioque* controversy during the Middle Ages. The Nicene-Constantinopolitan Creed (formulated at the Second Ecumenical Council in A.D. 381) originally declared simply that the Holy Spirit proceeds from the Father; the council did not deal with the question of whether he also proceeds from the Son. However, many theologians in both East and West spoke of the Spirit's procession from the Father and the Son, although the East more often used the expression "from the Father through the Son." The word *filioque* (Latin for "and from the Son") was added to the Western version of the creed sometime in the sixth or seventh century in Spain, and the altered version of the creed was in common use in the West by the early ninth century. The *filioque* controversy reached its peak in the middle of the ninth century, when the doctrinal question of the procession of the Holy Spirit was brought into what had already been a tense political battle between Rome and Constantinople.[23] Photius, who defended the Eastern claim that the Holy Spirit proceeds from the Father alone, declared the Western Church heretical because of its addition of the *filioque* to the creed. Two councils were held at Constantinople, the first in 869–70, which affirmed the *filioque,* and the second in 879, which rejected it. This dispute over the procession of the Holy Spirit was one of the key issues that led to the separation of Eastern and Western Christendom into what we now call the Orthodox Church and the Roman Catholic Church.[24]

The significance of the *filioque* controversy does not lie in the actual question of the Spirit's procession, since virtually no biblical evidence exists from which to draw any conclusion.[25] Rather, the controversy's major importance lies in the concepts of the Trinity behind the differing views on the Spirit's procession. At stake is the question of whether essence/nature or person is the fundamental constituent of God's existence. The Orthodox insist that in Western Trinitarian theology, essence is fundamental, and the three divine persons are reduced to little more than relationships within the one essence of God. Lossky writes,

> This is why the East has always opposed the formula of *filioque* which seems to impair the monarchy of the Father: either one is forced to destroy the unity by acknowledging two principles of Godhead, or one must ground the unity primarily on the common nature, which thus overshadows the persons and transforms them into relations within the unity of the essence.[26]

Of course, to acknowledge two principles of godhead would be virtually to say that the Father and Son are two separate gods, which no Christian does. Here Lossky is accusing the Western Church of the second mistake, losing sight of the distinct divine persons by concentrating so much on the essence of God.

Orthodoxy's rejection of the *filioque* reveals the same concern that lies behind its insistence on apophatic theology: the desire not to allow God to be turned into an abstract, philosophical idea. The essence of God is precisely that: an idea that has no concrete existence. God exists *only* as three eternal persons, each of whom possesses the same essence or nature and the same characteristics (attributes). But no entity called the essence of God exists. In this sense, the Orthodox are correct when they argue that the persons, rather than essence, are the fundamental constituent of God's being, and Western theology's emphasis on the essence of God runs the risk of losing sight of that fact.

On the other hand, though, the Orthodox understanding of the Trinity is fraught with risks as well, and Lossky admits that Eastern theology's insistence on the monarchy of the Father risks subordinating the Spirit and Son to him.[27] The danger in the West is that we will lose sight of the personal character of God as a fellowship of three divine persons, and the risk in the East is that we will lose sight of the equality of the three divine persons and will turn the Son and Spirit into some sort of lesser gods or semidivine beings. The explosiveness of the *filioque* controversy derived from the desire of both East and West to safeguard against the potential errors they saw in the other side's understanding of the Trinity.[28]

Clearly, theological discussions of the Trinity can become extremely complex, and a person can easily lose sight of the importance of the issue amidst the bewildering array of fine distinctions. Nevertheless, Western Christians should be aware of these differences in Trinitarian doctrine, for two reasons. First, even though most Orthodox people are unlikely to understand the theological issues behind the *filioque* controversy, they may nevertheless regard the idea that the Spirit proceeds from the Father alone as a rallying slogan, a way of defining themselves in opposition to the West. If we have much contact with Orthodox people, we are likely to encounter this slogan, and thus awareness of it is helpful.

Second, and vastly more important, Westerners need to realize that although both Western and Eastern understandings of the Trinity involve dangers, both concepts latch onto aspects of God's character that are crucial for Christian faith and life. Our Western emphasis on the unity of God helps to show that even though distinctions between the Trinitarian persons exist, and even though the Father does hold a certain priority, the three persons are equal and are in fact the same God, the same being. The one who entered the world for our salvation was not merely a semidivine being but was no less than the very Son of God, coeternal and coequal with the Father. Eastern theology will certainly affirm this fact with us, but the Western approach helps to guard against the danger of subordinationism and to preserve the crucial truth that the one who brought about redemption is the same God as the Father. On the other hand, Eastern theology's insistence on the persons as the constituent elements in God's being highlights the fact that God is not just a being who possesses such attributes as omniscience, omnipotence, and omnipresence. Rather, he is a society, a fellowship of three divine persons.[29] The love that the three persons share with one another is the basis for his creation of people to share fellowship with himself, and also the basis of his redemption of people. By maintaining the distinctions between the persons of the Trinity, Eastern theology avoids the Western temptation to turn God into a philosophical idea and highlights the personal, relational character of God, and thus the relational character of Christian life as well.

Although both the Eastern and Western approaches to the Trinity preserve important truths related to Christian salvation, the differences between these views are considerable, and they lead to somewhat different ways of understanding the person of Christ. Meyendorff points out that if one views the divine persons merely as relations within the one divine essence, then the person of the Son is not a concrete entity and therefore cannot be the subject of Christ's saving passion.[30] In order to unpack the significance of this extremely loaded assertion, I now turn to the Eastern and Western understandings of Christ's person.

The Person of Christ

All Christians are united in confessing that Christ is both divine and human, but throughout Church history, there has been significant debate about what Scripture means in asserting that he is both God and man. The debate about the person of Christ was at its most intense during events leading to the Councils of Ephesus in 431 and Chalcedon in 451. At Ephesus, the Church condemned Nestorius, who distinguished so sharply between deity and humanity in Christ that the Savior seemed to be little more than a man who was inspired and indwelt by God the Son. At Chalcedon, the Church condemned Eutyches, who appeared to have argued that Christ's humanity was fully absorbed into his deity and had, for all practical purposes, disappeared. The Council of Chalcedon declared that Christ is one person who is made known to us in two natures, united without confusion, without change, without division, without separation.[31] In this way, Chalcedon sought to emphasize that in contrast to what Eutyches asserted, Christ's deity and humanity were genuine and remained present in their integrity (united without confusion, without change), and in contrast to what Nestorius claimed, Christ's person was a unity (the natures were united without division, without separation).

The truths that Chalcedon sought to guard are of great importance in Christian theology because they preserve the possibility (and the actuality) of redemption. Christ must have been and was fully human and fully divine. Only if Christ was a genuine human being could the redemption that he effected avail for other human beings. At the same time, though, redemption was not something that the power of a mere man could accomplish; only one who was divine could achieve it. When Orthodox writers express this necessity that Christ be God and man, they argue that redemption must have originated in and been carried out by God, but that redemption must have extended to all aspects of human life. As fourth-century theologian Gregory of Nazianzus put it, "The unassumed is unhealed."[32] Christ assumed a full, complete human nature, because only then could he bring healing and salvation to every aspect of human life. When Western Christians (both Roman Catholic and Protestant) discuss the necessity that Christ be God and man, we normally emphasize that only one who was genuinely human could suffer and die on behalf of human beings, yet only a genuinely divine (and therefore infinite) person could die for many people at once. Chapter 6 addresses the different ways of looking at redemption in East and West, but for now the point is that all agree that Christ must have been fully divine and fully human.

In spite of the universal agreement that Christ was a single person made known in two natures, the Council of Chalcedon proved problematic, leading to the fracturing of Christendom into several factions. Subsequent events helped to resolve some of these disputes, but two splits were lasting: a visible rift within Eastern Christendom and a much more subtle disagreement between East and West about how to express our faith in Christ's person.

The first of these splits took place between what we now call the Chalcedonian and non-Chalcedonian Orthodox groups. Most of the non-Greek-speaking Eastern churches (which were located mainly in the Middle East and North Africa and came to be known as the Oriental Orthodox churches) believed that the Chalcedonian formula failed to safeguard adequately the true unity of Christ and therefore did not sufficiently reject Nestorianism. These churches preferred to use the expression "one nature" when talking about Christ in order to show that he was truly a unity. As a result of this expression, the churches adhering to Chalcedon's formula branded the Oriental churches as "monophysite" (a term derived from the Greek phrase meaning "one nature") and declared their leaders to be heretics. However, the monophysite groups clearly used the word "nature" in its older sense, a sense that Chalcedon covered using the word "person."[33] Thus, these churches were in effect saying that Christ was a single person, just as the Chalcedonian churches insisted. The problem was one of terminology, not of substance.[34] In fact, more than fifteen hundred years later, the Chalcedonian and non-Chalcedonian churches have recently healed their division by recognizing that they hold to the same faith in God the Son who has added humanity to himself.

The second disagreement, which is much less obvious but actually far more substantial than the first, concerns the way modern Eastern and Western theologians explain what Chalcedon meant by the "one person of Christ." Western theologians generally state that at the incarnation, divine and human natures were combined in an inexpressible union into a single person. This idea is connected to the Western way of describing the Trinity. Westerners emphasize the essence or nature of God to such a degree that we envision this nature as an entity in itself, which could be combined with a human nature to make the person of Christ.

Orthodox theologians are quick to point out, however, that this way of looking at the incarnation implies that in Christ we have the embodiment of the abstract idea of deity in a concrete man, Jesus. In contrast, they argue, one needs to remember that the divine nature or essence does not exist as an entity in itself, and so could not have been united to humanity in Mary's womb. What was united to a human nature, they argue, was the person of God the Son. Orthodoxy asserts that since the Son was already a single person before the incarnation, and since he remained a single person after the incarnation, then both before and after the incarnation he must be the same person. That is to say, the one person of Christ is not a product of the incarnation; his single person is the eternal person of God the Son. The incarnation was not a process of making a person out of two impersonal natures, but was an act by which God the Son added humanity to who he already was. He added human attributes and human experiences to what he already possessed as God. He took a full human nature into his divine person, without thereby ceasing to be God or changing from who he already was. The reason Jesus Christ possesses a divine nature is not that this nature was one of the building blocks of his person, but because he is God the Son, who has eternally shared the divine nature with the Father and the Spirit. Conversely, the reason he possesses a human nature is that this nature is what God the Son added to his divine person at the incarnation.

Accordingly, the real disagreement regarding the person of Christ is whether his one person is a composite created at the incarnation by uniting deity and humanity, or whether his person is the eternal person of the Son, who took humanity into himself at the incarnation. Meyendorff alludes to this disagreement in the previously cited passage (page 59). From the Orthodox perspective, an excessive emphasis on the essence of God leads one to think that the person of Christ is a composite. But as Meyendorff makes clear, only if the person of Christ is that of the Son himself can God be the one who was born for us, who redeemed us. Florovsky concurs when he argues, *"The incarnation is a phenomenon and action of God himself* and is his assumption and acceptance of humanity. God the *Logos* is *the only acting subject in the act of the Incarnation*; the *Logos* himself was born a man of woman."[35] Of course, the Orthodox do not deny Christ's full humanity, but they insist that this humanity is God's humanity, that it was God the Son who was born as a man, lived as a man, died as a man, and rose as a man for us. Only in this case, they argue, is salvation possible.

A great deal of disagreement remains among scholars about what the Council of Chalcedon itself intended,[36] but the important point for this discussion is that all Orthodox groups (both Chalcedonian and non-Chalcedonian) insist that God the Son has added humanity to his own person, whereas many modern Western theologians argue that the person of Christ is a composite created by the union of divine and human natures. The visible split between Chalcedonian and non-Chalcedonian groups largely resulted from a misunderstanding, whereas the deeper rift actually lies between different groups that claim to adhere to the Chalcedonian definition.

Western Christians might wonder about the necessity of probing extensively the Orthodox and Western understandings of God. Is it not enough to believe that God is both three and one and that Christ is both God and man? In one sense, of course, believing these truths is enough, but on the other hand, the differences between East and West significantly color the spiritualities that result. The difference between apophatic and cataphatic theology is especially significant. Western Christians, especially Protestants, think of God as one who is familiar, one whom we can describe, one of whose mercy we can be confident, and even one who is a close friend. Eastern Christians are much more likely to come before God with fear and awe, to plead for God's mercy rather than to consider it certain, to see him as a judge rather than a friend. Here, as always, these differences are not absolute. Orthodoxy does not consider God to be unpredictable or loath to grant mercy, and the Eastern Church does see him as one with whom we can share fellowship and even friendship. Although these differences are matters of emphasis rather than absolutes, they still produce discernibly different spiritual atmospheres, as even the most casual comparison of Western and Eastern church buildings and worship services attests.

Similarly, the question of whether one begins with the oneness or threeness of God helps to shape the sort of Christianity that is produced. Some critics say that if the Western churches dropped our belief in the Trinity and became Unitarian, we would not need to alter any other aspects of our doctrine. This statement is, of course, a great exaggeration, but it does make a point worth heeding. Our emphasis on legal standing, on salvation as a position of acceptance before God, our stress on the individual, and other typical Western theological ideas give little attention to the notion of communion between the divine persons and the way this fellowship flows to people whom God has created and redeemed. In contrast, the ideas of fellowship, of communion, and of the Church receive pride of place in Eastern theology; to some degree, these ideas derive from the Eastern understanding of God.

With respect to Christology, one can argue that the Orthodox way of describing the person of Christ actually corresponds more closely to what most conservative Western Christians believe than our own terminology does. Like the Orthodox, we believe that the incarnation resulted in a genuine, personal presence of God the Son on earth, not merely in the embodiment of a divine ideal or the divine essence in the man Jesus. Like the Orthodox, we see redemption as being largely a divine action: God himself, not a mere man, died for us. Accordingly, the differences in Western and Eastern ways of expressing our faith in the incarnation may actually mask the presence of a common belief that Orthodox and many Westerners share. This possibility receives more attention in chapter 8, but now we turn from the doctrine of God to the creation of humanity, where the differences between Orthodoxy and Western theology begin to be most apparent.

Chapter 5

Humanity: Creation, Vocation, and Fall

Western Christians normally regard humanity's initial created state as one of complete fellowship with God and see humankind's original purpose largely as fostering and enjoying that communion. In contrast, the Orthodox view of God's unknowability, combined with a stronger emphasis on human freedom than is typical among Westerners (although Western Christendom varies greatly on this issue), leads Eastern theology to a somewhat different vision of humanity's created state and original calling. This different vision in turn leads to a different view of fallen humanity and has important implications for the Orthodox doctrine of salvation. The differences between the Eastern and Western visions of Christian life become most apparent on this topic, which is the focus of chapters 5 and 6.

Humanity as Originally Created

One of the first major theological conflicts in the early Church was the battle against Gnosticism in the second century. Gnosticism was (among other things) intensely fatalistic, arguing that people were born into one of three distinct classes and that only those of the highest class could be saved. The Christian response to this sort of fatalism was led by Irenaeus of Lyons, who sought to defend human freedom by arguing that humanity was originally created in an unstable, immature condition and was called to progress to maturity.[1] While this approach was not the only way of looking at humankind's original condition among the early church fathers (nor even the only way that Irenaeus himself depicted the created state), this viewpoint has exerted a great influence on the subsequent development of Eastern theology.

Irenaeus's idea that humanity was originally created immature and called to achieve maturity in faith was developed by others in the early Church, most notably Pseudo-Dionysius.[2] Using Pseudo-Dionysius as his starting point, Lossky asserts that all creatures were originally called to perfect union with God and that achieving such union involved synergy, the cooperation of the divine and human wills. He writes, "In fact, because this union . . . presupposes 'co-operation', the agreement of wills and therefore liberty, it is possible to see in the initial state of the created cosmos an unstable perfection in which the fullness of union is not yet achieved and in which created beings have still to grow in love in order to accomplish fully the thought-will of God."[3] A little later, Lossky explains more fully,

> Creatures, from the moment of their first condition, are separate from God; and their end and final fulfilment lies in union with Him or deification. Thus the primitive beatitude was not a state of deification, but a condition of order, a perfection of the creature which was ordained and tending towards its end.[4]

Similarly, Greek theologian Panagiotes Chrestou describes humanity's created state as follows: "Perfection was not offered complete to him from the beginning which, in fact, would constitute coercion. But, rather, perfection was set before him as an objective to be attained."[5] Lossky and Chrestou might appear at odds with each other, since Chrestou insists that Adam and Eve were not perfect at creation, but Lossky uses the word "perfection" of their state. The two authors are referring to different types of perfection, however, as Lossky makes clear when he writes, "The perfection of our first nature lay above all in this capacity to communicate with God, to be united more and more with the fullness of the Godhead, which was to penetrate and transfigure created nature."[6]

Both authors display a strong emphasis on human freedom. God was not willing to coerce people into a relationship with him that they may not have wanted, so he did not create humanity in complete union with himself at the beginning. Rather, God created people immature, separate from him in some sense, and offered them the opportunity to use their freedom in order to attain union with him. One might think that the separation of which Lossky writes is simply the absolute, qualitative difference between Creator and creature. However, his statement that humanity's final fulfillment lies in union with God indicates that the separation which he has in view is not necessarily permanent, as is the Creator/creature distinction. Lossky and others seem to mean that humanity was initially separate in the sense of not having complete communion with God. Consequently, humanity's original "perfection" lay in the capacity to communicate with God and to be united with him, not in the actuality of such fellowship and union.

In support of this view of humanity's created condition, several early Church theologians (most notably, Irenaeus and Origen) distinguished between the words "image" and "likeness" in Genesis 1.[7] In verse 26 God says, "Let us make humankind in our image, according to our likeness," but the following verse reads, "So God created humankind in his image." Modern Eastern theologians, following Irenaeus and Origen, argue that the omission of "likeness" in the verse actually describing human creation indicates that the image of God is a created characteristic, but that the likeness is not. Chrestou explains this distinction:

> The image does not possess everything perfectly, as we have seen, but has a propensity towards perfection; the defect is amended by the faculty of likeness. . . . "In the likeness" refers to the tendency of the self-determining faculty to acquire perfection by painfully struggling in an endless course of progress. This means that man is not something perfected, but something which is formed with struggle.[8]

Leonid Ouspensky concurs by writing, "Man, created in the image of God, is consequently called to realize his likeness to God. To be in the image of God is to have the possibility of acquiring the divine likeness."[9] Moreover, Ware asserts,

> The image . . . denotes man's *potentiality* for life in God, the likeness his *realization* of that potentiality. The image is that which man possesses from the beginning, and which enables him to set out in the first place upon the spiritual Way; the likeness is that which he hopes to attain at his journey's end.[10]

These statements indicate that, in the Eastern mind, the image of God consists of those faculties that God gave humanity at creation in order to make union with him possible. On the other hand, the likeness consists of those perfections that God intended humanity to acquire by using free will to cooperate with God's grace and to grow to maturity and complete union with God. Chrestou's and Ware's assertions also emphasize that even in humanity's unfallen condition, life was understood as a journey, a path leading to perfection and union with God. God created a world in which people were immature but capable of growing into maturity by using the potential God had given them at creation.

Aghiorgoussis offers a more extended discussion, which helps to qualify the picture we have seen thus far:

> Man's being in the image of God means that man has a spiritual soul reflecting God (the Father) as a person. Man is capable of knowing God and being in communion with God. Man belongs to God, for being God's child and

image makes him God's relative. . . . The Fathers also make a distinction between the *image* of God in man, and his *likeness* to God: image is the potential given to man, through which he can obtain the life of *theosis* (communion with God). Likeness with God is the actualization of this potential; it is becoming more and more what one already is: becoming more and more God's image, more and more God-like. The distinction between image and likeness is, in other words, the distinction between *being* and *becoming*.[11]

One should notice here that the separation between God and people (to which Lossky refers in the earlier quotation) is not an absolute one. People were children of God from the beginning of their existence. Nevertheless, in a certain sense communion with God was not simply given to them at the beginning but was set before them as something to be obtained. Humanity's original calling, then, was to acquire the divine likeness, to aspire to union with God. Aghiorgoussis uses the Greek word *theosis* to describe this calling, and Lossky has called it "deification." Elsewhere, Lossky asserts that God called humanity "to a supreme vocation: deification; that is to say, to become by grace in a movement boundless as God, that which God is by nature."[12] Meyendorff writes that we must understand humanity in an open sense: people exist in order to ascend into the life of God.[13] What do the Orthodox mean by this crucial idea?

Humanity's Original Calling: Deification

In the early Eastern Church (and to some degree in the Western Church as well), the idea of deification (*theosis* or *theopoiesis* in Greek) was one of the primary concepts by which to describe humanity's calling. Modern Orthodoxy follows the early Church in emphasizing this idea, which is not always expressed with the word "deification." In fact, the Greek word *theosis,* so common in the early Church, has in modern times become somewhat of a technical theological term that Orthodox theologians use frequently but which is relatively rare in ordinary usage. The liturgy does not use this word, and many faithful Orthodox have never heard it. The ideas of transfiguration or transformation, acquiring the divine likeness, attaining union with God, sharing in divine life, and journeying to the kingdom are all ways of expressing the idea subsumed by the theological term *theosis.* Of course, to a Western Christian, the word "deification" sounds blasphemous, and even if other words are also used to describe *theosis,* we would be averse even to consider such a concept. Therefore, in order for us to move past our initial alarm and to be able to understand this central aspect of Orthodox thought, we need to examine first what the Orthodox do *not* mean by *theosis,* and then consider what they *do* mean by it, which will involve a consideration of the biblical roots of the concept.

The Orthodox do not intend by the word "deification" the same thing that Westerners take the word to mean. Meyendorff insists that *theosis* does not deny God's transcendence or imply that we actually become gods. Instead, he writes that God "*gives* us His own life. In receiving it, man does not 'possess' God, he does not become God in essence; he participates in that which is given to him and thanks God for His ineffable grace."[14] Lossky asserts that becoming partakers of God's nature does not imply becoming gods in essence, since that would mean God would be no longer a Trinity but a myriad of persons.[15] Elsewhere he explains further:

> The union to which we are called is neither hypostatic—as in the case of the human nature of Christ—nor substantial, as in that of the three divine Persons: it is union with God in His energies, or union by grace making us participate in the divine nature, without our essence becoming thereby the essence of God.[16]

These citations show that the Orthodox make a distinction between being God in essence and sharing in divine life, between being God by nature and becoming gods by grace. Lossky indicates that this distinction grows out of the difference between the essence and energies of God introduced in the previous chapter. To say that we become gods in essence or by nature would certainly be blasphemous, but the Orthodox assert instead that we become divine by grace, by participating in God's energies, and they insist that this participation does not blur the line between God and creation.

But if being God in essence is different from becoming divine by God's energies, what is that difference? In what sense do we become divine, according to Eastern Orthodoxy? Two key biblical passages on which the early Eastern Church concentrated were the statement in Psalm 82:6, "You are gods, children of the Most High," and the declaration in 2 Peter 1:4 that through God's promises we "may become participants of the divine nature." These passages indicate that there is some sense in which people are (or can become) divine, and they provided the justification for the use of the word *theosis* in the early Church (and thus in technical Orthodox theology today). These passages do not, however, constitute the major biblical source of the idea, even if they did supply the Eastern Church with the word. Rather, the ultimate source of the concept is God's revelation to Moses on Mount Sinai (which, we have seen, was also the source of Orthodoxy's apophaticism). What we find in the account of Sinai is not simply darkness, but also light. The mountain was shrouded in darkness, but when Moses came down from the mountain to the people, his face shone with the glory of the Lord, so much so that he was forced to veil his face to keep the people from seeing it (Exod. 34:29–35). The Eastern Church finds here its paradigm for the transformation to which humanity is called. In the midst of divine darkness is divine light, and God reveals himself as divine light to people who, like Moses, are prepared to see him. People to whom the revelation is given are thereby transformed so as to become the ones through whom it is given, just as the light revealed to Moses transformed him so that his face shone with glory.

These ideas of light and darkness, revelation and transformation, find their preeminent biblical expression in the narrative of Jesus' transfiguration (Matt. 17:1–8; Mark 9:2–8; Luke 9:28–36). Here again we find a cloud overshadowing the scene, again we find light emerging from the darkness, and again Moses himself is present. This time, though, the light is not God's glory reflected in Moses' face; the light is God's glory emanating from Christ's face. The glory of God that Moses saw, and that caused his face to shine, is the glory that comes forth from Christ's face and that Peter, James, and John see.[17] The Eastern Church (both patristic and modern) emphasizes that Jesus did not change at the transfiguration. He had always been God, and as such he had always possessed the radiance of divine glory. After the incarnation, that glory was veiled from the sight of most people, but Peter, James, and John were granted the ability to see it. Moses saw God's glory on the mountain; the apostles saw the same glory in Jesus, the Son of God. What enabled them to see the divine glory, the Orthodox assert, was the transformation they underwent. Another biblical passage underlying the idea that a person's transformation enables him or her to see divine light is Paul's ecstatic vision of 2 Corinthians 12:2–4, when he was caught up into the third heaven.

The transfiguration and Paul's vision are the two foci of Gregory Palamas's theological writing. We have already seen that Palamas played the pivotal role in developing the Eastern distinction between essence and energies, and he was also the key Eastern father who developed the idea that the goal of transformation is the vision of divine light.[18] Following Palamas and other Eastern fathers, the Orthodox make the transfiguration the central paradigm for understanding humanity's vocation.[19] Human beings were called at creation (and are still called today) to purify ourselves in preparation to see the divine light. As we are united to God and enabled to see his divine glory, we become transformed and are able to radiate that glory to the rest of creation. This transformation makes us participants in the divine nature.

Under this broad umbrella of *theosis* as the vision of divine light are three related ideas that help to fill out the Orthodox understanding of humanity's calling. These ideas are developing godly qualities, sharing in divine immortality, and sharing communion with God. First, divine light shines forth from God and enables people to see him as he is and to acquire those characteristics that he reveals to people who see him. As explained in the previous chapter, God's energies are his divine life outside of his essence, his character as revealed in his giving himself to his creation. Thus God's energies include qualities such as love, justice, mercy, and compassion. God shares these qualities with people as we purify ourselves so as to see him. Ouspensky affirms that achieving the divine likeness is a cooperative process between God's grace and human effort "to acquire the virtues of which love is the highest, the supreme trait of the likeness of God."[20] Ware asserts that people were created with the calling "to advance in love from the divine image to the divine likeness."[21]

This aspect of *theosis* is somewhat similar to what Western Christians would call "becoming godly" or becoming "conformed to the image of his Son" (Rom. 8:29). In fact, the expression "participants of the divine nature" in 2 Peter 1:4 comes at the beginning of a discussion of godly characteristics that people should strive to acquire: goodness, knowledge, self-control, endurance, godliness, mutual affection, and love (2 Pet. 1:5–7). Therefore, deification to the Orthodox consists partly of becoming united with God in his energies, partaking by grace and one's own action of those qualities that God shares with humanity.

A second aspect of deification is human participation in God's immortality, sharing in his eternal existence. Second Timothy 1:10 describes Christ as abolishing death and bringing life and immortality to light. Similarly, 2 Peter 1:4 describes partaking of the divine nature as escaping corruption, and one of the major ideas of the early Church was that humanity was called to move from a mortal, corruptible state to an immortal, incorruptible one. Greek theologian Christophoros Stavropoulos writes that *theosis* "means the elevation of the human being to the divine sphere, to the atmosphere of God. It means the union of the human with the divine." He emphasizes that this elevation does not constitute a transformation of our essence into that of God, but "the union of the whole person with God as unrestricted happiness in the divine kingdom."[22] Similarly, Florovsky writes that deification is a sharing of life everlasting and incorruptible—not an ontological becoming God, but a personal communion with God forever.[23] In this sense, divine life is life that cannot be destroyed. With respect to Lossky's comment about becoming by grace what God is by nature, Orthodoxy argues that God is naturally immortal and incorruptible, whereas we were created naturally mortal and corruptible and therefore can possess incorruption only by grace. This incorruptible life is the goal to which God called people when he created them. This aspect of deification corresponds to what Western Christians might call "eternal life," sharing God's immortality and enjoying his presence eternally.

Following directly from this aspect of *theosis* is a third component, namely, communion with God. The divine light reflects the inner relationships between the persons of the Trinity, and as we see the divine light, we share in the fellowship of the Trinity. In the statement I have just cited, Florovsky links everlasting life with enjoying personal communion with God. In another work, he affirms that deification is "an intimate communion of human persons with the living God. To be with God means to dwell in Him and to share His perfection."[24] Likewise, Meyendorff states that the ultimate destiny of humanity is communion with God.[25] This aspect of *theosis* corresponds to some degree with what Westerners might call sharing fellowship with God, but the Orthodox understanding is deeper than ours. Zizioulas writes that *theosis* "means participation not in the nature or substance of God, but in His personal existence. The goal of salvation is that the personal life which is realised in God should also be realised on the level of human existence."[26] What Zizioulas means by God's personal life is the communion that the persons of the Trinity share with one another. God created humanity with the calling to aspire to mystical participation in that very life, that communion which God has within himself. This aspect of deification is the most important and the ultimate goal of humanity. When the Orthodox speak of becoming children of God (one should remember that Ps. 82:6 links being "gods" with being "children of the Most High"), they are referring to people's sharing in the sonship that God the Son has with his Father, the communion within the Trinity.

One other point worth making is that people's calling is not simply to be united individually to God through *theosis,* but to unite the entire world to God. Auxentios writes that people were originally called to unite all aspects of the created universe in themselves. He continues,

> By uniting these diverse elements within himself—thus uniting the whole of creation—and simultaneously surrendering himself to God "in a complete abandonment of love," man would have expressed the willful self-offering of the whole of the creation unto the Creator. God, in his turn, would have given himself unto man, and thus effected the deification of the whole of his creation in and through his last creature (man). This is the potential, the divinely appointed function that was given to man.[27]

This passage clearly indicates that humanity's calling was one that would have been achieved through a synergy of divine and human action, and also that this task was in part to offer the entire universe to God. Similarly, during a discussion of Maximus the Confessor, Aghiorgoussis writes,

> Man has to overcome all kinds of distinctions within God's creation, before man brings God's creation back to God: man was called to overcome the distinction between male and female, inhabited earth and paradise, heaven and earth, visible and invisible creation, and finally, the division between created and uncreated, thus unifying God's creation with the Creator.[28]

These two citations do not offer much hint as to how humanity was to unite the whole universe within itself, but one should remember that like Moses, people who are able to see divine light become the means through which the light is communicated to others. Clearly deification is not simply an individual matter. God gave this task to humanity to involve the entire world.

This brief treatment of *theosis* should reveal that the idea is not at all foreign to Western Christian thought. The word "deification" itself may provoke strong reactions, but before we are too quick to reject the Orthodox view of humanity's calling, we need to remember that the word *theosis* is rarely used in Orthodoxy outside of technical theological writings, and also that the idea behind the word is one with which we should have a great deal of sympathy. As we are purified, we are united more and more with God and therefore are able more and more to see God as he is. As we see him, this vision of divine light in turn transforms us so that we become more like God, share more in his immortal life, and share in the communion between the Father, Son, and Spirit.

Significantly different from Western Christian thought, however, is the Orthodox idea that people were created with a vocation to obtain union and fellowship with God, rather than being created already in such fellowship. The Western juridical approach to theology tends to emphasize the state in which humanity was created, whereas the Eastern mystical and personal emphasis leads Orthodoxy to focus on the goal to which human beings were called. In Eastern thought, humanity's original condition was not as significant as the journey that humankind should have undertaken, a journey leading to God. Thus the different ways of depicting humanity's original condition in East and West reflect the differences in perspective noted previously.

The Fall

The Eastern vision of humanity's created state and calling leads directly to a different view of the fall than that which is typical in Western Christianity. Shortly after Auxentios describes humanity's vocation in the passage quoted earlier, he writes, "For Orthodoxy, man's fall, the *lapsus,* was like a wayfarer departing from the path, indeed the only path, that led to his rightful home.

The fall was not a departure from an originally static and perfect nature; it was the interruption—the cessation of a priceless process."[29] One should notice here that Auxentios rejects the idea that humanity's prefall state was "an originally static and perfect nature." This sort of state or condition is what he believes (correctly) that Western Christianity stresses. His Eastern emphasis on life as a journey, rather than on pre- and postfall states, contributes to his interpretation of the fall as a departure from a pathway. Similarly, Lossky asserts, "Adam did not fulfill his vocation. He was unable to attain to union with God, and the deification of the created order."[30] Aghiorgoussis calls the pathway from immaturity to maturity a test and argues that the fall consisted of Adam's failing that test.[31]

Zizioulas makes the same point even more forcefully when he writes, "For the Greek Fathers, the fall of man—and for that matter, sin—is not to be understood as bringing about something new [that is, a new condition or state] . . . , but as *revealing and actualizing the limitations and potential dangers inherent in creaturehood, if creation is left to itself.*"[32] This statement strikingly reveals what is implicit in the other cited passages. As God originally created the universe, it was limited and even dangerous, precisely because it was not yet in union with God. (The clause "if creation is left to itself" refers to creation that does not take part in *theosis,* creation that is not brought into union with God.) The task of humanity was not to remain in and enjoy a perfect universe, to maintain an already-perfect fellowship with God. Rather, the prospect of gaining union with God was a goal set before people, and their fall was a "departure from a path" or a "failure to achieve their vocation." This fall simply revealed what was already present in creation; the fall did not bring people into a substantially new condition. As a result, the notion of a drastic fall from a state of blessedness is absent from Eastern thought because Orthodox theologians do not believe humanity was yet in such a perfect state. This approach, again, does not mean people had no relationship with God before the fall. They were his children in some sense, but the Orthodox emphasis in dealing with the fall is not that people lost a condition or state they had previously possessed; rather, they failed to accomplish a task that God had set before them.

A corollary of this view is that Orthodoxy holds a somewhat different concept of sin than that of Western Christians. Zernov writes, "The East regards sin as only a temporary malady which hurts man but does not annihilate his God-like image."[33] While Westerners also affirm that people still bear the image of God in spite of sin, we insist that sin is much more than simply a "temporary malady." Auxentios offers a similar explanation of sin: "Man did not 'fall' into a state where his nature became sinful. He chose to remain and indulge in his own undeified nature." He continues, "As man approaches Christ he comes as a somewhat crippled creature, not as one thoroughly destroyed. His fall was not from the heights of heaven, but from a precious road; so, man 'is not to be judged too harshly for his error.'"[34]

These statements might lead one to believe that the Orthodox hold a low view of sin. A more accurate conclusion, however, would be that they understand sin differently from the way Western Christians do. Schmemann writes, "In our perspective, however, the 'original' sin is not primarily that man has 'disobeyed' God; the sin is that he ceased to be hungry for Him and for Him alone, ceased to see his whole life depending on the whole world as a sacrament of communion with God."[35] Ware argues that original sin means not that we have inherited guilt but that "we are born into an environment where it is easy to do evil and hard to do good."[36] These assertions show that in Eastern thought, sin has less to do with disobedience and consequent guilt than it does with the failure to pursue the calling of deification (being hungry for God alone). Such an idea is consistent with the fact that Eastern theology views reality less in legal categories and more in terms of life and relationship than does Western theology. From a Western perspective, a view of sin with less emphasis on guilt may not be as severe a view of sin as ours, but one should not conclude that the Easterners have a low view of sin. To the Orthodox, sin is still very serious.

The major consequence of the fall and of humanity's sinfulness, according to Orthodox thought, is that people are now unable to become united to God. The task that God set before people at creation has become one which we are not capable of fulfilling. Lossky again offers the clearest explanation:

> The infinite distance between the created and uncreated, the natural separation of man from God which ought to have been overcome by deification, became an impassable abyss for man after he had willed himself into a new state, that of sin and death, which was near a state of non-being.[37]

This statement aptly summarizes the major aspects of the Orthodox vision presented in this chapter. People were created without complete communion with God, but with the capacity to achieve union with him through deification or transformation. The fall constituted a departure from the road that would have led to such union, and the result is that humanity became unable to pursue *theosis*.

If we remember that one of the major aspects of union with God in Orthodoxy is partaking in divine life, incorruption, and immortality, we will not be surprised that Eastern Christianity describes humanity's inability to undergo *theosis* by saying that people have become slaves to death. Lossky asserts in this passage that fallen humanity is in a state of sin and death, and Meyen-dorff argues that the result of the fall for humanity was that "he abandoned his own destiny, the proper aim of his nature, and became enslaved to the power of death because he did not possess immortality as a property of his own."[38] This idea of enslavement to death, taken in part from Hebrews 2:14, is the primary way by which Orthodoxy expresses the change that took place at the fall. The failure to achieve humanity's vocation led people to become unable to fulfill that calling. They became slaves to the death and corruption that they could have overcome if they had followed the path to union with God. People did not become mortal with the fall, for we already were mortal. Instead, we lost the ability to transcend our mortality.

This chapter has revealed perhaps the heart of the differences between East-ern and Western Christianity. At the risk of oversimplifying, I suggest that the different understandings of humanity's creation, vocation, and fall can be schematized into two distinct pictures of the overall structure of human life and salvation. The first of these, that which most Western Christians espouse, can be called a three-act scheme of salvation. The first act is God's act of cre-ation, by which he placed people in a condition of perfect fellowship with God and each other. The second act is the fall, which produced a condition in which the fellowship with God was lost altogether and people's relationships with each other and with the natural world were disrupted. The third act is God's redemption of humanity, by which he places us in a condition basically sim-ilar to the original state. In this understanding, God's actions to redeem and save people constitute a restoration of humanity to a state resembling the orig-inal created condition.

The second picture, which I call a two-act salvation scheme, is that of the Orthodox. In the Eastern model, the first act is that of creation, and God cre-ated humanity not so much in actual fellowship and union with God, as with the potential for such union. People were called to achieve *theosis,* to become partakers of the divine nature. In this model, the fallen state is not drastically different from the original created state; the fallen state is the condition of people who have turned aside from the path they were to follow. Accordingly, the fall does not constitute a separate act in the drama, the way it does in the Western model. Rather, the second act is that of raising humanity to a new level altogether, a level of complete fellowship with God and sharing in divine life. This fellowship is the goal of the journey, not a state that people have pos-sessed before. In this scheme, salvation is not a restoration, but an elevation to an entirely new sphere of life. In fact, the Orthodox do not regard "salva-tion" as the best word for describing this process, since it is a negative term that implies that one must be saved from something and that denotes merely the removal of the obstacles preventing people from achieving our vocation. In Orthodoxy, "vocation" is the key term. In summary, then, a three-act scheme emphasizes *salvation* as a *restoration* to the original beatitude, the state that had been lost with the fall. A two-act scheme stresses *vocation* as an *elevation* to a new level of beatitude, something never before experienced by humanity.

We have seen that these different understandings of vocation/salvation grow out of the different mindsets with which East and West approach reality. Equally important, we have seen that the differences between them are often matters of emphasis, not absolute contradictions. Few (if any) Western theologians would assert that the redeemed condition is exactly the same as humanity's state before the fall; we as well would affirm that salvation is something more than this. All Eastern theologians would say that the fall was a serious matter, that significant changes took place when humanity failed in the task of *theosis*. Nevertheless, the differences in emphasis are striking. Now the time has come to address the issues of redemption and salvation, as we look at the way Eastern theology continues to develop its idea of union with God or *theosis*.

Chapter 6

Salvation: The Path of *Theosis*

Once humanity had fallen, the human vocation of aspiring to union with God became impossible, and if we were to resume that vocation, God would need to intervene directly in history to redeem us. Lossky explains,

> The way to deification, which was planned for the first man, will be impossible until human nature triumphs over sin and death. The way to union will henceforth be presented to fallen humanity as *salvation*. This negative term stands for the removal of an obstacle: one is saved from something—from death, and from sin—its root. The divine plan was not fulfilled in Adam; instead of the straight line of ascent towards God, the will of the first man followed a path contrary to nature, and ending in death. God alone can endow man with the possibility of deification, by liberating him at one and the same time from death and from captivity to sin. What man ought to have attained by raising himself up to God, God achieved by descending to man.[1]

In this passage, one can see clearly the relation between vocation and salvation in Orthodox theology. Humanity's vocation was (and after the fall, still is) to aspire to union with God. Salvation, which becomes necessary only after the fall, is the negative side of vocation. Salvation removes the human captivity to sin and death, a captivity that prevents people from achieving the vocation of *theosis*. One should also notice that God does not fully accomplish deification for people through Christ's redemptive work; instead, he endows us anew with the possibility of achieving *theosis*. This statement encapsulates the Orthodox view of the incarnation and Christ's atoning work, and I now examine this view in more detail.

Redemption and Atonement: Three Major Views

In Christian theology, attempts to describe the atonement that Christ effected for humanity fall into three broad categories. The first (the "classic" or "incarnational" view of the atonement) sees Christ's incarnation, life, death, and resurrection as a victory over sin and death. Since the incorruptible Son became a man and died, he overcame the powers of death and corruption, thus enabling people to gain immortality and eternal life. This view usually asserts that because of people's sinfulness, we were slaves to the devil, who held the power of death (see Heb. 2:14). Through the incarnation, God the Son himself invaded the dominion of Satan in order to defeat him and end his power over people. Through Christ's life, he taunted the devil into killing him, even though Satan had no power over a sinless person. Christ's death was a ransom by which God enticed Satan to go beyond his authority and kill someone whom he had no right to kill.[2] In killing Jesus, the devil forfeited his power over death, and Christ thus secured a victory over the powers of sin and death for all people. Christ's resurrection was a proclamation of this victory, which he won through his death. This view emphasizes the incarnation more strongly than other aspects of Christ's life, because the incarnation was the entrance of God into the kingdom of death, which ensured that victory would be won.

The second understanding (the "Latin" or "juridical" view) emphasizes Christ's payment of the penalty for human sin. In this view, Christ's incarnation and life are seen as the qualifications necessary for the offering of a perfect sacrifice: he was sinless so that he could offer himself in place of sinners. On the cross, Jesus suffered the wrath of God as a substitute for sinners who deserved such suffering, and in doing so he turned away God's hatred toward sin and eliminated people's guilt by paying the penalty completely. As a result, he made possible God's acceptance of humanity. Jesus' resurrection constituted the evidence that God the Father had accepted the Son's sacrifice, and the ascension into heaven placed Christ in a position from which he could intercede for his people. This view places most of its emphasis on the death of Christ as the event that actually constituted the atonement.

The third model (the "exemplary" or "moral influence" view) sees Jesus primarily as an example to fallen humanity. Jesus' purpose while on earth was to demonstrate perfectly the life of selfless devotion that God desired from people. He repeatedly laid down his own desires and rights in order to live a life of love. His death was the ultimate example of such selflessness, given that he did not attempt to defend himself from the false charges leveled against him. Christ's resurrection serves to awaken in us a desire to emulate him and, in so doing, to overcome our sinfulness. This view emphasizes the life and earthly ministry of Christ more strongly than other events.

During the first millennium of Christian history, various forms of the classic view dominated the Church's attempts to explain the atonement, and the Eastern Orthodox Church has continued to adopt this view. Beginning with Anselm of Canterbury's revolutionary work *Why God Became Man* (written ca. 1100), the juridical view of the atonement has dominated the Western Church. The exemplary view rose to prominence in the West with the writings of Abelard in the early twelfth century, but only in some Protestant circles has it become more common than the juridical view. In general, modern Eastern Orthodoxy emphasizes the classic view and modern Western Christianity the juridical view. That the juridical model dominates the Western view of the atonement is consistent with the previously discussed Western emphases on individuals and on juridical categories. These emphases lead us to see the issues of individual guilt and punishment as the major problems the atonement must solve. In the same way, the Eastern idea that enslavement to the power of death is what prevents fallen people from achieving union with God leads the Orthodox Church to place most of its emphasis on the atonement as a victory over death.

Because of these differences of emphasis, Western Christians are likely to be critical of the Orthodox understanding of the atonement, because it seems to ignore the substitutionary, juridical elements that we believe are central to the work of Christ. However, asserting that the Orthodox ignore these elements is not completely accurate. Orthodox theology does recognize—but does not strongly emphasize—the substitutionary aspects of the atonement that are so crucial to Western thought. The major difference between Western and Eastern atonement theory lies not in the exclusive adherence to a single view, but in the way Eastern Christendom links the atonement to humanity's purpose of *theosis*.

Classic and Juridical Elements in the Orthodox View of the Atonement

That both classic and juridical elements are present in the Orthodox understanding of the atonement is clear from the liturgy itself. The classic view is extremely prominent in, for example, the service in celebration of the resurrection. At various points in the service, the priest makes affirmations about Christ, such as the following: "When You descended unto death, O Life immortal, You destroyed Hades with the splendor of Your divinity. . . . The Lord has shown the power of His reign: He has conquered death by death. . . . Death has been vanquished, Christ our God has risen, granting to the world great mercy."[3] The image here is of a powerful king battling victoriously against the forces opposing his people. These forces are led by death, and the victory is thus understood mainly in terms of life.

At the same time, the office of preparation (in which the priest prepares the elements for the Eucharist) includes a prayer that links both classic and juridical aspects of the atonement: "O God, cleanse Thou me a sinner, and have mercy upon me. By Thy precious blood hast Thou redeemed us from the judgment of the Lord, for Thou wert nailed to the Cross and pierced with the spear. Upon mankind hast Thou poured immortality as from a fountain, O Redeemer. Glory be to Thee."[4] This prayer includes both legal terminology (the idea of redemption from judgment) and the ideas of life and victory over death (the idea of pouring out immortality on people). While the classic emphasis is prominent in the liturgy, the juridical element of the atonement is mentioned as well.

Among Orthodox theologians, Lossky most cogently illustrates the link between the classic and juridical emphases in the Orthodox vision of the atonement. He gives an overview of the atonement by asserting that the incarnation removes the division between the divine and human natures, Christ's death removes the obstacle of sin separating people from God, and Christ's resurrection removes the sting of death.[5] This statement reveals both the idea of Jesus' suffering the penalty of our sins and the idea of victory over death. Later in his discussion, Lossky emphasizes the juridical aspects of the atonement: "Through dereliction, through accursedness, an innocent person assumes all sin, 'substitutes' Himself for those who are justly condemned and suffers death for them."[6]

However, Lossky argues that this understanding is not complete in itself, declaring that although the legal aspects of the atonement are strongly present in Scripture, they do not constitute the only image of the atonement the New Testament offers.[7] He writes that the atonement was also a ruse on God's part against the devil. By consenting to death, Christ enticed Satan to pursue him even though he was innocent (and thus the devil had no power over him). Because Satan had no right to kill Jesus, in doing so he lost his authority over Christ and all those who were subject to the power of death. (This understanding derives from Jesus' statement in Matthew 20:28 that he would give his life as a ransom for many.) In this way, Christ's death was a victory that freed us from the power of death and the devil. Lossky concludes that the atonement was both a debt to God (which stresses the juridical aspect) and a debt to the devil (which emphasizes the atonement as a victory over death, since the devil had authority concerning death).[8]

In light of Lossky's balanced discussion, one might ask why the classic view of the atonement alone came to be identified with the Orthodox Church. The answer seems to be that Orthodoxy emphasizes this view so strongly because it is reacting against the notion that the atonement consisted exclusively of

Christ's payment for our sins. In fact, in another work Lossky criticizes Anselm for giving the impression that Christ's victory over death held no place in the atonement. Lossky argues that, in contrast, Athanasius had earlier balanced the juridical view with a view of the atonement as a triumph over death.[9] Lossky concludes that the juridical view of redemption is one of the images the New Testament uses to describe the atonement, but not the only one.

Similarly, Florovsky writes that the cross cannot be explained in terms of vindicatory justice: it is the symbol not of justice but of divine love.[10] At first Florovsky seems to be rejecting the juridical view of the atonement altogether, but he continues, "The death of our Lord was the victory over death and mortality, not just the remission of sins, nor merely a justification of man, nor again a satisfaction of an abstract justice."[11] Florovsky's use of the phrases "not just" and "nor merely" indicates that he does not reject these elements of the atonement outright, but rejects a view that would limit the atonement to these aspects. Florovsky joins Lossky in insisting that Christ's death also achieved victory over death and mortality. Moreover, his assertion that the cross cannot be explained in terms of "vindicatory justice" shows that the view against which he is arguing is one that so strongly emphasizes God's wrath toward sin that it neglects his love for those whom he is justifying by means of the cross. Florovsky argues that love, not simply justice, motivated Christ's sacrifice.

Lossky's and Florovsky's discussions show that the Orthodox do not adhere solely to the classic view of the atonement. Lossky's treatment contains elements of the juridical view, and an examination of Florovsky's statements shows that he is arguing against an extreme form of the juridical view, not against the substitutionary aspect of the atonement itself. Moreover, Bulgakov also stresses the juridical aspects of the atonement by writing that Christ bore the weight of human sin and "offered to the God of justice a sacrifice of propitiation."[12]

Kallistos Ware offers an interpretation of Christ's suffering that may appear to be at odds with Lossky and Florovsky, but which is actually in agreement. Ware affirms that Christ's suffering has done something for us that we could not have done without him, and he continues,

> At the same time, we should not say that Christ has suffered 'instead of us', but rather that he has suffered *on our behalf.* The Son of God suffered 'unto death', not that we might be exempt from suffering, but that our suffering might be like his. Christ offers us, not a way *round* suffering, but a way *through* it; not substitution, but saving companionship.[13]

This assertion seems to contradict directly Lossky's insistence that Christ has substituted himself for us, but one should remember that according to Lossky, what Christ assumed in our place was dereliction and accursedness. Christ suffered God's rejection in our place; we do not and will not suffer that. Ware is seeking to emphasize that Christ's death does not exempt us from suffering in general, but rather offers us Christ's companionship as we suffer. By definition, when we suffer with God's companionship, we are not suffering God's rejection. Therefore, Ware is apparently arguing against a form of the substitutionary view which claims that because of Christ's substitutionary suffering, Christians do not need to suffer at all. Again we find that the Orthodox reject a distorted or extreme version of the substitutionary view, or a view that would limit the atonement to its substitutionary aspects. They do not deny the idea that Christ has suffered separation from God the Father in our place.

Ware's passage is also significant because he links Christ's suffering to a way through our suffering and asserts that we will have saving companionship as we suffer. Here again we see the Orthodox emphasis on Christian life as a journey. The journey will involve suffering, but Christ is our guide and fellow traveler as we make that journey. Ware's comments link the atonement to the human vocation of *theosis,* and I now examine this link.

The Atonement and *Theosis*

When one considers the link between redemption and the task of achieving union with God, the key event is the incarnation. We saw in chapter 4 that the Orthodox understand the incarnation not as a fusion of divine and human natures to make the person of Christ, but as the Son's taking humanity into his own person. Ware explains this understanding as follows:

> In his outgoing or "ecstatic" love, God united himself to his creation in the closest of all possible unions, by himself becoming that which he has created. God, as man, fulfills the mediatorial task which man rejected at the fall. Jesus our Saviour bridges the abyss between God and man because he is both at once.[14]

Shortly after this, he continues,

> The Incarnation of Christ . . . effects more than a reversal of the fall, more than a restoration of man to his original state in Paradise. When God becomes man, this marks the beginning of an essentially new stage in the history of man, and not just a return to the past. The Incarnation raises man to a new level; the last state is higher than the first. . . . Christ is the first perfect man—perfect, that is to say, not just in a potential sense, as Adam was in his innocence before the fall, but in the sense of the completely realized "likeness." The Incarnation, then, is not simply a way of undoing the effects

of original sin, but it is an essential stage upon man's journey from the divine image to the divine likeness.[15]

These statements clearly reveal the pattern of the Orthodox vision of redemption. People were called to union with God but failed to achieve this union and thus lost the capacity to do so. By taking humanity into his own person, God the Son brought about perfect unity between deity and humanity; he "bridged the abyss" between the two in himself. As a result, the incarnation did not simply restore humanity to its prefall condition; the incarnation brought about something new, the union of one man, Christ, to God, which opens the way for all people to pursue the calling of transformation or *theosis*. Meyendorff concurs by writing that people's ultimate destiny is *theosis*, and the foundation of this deification is the hypostatic union of divinity and humanity in Christ.[16] Similarly, Florovsky writes that redemption is seen as union between God and people, and thus the Redeemer needed to belong to both sides.[17]

From these statements, one might conclude that the Orthodox believe the union of divine and human natures in Christ has fulfilled the human vocation of deification, partaking of God, but such a conclusion would be mistaken. Lossky comments that the essence of Christianity is "an ineffable descent of God to the ultimate limit of our fallen human condition, even unto death—a descent of God which opens to men a path of ascent, the unlimited vistas of the union of created beings with the Divinity."[18] Elsewhere he writes that after the fall, humanity's task is still deification and that Christ does not fulfill that task for people. Instead, his life, death, and resurrection serve to unite creation to God "in order to return to man the possibility of accomplishing his task."[19] Here one can see that the incarnation alone does not accomplish redemption: God must have descended and did descend not merely to human life, but even to death.[20] The entire life and work of Christ contributed to that descent. Furthermore, the role of the atonement is clearly to make possible our becoming united to God. Christ did not complete the human vocation for us; he completed it in himself so as to guide and accompany us as we walk the pathway to eternity.[21] Therefore, the purpose of Christ's incarnation and work was to enable people who had lost the capacity for *theosis* to embark once again upon the road to union with God. This understanding of the atonement as restoring the possibility of deification is concisely summarized by Athanasius's statement in the fourth century (a statement that Orthodox authors quote frequently), "God became man in order that we might become divine."[22]

This concept of redemption raises two important questions, the first of which is how the atonement restores the capacity for deification. From the previous discussion, what prevents fallen humanity from undergoing *theosis* appears to be a combination of personal sin and enslavement to the powers of sin and death. (Of course, Orthodoxy emphasizes the latter of these more strongly than the former.) Accordingly, the atonement (as a victory over the powers of sin and death) removes these obstacles and thus restores people's ability to pursue deification. Another important question is how people are deified after the fall. We have seen that as sinners, we are unable to undergo the process of *theosis* ourselves and that the work of Christ does not automatically fulfill humanity's calling to transformation. So what is necessary in order for us to become united to God now? I turn to this question in the next section.

Salvation by Grace through the Holy Spirit's Action

In a helpful summary of Orthodox soteriology,[23] Aghiorgoussis lists seven keys to understanding the Eastern perspective on salvation. First, the treatment of Christ's work is not limited to the cross, but focuses on the incarnation and the person of Christ. Second, the essence of salvation is communion with Christ, participation in divine life, and sanctification by the energies of God. Third, the atonement is seen not as satisfaction but as the death of the Son so that human death might be reversed. Fourth, Christ achieves salvation, but it is applied to people by the Holy Spirit. Fifth, people have real choices to accept salvation and to actualize it through love. Sixth, the Church is the ark through which salvation in Christ and the Holy Spirit comes, and sacraments play a crucial role in bringing salvation to people. Finally, salvation will be completed with the return of Christ and the last judgment.[24] I have already covered the first three of these key ideas, and I have alluded to the last one by emphasizing that Orthodoxy sees salvation as a journey focused on the end, the goal. The remaining sections of this chapter focus on the fourth, fifth, and sixth of these ideas, all of which pertain to the means of achieving union with God.

As Aghiorgoussis's summary suggests, the Orthodox regard *theosis* as being, first and foremost, the result of the Holy Spirit's activity in people. Lossky writes, "The Son has become like us by the incarnation; we become like Him by deification, by partaking of the divinity in the Holy Spirit."[25] Similarly, Stavropoulos affirms that *theosis* is offered by Christ, but realized only with the Spirit: "Only in the Holy Spirit will we reach the point of becoming gods, the likenesses of God."[26] Thus, the Holy Spirit gives us God's own energies, granting us the transformation that Eastern Christendom associates with salvation.

As mentioned in chapter 2, the Orthodox associate the gift of the Holy Spirit with the sacrament of chrismation (anointing with oil), which comes immediately after baptism. Schmemann asks rhetorically, "Are we able to understand that the *impossible uniqueness* of this personal Pentecost is that we receive as *gift* Him Whom Christ and only Christ has by *nature*: the Holy Spirit?"[27] Shortly after this query, he continues, "Prepared and made possible by Baptism, which thus is fulfilled in it, it [chrismation] takes man beyond Baptism, beyond 'salvation': by making him 'christ' in Christ, by anointing him with the Anointment of the Anointed One, it opens to man the door of *theosis,* of *deification.*"[28] One should remember, as we saw in chapter 5, that to become divine is to share by grace in that divine life which God possesses by nature. Schmemann indicates that the reception of the Holy Spirit makes this sharing possible. Christ possesses the Holy Spirit by nature, since he is the Son of God and shares the communion of the Trinity. We receive the Holy Spirit as a gift, and his presence in us opens the door to *theosis.* Notice also that Schmemann uses the word "salvation" only negatively, to refer to the removal of obstacles to *theosis* by the atonement. Reception of the Holy Spirit takes us beyond mere "salvation," to the possibility of union with God.

This action of the Holy Spirit in granting people deification is a function of God's grace. Ouspensky writes, "Orthodox theology insists on the uncreated character of grace and defines it as natural processions, as the energy characteristic of the common nature of the three divine persons. By these energies, man surpasses the limits of the creature and becomes a 'partaker of the divine nature.'"[29] Lossky offers a further description of grace: "In the tradition of the Eastern Church grace usually signifies all the abundance of the divine nature, in so far as it is communicated to men; the deity which operates outside the essence and gives itself, the divine nature of which we partake through the uncreated energies."[30] Later, he writes similarly, "Grace is uncreated and by its nature divine. It is the energy or procession of the one nature: the divinity (*theotes*) in so far as it is ineffably distinct from the essence and communicates itself to created beings, deifying them."[31] We have already seen the Orthodox distinction between God's essence and his energies in connection with the Eastern belief that God is unknowable in his essence. Here Ouspensky's and Lossky's statements indicate that the energies (in which we can participate) constitute grace.

In the Eastern understanding, therefore, to assert that salvation is by grace means that people are transformed as a result of God's communicating his energies, those aspects of his divine life that he chooses to share with people. The energies of God are thus connected with divine light, and one should remember that Palamas most fully developed both the idea of divine light and the essence/energies distinction. The energies of God are the light of grace that shines forth from his essence. As we are enabled to see that divine light, we are more and more transformed by grace, by light, by the energies of God. As we are transformed, we are more fully united to God, more fully deified.

This belief that grace is the energies of God, which can be communicated to people and which lead them to union with God, contrasts markedly with the typical Western understanding. When we use the word "grace," we normally have in mind an attitude of God toward people, on the basis of which he grants salvation to us as a gift. We usually understand grace in contrast to merit or to humanity's natural capacities: God gives us what we do not deserve or does something for us that we could not have done ourselves. In the East, grace is understood as God's giving us himself (that is, his own Spirit who communicates his own energies to us), so that we may be united to him.

The Locus and Means of the Holy Spirit's Action

To the Orthodox, the locus or sphere in which *theosis* takes place is the Church, and the primary means by which the Holy Spirit works to give grace and to deify people are the sacraments and human effort to cooperate with God's gracious action. Florovsky explains the centrality of the Church as follows:

> He [Christ] lives and abides ceaselessly in the Church. In the Church we receive the Spirit of adoption. Through reaching towards and accepting the Holy Ghost we become eternally God's. In the Church our salvation is perfected; the sanctification and transfiguration, the *theosis* of the human race is accomplished.[32]

Aghiorgoussis concurs when he asserts, "Acquisition of the Holy Spirit, and the life of *theosis,* in communion with God, healing and transfiguration of the human nature, is the ultimate purpose of the Christian life. The grounds upon which this process is possible and actually takes place is the grounds of the church of Christ."[33] Notice from these two passages that in Orthodoxy, reception of the Holy Spirit is a process. We have seen that one receives the Spirit at chrismation, but one also continues to receive him more fully throughout Christian life, and this continual acquisition of the Holy Spirit takes place in the Church. The Church is the realm in which Christian life is born, is nurtured, grows to maturity, and reaches its ultimate goal of participation in the divine nature.

How then does one progressively receive the Holy Spirit in the Church? Stavropoulos writes that reception of the Holy Spirit and union with God come about through the Christian life, and that "the Christian life comes into being with the Sacraments and with holy works, those virtuous works which are done with a pure and holy motive in the name of Christ."[34] He writes further that divine grace strengthens people to walk the road to *theosis,* and that this grace is transmitted and actualized in the sacraments, especially baptism, penance, and the Eucharist.[35] We have seen in chapter 2 that these three sacraments are a major component of the Church's expression of tradition. That they are instrumental in the process of salvation should not be surprising. Baptism is the means by which God begins the process of *theosis* in a believer, since it brings him or her into the life that the Church possesses. Penance is the continual act by which a person returns to that life, and the supreme means of *theosis* is the Eucharist, because it is the sacrament through which people become the body of Christ, actualizing their union with the head of the Church through the Holy Spirit whom they receive.

One should not take this emphasis on the Church and sacraments as an indication that the Church controls the Holy Spirit or dispenses grace itself. Meyendorff corrects this potential misconception by writing, "It is not the Church which, through the medium of its institutions, bestows the Holy Spirit, but it is the Spirit which validates every aspect of Church life, including the institutions."[36] The belief that the Holy Spirit "validates every aspect of Church life" grows directly out of the Orthodox understanding of the Church. Eastern Christianity asserts that the Church is, by definition, the activity of the Holy Spirit among people. Therefore, even though the Church itself does not convey grace, one can be confident that one does receive grace by means of the sacraments, precisely because the Holy Spirit works through the Church. Bulgakov affirms this belief when he writes that the mode of transmission of the Holy Spirit is sacraments administered by a priest of the apostolic succession.[37]

Furthermore, the Eastern stress on the sacraments as the means of deification is linked to the idea that the Church is primarily a sacramental community. Humanity's purpose is to be transformed, and the Church is the Holy Spirit's life in the world, which exists primarily for the purpose of celebrating the sacraments. The Church, through the sacraments, is thus the means by which the Holy Spirit transforms people. Accordingly, the Orthodox concepts of the Church and of deification depend closely on each other, and the Eastern emphasis on the Church as the locus of salvation grows out of this interconnection of ideas.

In addition to the sacraments, the other means by which the Holy Spirit deifies people is human effort. In the passage quoted above, Stavropoulos indicates that the Christian life comes into being not only through the sacraments, but also through holy works. He continues by asserting that the true purpose of the Christian life is the reception of the Holy Spirit, who divinizes people. Prayer, fasting, and other works are not the purpose of life, but they are the *"necessary means* for the achievement of the purpose."[38] Lossky argues that good works are necessary because our sin renders grace inoperative in our lives. He writes, "The sacramental life—'the life in Christ'—is thus seen to be an unceasing struggle for the acquisition of that grace which must transfigure nature; a struggle in which victories alternate with falls, without man ever being deprived of the objective conditions of salvation."[39] By "the objective conditions of salvation," Lossky means both the work of Christ and the presence of the Church, which provides the locus and the means (the sacraments) for receiving grace.

It should be clear that in Orthodoxy, the reception of grace is a continual, active process in which one's own striving after virtue plays a major role. In fact, Ware emphasizes the active, struggling nature of Christian life by describing it in terms of three steps. The first of these (*praktike*: the practical phase) involves struggling with one's passions in order to obtain purity of heart. The second step (*physike*: the natural phase) involves the contemplation of nature in order to see God's presence everywhere. The third step (*theologike*: the theological or purely contemplative phase) is the direct vision of God and union with him. Ware emphasizes that these steps should not be understood in a strictly consecutive way. No one fully passes beyond the first in this life, but one can take part in the other steps without achieving full purity of heart.[40] This division of Christian life into three steps shows clearly the Orthodox emphasis on human effort and struggle as an important means of receiving grace, receiving the Holy Spirit. One should remember from the discussion of deification in chapter 5 that people who are purified are the ones who can see divine light and be transformed. Here we see more specifically the steps involved in that process of purification.

However, virtuous works alone do not enable people to earn union with God. Stavropoulos stresses that the Holy Spirit deifies people by means of those works. Bulgakov likewise emphasizes that good works do not merit transformation: "Good works do not constitute merit—no one merits or can merit salvation by human works. They represent man's personal participation in achieving salvation, beyond any reckoning or compensation."[41]

Lossky gives the theological reason for the Orthodox emphasis on human effort in *theosis*: "God becomes *powerless* before human freedom; He cannot violate it since it flows from His own omnipotence. Certainly man was created by the will of God alone; but he cannot be deified by it alone."[42] This statement reflects the same emphasis on human freedom that, as we saw in chapter 5, leads Orthodox theologians to deny that people were originally in complete fellowship with God. According to Eastern theology, God's respect for freedom led him to create people with only the possibility of union with him, rather than coercing them into a communion with him that they may not have desired. In the same way, Orthodoxy asserts, God lays down his power before human freedom by refusing to deify people without their active consent and participation. Florovsky concurs with this emphasis on human participation in *theosis*: "God has freely willed a synergistic path of redemption in which man must spiritually participate."[43] In general, Eastern theology places much more emphasis on human freedom and less on God's sovereignty than do the Augustinian and Reformed strands of Western theology, although some branches of Western Christianity, such as Wesleyanism, hold a view of human free will closer to that of the Orthodox.

This discussion demonstrates that the process of transformation is the result of both the Holy Spirit's action (performed by means of the Church's sacraments) and of human striving to acquire virtue, grace, and the Holy Spirit. For the Orthodox, no dichotomy exists between grace and works, and the question of whether salvation is by faith or works does not arise. As we have seen, Eastern Christians do not think in categories of merit or lack thereof, and they see grace not as an expression of the undeserved nature of salvation, but as the energies of God that can be communicated to people.

Theosis as a Process

In the Eastern understanding of salvation, the emphasis clearly lies on the process of becoming united to God through deification. As noted previously, Orthodoxy possesses a forward-looking spirituality, not a backward-looking one as in much of Western Christendom. Life is a journey from this world to the next, and the emphasis on the goal is so strong that American Orthodox writer Paul O'Callaghan can claim, "Christians are not fully saved until they enter the heavenly kingdom."[44] Of course, Westerners could make this claim as well, but we rarely use the word "salvation" to refer to the final glorification of believers. The Orthodox use the word "salvation" (or better "vocation") primarily for that final event, the goal to which we are called.

Because *theosis* is a process rather than an instantaneous change, the Eastern understanding of salvation carries with it the corollary that people will not be completely united to God by the time they die. Accordingly, Orthodox theology affirms continued progress in transformation after a person's death. Zernov asserts that a Christian's rewards come not immediately after death but at the end of history and that as a result, further improvement is possible.[45] This idea does not lead, in Orthodox thought, to a fully developed concept of purgatory like that of traditional Roman Catholicism. Bulgakov cautions that the Orthodox do not recognize a place of purgation, but they do acknowledge the possibility of a state of purification after death.[46] Naturally, this idea leads to the belief that prayers for believers who have died can help them to complete the process of *theosis*. Such prayers are a major part of Orthodox piety and occupy a significant place in the liturgy.

As a result of this emphasis on the process of becoming united to God, Orthodox theology places little stress on that aspect of salvation which Western Christians most strongly emphasize: the change that takes place in a person's standing before God when he or she begins to believe. Both Roman Catholics and Protestants emphasize the importance of the believer's status in God's eyes, although Roman Catholics generally use the expression "state of grace" to refer to this status, whereas Protestants call this state "justification." In fact, if one were to use Protestant terminology, one could generalize that the Orthodox understanding of salvation consists mainly of elements related to what we would call the process of sanctification (becoming Christ-like), whereas the Protestant understanding consists largely of elements related to justification (understanding the word "justification" in the Protestant sense of God's declaring a person righteous and acceptable before himself, because of the righteousness of Christ).

Aghiorgoussis explains this difference of emphasis by asserting that in Romans 8:28–30, when Paul writes of predestination, calling, justification, and glorification, these are all stages in one process, that of deification or sanctification. "In other words," he continues, "justification is not a separate act of God but the negative aspect of salvation in Christ, which is freedom from sin, death, and the devil; whereas sanctification is the positive aspect of God's saving act, that of spiritual growth in new life in Christ communicated by God's Holy Spirit."[47] This explanation makes clear that the emphasis falls on the process of spiritual growth, and in fact, Aghiorgoussis's definition of justification does not even include the idea of being declared righteous at the beginning of faith, a pivotal idea in virtually all Protestant thought that is also present in Roman Catholic thought, albeit expressed with different terminology. Florovsky explains more completely when he critiques Luther's view of justification. He writes, "For Luther 'to justify'—*dikaioun*—meant to declare one righteous or just, not 'to make' righteous or just—it is an appeal to an extrinsic justice which in reality is a spiritual fiction."[48]

From these statements the absence of legal categories in Orthodox thought is again apparent. To Westerners the issue of a person's status before God is one of the most critical of all questions. To Easterners this question hardly arises at all, in light of the overriding emphasis on the process of actually becoming righteous through *theosis*. As a result, the Eastern conception of Christian life is substantially different from that which is common in the West. To Westerners (especially Western Protestants), the most important element of salvation is acceptance before God (or being declared righteous). Acceptance is accomplished at the beginning of faith, and the process of sanctification grows out of this change in status before God. To the Orthodox, the process of sanctification or transformation is the means to the ultimate goal of union with God.

However, one should not assume that Orthodox theology places no emphasis at all on the beginning of Christian life. Schmemann describes the relation between faith and what he calls the cult (that is, the liturgical and sacramental life of the Church):

> A New Aeon is entering into the world as a result of this fact [the fact that Christ is preached], is being revealed in the world; faith is what brings man into the New Aeon. The cult is only the realization, the actualization of what the believer has already attained by faith, and its whole significance is the fact that it leads into the Church, the new people of God, created and brought into being by faith.[49]

Notice in this passage that despite the lack of legal terminology, Schmemann clearly indicates that the decisive event in Christian life comes at the beginning and takes place through faith. Faith makes one a citizen of the coming age; faith brings one into the Church. Similarly, Ware writes, "Through our faith in Christ, we possess here and now a living, personal relationship with God; and we know, not as a hypothesis but as a present fact of experience, that this relationship already contains within itself the seeds of eternity."[50] Here the language is of relationship, and the emphasis on the beginning of Christian life is unmistakable. Ware insists that we already have a personal relationship with God, and any Western Christian should be able to agree with what he writes. One clearly does not have to adopt a juridical approach to Christianity in order to emphasize adequately the changes that take place in a believer at the beginning of faith.

Schmemann's and Ware's comments show that Orthodox theology at its best does pay attention to the beginning of faith, and even though its spirituality is forward-looking, Orthodoxy does base spirituality on the change that God has already made in a believer's life. Once again, the difference between Eastern and Western visions of Christian life is a difference of emphasis, not an absolute contradiction. Nevertheless, on this issue, probably more than on any other, a difference of emphasis can easily turn into an absolute difference in the hands of less able theologians than Schmemann and Ware. The Western stress on the beginning of Christian life can easily lead one to think that as long as one has "received Christ" or "prayed the prayer" or been baptized, that person is saved, regardless of whether he or she continues in faith or not. In fact, this is a very common Orthodox caricature of Protestantism, and perhaps more truth resides in this caricature than we like to admit. On the other hand, the Orthodox sometimes easily forget that Christians seek to be holy because God has already made us his children; we do not seek sanctification in order to become acceptable before him. Once one loses sight of the change in a person's relationship to God when he or she begins to believe, one will be prone to turn Christian life into a dark existence, full of uncertainty about God's acceptance or even terror of God's judgment, but noticeably lacking in joy at what God has done in saving a person.

Again I repeat that the best expressions of Western and Eastern Christian visions do not fall into these traps, and because I am here trying to deal with Eastern Orthodox theology at its best, in its renaissance expression, I now simply note the differences in emphasis. I return to these differences when evaluating the relation between Eastern and Western theology in chapter 8 and as I look at the more popular expressions of Orthodoxy in part 3.

In this chapter we have seen several rather startling differences between Eastern and Western understandings of redemption and salvation, and some readers (especially Protestants) may be somewhat alarmed at the degree of emphasis given to human freedom, at the prominence of the Church in the doctrine of salvation, and above all at the lack of emphasis on God's declaring sinners righteous when they begin to believe. As disconcerting as these ideas may be to some of us, Orthodox soteriology is thoroughly consistent with the other aspects of Eastern thought discussed previously.

The two-act understanding of humanity's vocation lends itself naturally to a soteriology that focuses on the goal of union with God and sees salvation as a process, not a state. In contrast, the three-act Western view of salvation lends itself to an emphasis on the beginning of Christian life, to the change in a believer's condition and status before God. The soteriological emphasis on human striving is consistent with the overall emphasis on human freedom in Eastern thought, an emphasis that has also led Orthodox theology to describe humanity's original created condition as one of immaturity and opportunity, not the reality of union with God. The role of the Church in Orthodox salvation doctrine should not be surprising, given the prominence of the Church in the Eastern understanding of tradition as the source of its vision of Christian life. In fact, the roles of the Church in making people the body of Christ and in assisting people in gaining union with God are virtually one and the same. *Theosis* is not an individual matter; it involves the entire Church, and indeed the entire universe. No one aspires to become a partaker of the divine nature alone; people pursue transformation as the community of saints.

This last idea of the community of saints is crucial to Orthodox salvation doctrine, and one could easily argue that my presentation of the means of *theosis* has been notably incomplete, since I have thus far written so little about that role of the saints in salvation. As we shall see in the next chapter, the divergences between Orthodoxy and the bulk of Western Protestantism become most prominent here.

Chapter 7

Salvation and the Communion of Saints

To Western Christians, perhaps the most obvious aspects of Eastern Orthodoxy are its attention to the saints and its use of icons in worship, which are the subjects of this chapter. These aspects of Orthodox life are likely to stand out to both Roman Catholic and Protestant observers, for very different reasons. The typical Protestant reaction to Orthodox (or for that matter, Roman Catholic) veneration of the saints is that it is tantamount to blasphemy because it denies the uniqueness of Christ as the one mediator between God and humanity (see 1 Tim. 2:5) and offers worship to others besides the Trinity. This criticism stems from the Protestant perception that Orthodox (and Roman Catholic) Christians believe God is too remote and aloof from them to be accessible and that the saints fill the gap between people and God. This reaction is frequently so strong that it completely colors Protestants' understandings of the issues related to veneration of the saints. In contrast, Roman Catholics have no aversion to the idea of venerating saints but nevertheless find that the saints do not function in the same way in Orthodoxy as in their own practice, and they will find Orthodox veneration of saints to be puzzling. In this chapter, I first outline the Orthodox response to Protestant criticism and then attempt to explain the Eastern understanding of the way Mary and the saints contribute to people's achievement of our divine calling.

The Saints as Intercessors

The Orthodox answer Protestant criticism of their attention to the saints in two primary ways. First, the Orthodox claim that the Protestant aversion to veneration of saints is largely the result of an individualistic outlook. In the Eastern corporate understanding of reality, veneration of saints is not a threat to the unique place of Christ but actually affirms Christ. The saints are saints precisely because of their relationship to Christ, and paying honor to them constitutes giving honor to Christ and to the fullness of his Church. Thus Ugolnik can write, "The Russian sees the saint, just as the Russian sees identity itself, as a function of constant and reflective inter-relationship with a Triune God."[1] Just as God is not "individualistic" but is a fellowship of three eternal persons, so also all of life reflects communion between persons. Honoring saints who are a part of this communion does not, the Orthodox argue, dishonor God in any way at all. Moreover, Bulgakov declares that people who reject the veneration of saints traverse the road to salvation alone, without knowing communion with others.[2] Honoring the saints is a way of gaining encouragement as we follow their footprints along the path to deification; we do not walk where no one has ever trod before.

The second major way the Orthodox answer Protestant objections is by insisting that the saints are not mediators between people and God. Instead, they are intercessors who pray for believers on earth. As early as the end of the fourth century, Eastern theologians such as the three Cappadocians and John Chrysostom argued that departed saints continued to pray for people just as believers on earth prayed for each other.[3] Consequently, when Christians invoke the aid of departed saints, this act is no different from asking other living believers to pray for them.[4] In fact, Schmemann argues that asking for the intercession of departed Christians was a common practice from the earliest days of the Church. Early Christians (he asserts) believed that death did not destroy the communion of the saints, because in Christ no one was actually dead; all were alive.[5] This historical argument may represent a leap of logic: just because the earliest Christians believed in the communion of living and dead believers does not necessarily mean that they believed one should pray to departed saints. Nevertheless, this understanding of the saints as intercessors preserves the uniqueness of the Trinity as the sole focus of worship and the exclusive place of Jesus Christ as the one mediator between God and people.

These responses to Protestant criticism show that Orthodox writers are aware of how veneration of saints appears to some other Christians. Moreover, this practice clearly does not (at least in its theologically developed form) constitute worship of others besides God or an attempt to introduce mediators between humanity and a distant Father. On the contrary, Orthodox attention to the saints points to the unity between Christ and his people and (at least in theory) stresses the nearness of God to this world. Thus, the initial Protestant reaction to veneration of saints is based on an incomplete understanding of the practice. In order to make a more accurate assessment, let us consider the way veneration of the saints is related to other aspects of the Orthodox vision.

Saints and the Process of *Theosis*

In Orthodox thought, the attention given to the saints is a result of their understanding of *theosis,* because the saints are those people who Eastern Christians believe have most fully achieved union with God. The saints are often grouped into six major categories, in order of importance. Foremost are the apostles, who were the first to spread the good news of Christ. Second are the prophets, who predicted the coming of Christ. Third are the martyrs, who gave their lives for the confession of Christ as Savior. Fourth are the fathers of the Church, who excelled in explaining and defending the Christian faith. Fifth are the monastics, who dedicated their lives to spiritual exercise, so as to reach perfection in Christ. The final group is the just, people who lived in the world and led exemplary lives as clergy or laity.[6] These different categories show that transformation can take different forms; the paths to union with God are not identical.

Zernov explains the relation between the saints and *theosis* by asserting that the saints are not mediators but guides: "All mankind is involved in the process of deification and the saints are those who, having advanced nearer to the ultimate goal, can uplift the rest."[7] The way the saints "uplift the rest" is through their example (to be discussed later in this chapter) and their prayers. Bulgakov writes that the saints "surround us in a cloud of prayer, a cloud of the glory of God."[8] Because the saints are the most fully united with God, the Orthodox believe that their prayers are especially helpful in enabling people to make progress toward such union. Therefore, praying to saints in order to ask them to pray for oneself is believed to be one of the major ways a person advances along the road of *theosis*.

Florovsky asserts that in addition to enabling people to gain help and intercession, prayer to the saints deepens the believers' consciousness of the Church's unity.[9] Veneration of the saints and praying to them thus reflect the Orthodox belief that all Christians are advancing together toward deification: those who are most united with God are emblems of the Church's unity (*sobornost*) and act as intercessors, helping others attain the same state.

The Special Veneration of Mary

Of all the saints whom the Orthodox venerate, easily the most honored is Mary, the mother of Jesus. The Eastern attention to Mary is so strong that Bulgakov can assert,

> Love and veneration for the Virgin is the soul of Orthodox piety, its heart, that which warms and animates its entire body. A faith in Christ which does not include His virgin birth and the veneration of His Mother is another faith, another Christianity from that of the Orthodox Church.[10]

Similarly, Lossky writes that the veneration of Mary is one of the most widespread and precious aspects of Church tradition, despite the absence of special veneration accorded her in Scripture.[11] (Remember that to the Orthodox, Scripture is one of the forms for expressing tradition, and valid truth can come from other expressions as well.)

The Orthodox veneration of Mary shows itself clearly through the prominent position she holds in the liturgy. The liturgical prayers typically end with the formula, "Remembering our most holy, pure, blessed, and glorious Lady, the Theotokos and ever virgin Mary, with all the saints, let us commit ourselves and one another, and our whole life to Christ our God."[12] During the liturgy of the faithful, just after the priest asks God to transform the bread and wine into the body and blood of Christ, prayers are offered in memory of the saints. During these prayers, Mary is praised with the following adulation: "It is truly right to bless you, Theotokos, ever blessed, most pure, and Mother of our God. More honorable than the Cherubim, and beyond compare more glorious than the Seraphim, without corruption you gave birth to God the Word. We magnify you, the true Theotokos."[13] Finally, the prayers for forgiveness during the liturgy are linked to the intercession of Mary and the saints: "Wash away, Lord, by Your holy Blood, the sins of all those commemorated through the intercessions of the Theotokos and all Your saints."[14]

These passages from the liturgy include the three major titles by which the Orthodox honor Mary. The first of these titles is *Theotokos,* which literally means "bearer of God" but is rendered "Mother of God" in English, Russian, and other languages. This title was given to Mary at the Third Ecumenical Council in 431 as a way of safeguarding the true deity of Christ (explained more fully below). The second title is *Aeiparthenos,* which is translated "ever virgin." This title was given at the Fifth Ecumenical Council in 553. Florovsky explains that the term refers to purity of heart and the absence of erotic or selfish desires, as well as to perpetual physical virginity. To be the "handmaid of the Lord," he insists, is to be free from any fleshly preoccupations.[15] The third major title is *Panagia,* which means "all holy" (or "most holy," as it is rendered in the translation of the liturgy cited above). This title indicates that Mary was free from actual sin (although some Orthodox writers dispute this point), although the title does not imply that she was free from the inclination to sin. Traditional Roman Catholicism asserts that Mary, like Christ, was miraculously conceived, and thus she did not inherit the sin nature with which all other people are born. Bulgakov comments that even though the Orthodox deny this Roman Catholic dogma, they affirm that Mary had no personal sin at all.[16] Lossky agrees when he argues (during a discussion of Gregory Palamas's teaching on Mary) that she was not exempt from the inclination to sin, but she was kept from the taint of sin without any impairment of her freedom.[17]

In addition to her place in the daily liturgy, Mary also figures prominently in the yearly calendar of feasts. We have already seen that five of the twelve major feasts are dedicated to Mary. Of these feasts, two (the Annunciation and the Meeting of our Lord—Mary and Joseph's presentation of Jesus to Simeon and Anna in the temple) are based on biblical events. The Feasts of the Nativity of the Mother of God and of the Presentation of Mary in the Temple are based on a second-century pseudepigraphical work called the *Protoevangelion of James*. This book describes allegedly historical events related to Mary's birth and early years and asserts that her parents consecrated her to God while she was a young child. According to this book, she was given to serve in the temple at age three. Zacharias placed her in the Holy of Holies, where she was fed by an angel until the age of twelve. At that time, she was betrothed to Joseph.[18] The Feast of the Dormition (death) of Mary is based on a tradition that just before her death, Mary lived at John's house on Mount Zion. All of the apostles (except Thomas), as well as Paul, Dionysius, Herotheus, and Timothy, were allegedly carried miraculously from where they were preaching to this house to see her before she died. Christ descended from heaven in their presence to take her soul to himself, and three days later he raised her body from the dead.[19] Regardless of how many Orthodox people regard these stories as historical, Eastern Christendom insists that Mary's entire life, even from earliest childhood, was one of complete devotion to the Lord. This dedication is the object of the major feasts that Orthodoxy celebrates in Mary's honor.

Rationale for the Veneration of Mary

There are two general reasons for such strong devotion to Mary in Orthodoxy. The first is that she is the greatest of the saints and therefore deserves the most veneration, and the second concerns her unique position as the Bearer of God.

If the saints, in Orthodox thought, have advanced nearest to the goal of deification, Mary is the saint who has most completely achieved this goal. Lossky affirms that Mary is the fulfillment of humanity's vocation, the completion of the holiness to which the Church is called.[20] Elsewhere, he elaborates,

"Mary the mother of Jesus" (Acts 1, 14) made actual the unique relationship, which linked Her to Her Son, by manifesting it in Her personal sanctity. But this sanctity can be no other than the "total-sanctity", the plenitude of the grace conferred on the Church—the complement of the glorious humanity of Christ. But whilst the Church still awaits the advent of the world to come, the Mother of God has crossed the threshold of the eternal Kingdom; and, as the sole human person deified—token of the final deification of creatures—She presides, at Her Son's side, over the destinies of the world which yet unfold in time.[21]

In this passage, we see that the grace which leads the entire Church to holiness and *theosis* rested on Mary in a unique way. According to the Orthodox, she is the only person whose final deification does not need to wait for the return of Christ and the advent of the kingdom of God. Instead, she is fully transformed, fully united to Christ now.

The idea that Mary has already completed the process of deification and "crossed the threshold of the eternal Kingdom" is closely related to the Orthodox idea that she was bodily resurrected after her death and burial, rather than waiting for the general resurrection as other believers do. Lossky explains the link between this "dormition of the Mother of God" (which Roman Catholicism calls the "assumption of Mary") and her deification:

The glorification of the Mother is a direct result of the voluntary humiliation of the Son: the Son of God is incarnate of the Virgin Mary and is made "Son of Man", capable of dying, whilst Mary, becoming the Mother of God, receives the "glory which belongs to God" and is the first among human beings to participate in the final deification of the creature.[22]

Because Mary is in complete union with God, the Orthodox believe that she is the chief intercessor for all people as we attempt to achieve such union ourselves. Bulgakov writes that she prays for the whole human race, so the Orthodox pray to her, invoking her aid.[23] As a result, Mary represents the summation of the relationship between deification and veneration of the saints. Humanity's purpose is to partake of God's nature, and those who have done this most fully are able to help others progress along the road of *theosis*. Accordingly, the saint who is believed to be most completely deified is able to offer the most aid to those seeking union with God. Since Mary is allegedly "the first among human beings to participate in the final deification of the creature," as Lossky writes, she is supremely venerated and constantly invoked in prayer.

Veneration of Mary also derives from her unique role as *Theotokos*. In Orthodox theology, this expression is an attempt to safeguard the true deity of Christ. Florovsky explains that to refuse to call Mary *Theotokos* is to misinterpret the Son. The term *Theotokos* stresses that the child she bore was the only begotten Son of God, not simply a man.[24] Schmemann elaborates on the unique relationship between Mary and Jesus:

> If God had chosen a Man to be His Temple in the future, then the Virgin Mary was such a temple of God in a most particular and literal sense, "for what was born from Her is holy." Her body was a temple erected by the Old Testament itself, by all its sacredness, its expectation of salvation, its faithfulness to God, which made possible the union of God with Man, and in this sense She is the fruit of the Old Testament Temple, of that link with God which the Temple expressed. If this is so, then reflection reaches out to the relationship between this living temple and that other one whose significance, as the only center and source of salvation and union with God, Christ came to "fulfill" by His Incarnation.[25]

This passage makes clear that in Orthodoxy, just as Christ is the temple of God, so also Mary is the temple of Christ. The Old Testament temple's symbolism of the presence of God pointed to Christ, and in a sense, Mary was the fulfillment of Old Testament hope and piety, because she was the temple through whom God brought the supreme temple into the world. Thus, Mary stood in a unique position at the juncture of the Old and New Testaments. She was the greatest expression of the hopeful patience with which Old Testament saints waited for the Messiah, and she was the bearer of that Messiah who was God himself. This unique position leads the Orthodox to offer her unique honor.

In Orthodox thought, Mary's complete achievement of deification and her unique relationship to Christ are inseparably linked. Bulgakov asserts, "Mary is not merely the instrument, but the direct and positive *condition* of the Incarnation, its human aspect."[26] By this he means that in order for the incarnation to take place, it was necessary for Mary to be fully united to God. The Orthodox find expression of this union, this deification, in her words to the angel after the annunciation: "Here am I, the servant of the Lord; let it be with me according to your word" (Luke 1:38). Furthermore, the Orthodox regard their special veneration of Mary as the fulfillment of Mary's words to Elizabeth: "from now on all generations will call me blessed" (Luke 1:48).[27]

Orthodox veneration of the saints does not consist solely in praying to them. Strong emphasis is also placed on the way Christians can profit from the example and holiness of departed saints, and this emphasis is closely tied to the use of icons in worship. The remainder of this chapter addresses this issue. As with the veneration of saints, the Orthodox attention to icons provokes a strong reaction from many Protestants, which the Orthodox defend as follows.

Icons, Vision, and the Second Commandment

In the introduction to this book, I asserted that one of the prominent differences between the way Easterners and Westerners view the world is that Westerners are (or at least were) more text-oriented, whereas Easterners are more image-oriented. In chapter 3, we saw that the Orthodox believe tradition is expressed through visual as well as textual means.[28] Ugolnik offers a lucid explanation of this difference between Eastern and Western orientations by using American and Russian cultures (his own two cultural worlds) as illustrations. He writes,

> The American Protestant mind is culturally and literarily disposed to envision the Word in terms of a book, the "text" of creation. The Russian Orthodox mind, through the veil of its own culture, interprets the Word in the light of the images that reflect it. American Christians obey the Augustinian injunction "Take up and read!" Their Russian counterparts are apt to concentrate upon the insight that follows the imperative "Look up and see!"[29]

Here Ugolnik alludes to the famous passage from Augustine's *Confessions* (book 8, chap. 12), in which he describes his conversion. While in his garden searching in vain for some indication of God's forgiveness, Augustine heard a child saying the words (presumably as part of a game), "Take up and read." He immediately went inside, opened his Bible at random to Romans 13:14, and resolved to leave his immoral lifestyle and follow Christ. Ugolnik argues that this event profoundly shaped Western Christianity's subsequent approach to spirituality, giving it a text-based orientation that it would never lose. Furthermore, Ugolnik argues here that both the Western text-oriented approach and the Eastern image-oriented approach are cultural heritages, and the implication is that both of these ways of approaching Christian life are acceptable.

In response to this idea, Western Protestants often charge that Orthodoxy's visual approach to reality is an inheritance from the paganism of the Greco-Roman world, not an appropriate way to worship the true God of the Bible. Orthodox theologians meet this charge by pointing out that not everything in paganism is necessarily wrong. Ouspensky writes that the role of the Church in the world is to gather those elements of pagan culture that are true and to bring them together. He continues,

> This process of gathering is not the influence of the pagan world upon Christianity, but the influx into Christianity of those elements of the pagan world, which by their very nature had to flow into it; it is not a penetration of pagan customs into the Church, but their "churchification", not a "paganisation of Christian art", as is often thought, but the Christianisation of pagan art.[30]

Schmemann concurs, writing that "even natural religion—even paganism itself—is only a distortion of something by nature true and good."[31] These statements make a point that Westerners need to hear. Not all culture is neutral and can acceptably be imported into Christian life, but neither is any influence of a group's cultural surroundings on that group's practice of Christianity *de facto* wrong. In fact, we have seen throughout this book that one's cultural perspective necessarily influences the way one looks at Scripture and views Christian life. For Protestants to accuse the Orthodox of having allowed pagan influences to slip into their worship, while remaining unaware of the Western cultural inheritances that have helped to shape *our* Christianity, is naive and irresponsible. We need at least to take seriously the Orthodox contention that visual representations are an acceptable part (and, they would argue, even a necessary part) of Christian worship.

However, even if Protestants are willing to grant that a certain practice is not necessarily wrong simply because it is found in paganism, we are still quick to cite the Second Commandment (which prohibits making idols) and to argue that the Eastern emphasis on icons is essentially idolatry. In response to this criticism, the Orthodox state quite clearly that Christian icons are not the same thing as idols. Icons are not themselves gods that are to be worshiped, as pagan idols are. Ouspensky asserts, "If the icon were identified with the person it represents, it would be impossible for an even slightly developed religious conscience to venerate icons."[32] Instead, he declares, "Icons are intermediaries between the represented persons and the praying faithful, causing them to commune in grace."[33] In keeping with this distinction between the icon and the one whom it represents, Orthodox theology also distinguishes between worship and veneration or honor. As we saw in chapter 3, worship or *latreia* is due only to the Trinity, but veneration or *proskynesis* can be given to saints and to icons as well. Through these two distinctions, the Orthodox show that images are not actually gods and that venerating icons does not constitute worshiping them. The use of icons in worship is not (at least in its correct theological understanding) a violation of the Second Commandment.

In fact, the Orthodox find their justification for the creation and use of icons precisely in the Old Testament's prohibition of idols. Just before the second listing of the Ten Commandments, Moses gives a more complete form of the prohibition of idolatry, which the Second Commandment summarizes. He tells Israel:

> Since you saw no form when the LORD spoke to you at Horeb out of the fire, take care and watch yourselves closely, so that you do not act corruptly by making an idol for yourselves, in the form of any figure—the likeness of male or female, the likeness of any animal that is on the earth, the likeness

> of any winged bird that flies in the air, the likeness of anything that creeps
> on the ground, the likeness of any fish that is in the water under the earth.
> Deut. 4:15–18

Drawing on this passage, Ouspensky reasons that the prohibition against images was related to the fact that in the Old Testament, God revealed himself only by word; the people saw no form. According to Ouspensky, this prohibition implies that when God did reveal himself in visible form, no further injunction would be in place against making images of him.[34]

In addition to these arguments, the Orthodox assert that iconoclasts (people who oppose icons) divide too sharply between the material and spiritual realms. During the major controversy over icons in the eighth and ninth centuries, Eastern theologians argued that the iconoclasts were separating these two realms so completely that they were, in effect, denying the goodness of matter. Because deification includes the entire universe, material as well as spiritual, using material images in worship is not inappropriate.[35] In these ways, Orthodox scholars attempt to respond to the common objections that the use of icons is pagan and violates the Second Commandment. They argue that not only is a visually oriented approach to the world appropriate, but even more important, icons are celebrations of the fact that God himself has assumed visible form at the incarnation.

Icons as Emblems of the Incarnation

The fact that God has become visible as a man is the primary reason for the existence of icons in Orthodox life and worship. Ugolnik calls the icon "an emblem of the Incarnation,"[36] and Florovsky writes that the icon of Christ is a continual witness to the incarnation, the basis of faith. God has become visible, so having a true image of God is now possible.[37] In the same way, Ouspensky affirms, "The Church declares that the Christian image is an extension of the divine incarnation, that it is based on this incarnation and that, therefore, it is the very essence of Christianity, from which it is inseparable."[38] Therefore, in Orthodoxy, the incarnation does not simply make icons permissible. Rather, icons actually represent the incarnation; they bear witness to the truth that the Word has indeed become flesh. As a result, one can even say that they are "inseparable" from the incarnation and "the very essence of Christianity."

Ouspensky elaborates further on this idea by quoting from Theodore the Studite (752–826):

> "In so far as He proceeded from a Father Who could not be represented,"
> says St. Theodore the Studite, "Christ, not being representable, cannot have

an image made by art. In fact, what image could correspond to the Divinity, the representation of which is absolutely forbidden in divinely-inspired Scripture? But from the moment when Christ was born of a representable Mother, he clearly has a representation which corresponds with the image of His Mother. And if He had no image made by art, that would mean that He was only of the Father; but this contradicts His whole economy." Thus, once the Son of God became Man, it was necessary to represent Him as man. This thought is the main theme of all the fathers who defended the veneration of icons.[39]

This statement provides the rationale for the great importance Orthodoxy attaches to icons: they are the means by which the Eastern Church affirms the truth that Christ was genuinely and visibly human. His humanity can be (and, they argue, must be) represented visually.

Because of this link between the incarnation and icons, Orthodoxy views them as an indispensable element of Christian faith. Ouspensky explains,

> In the eyes of the Church the denial of the icon of Christ appears as a denial of the truth and immutability of the fact of His becoming man and therefore of the whole Divine dispensation. Defending the icon in the period of iconoclasm, the Church was not defending merely its educational role, and, still less, its aesthetic value; it was fighting for the very foundations of the Christian faith, the visible testimony of God become man, as the basis of our salvation.[40]

So strong is the link in the Eastern mind between icons and the Christian faith that the Orthodox Church celebrates the final resolution of the iconoclastic controversy (on March 11, 843, when an imperial edict was issued restoring icons to the churches) as "the triumph of Orthodoxy."

Icons and the Calling to Union with God

Such belief in icons as representations of the incarnation is understandable with respect to images of Christ, but we have seen in chapter 3 that Orthodox churches are also filled with images of Mary, John the Baptist, and other saints. The significance of these icons is found (once again) in relation to the concept of *theosis*. Zernov writes that icons are depictions of people restored to their proper image of God, "pledges of the coming victory of a redeemed creation over the fallen one."[41] Ouspensky explains more completely,

> If transfiguration is an illumination of the entire man, the enlightenment through prayer of his spiritual and material constitution by the uncreated light of Divine Grace, the manifestation of man as a living icon of God, then

the icon is an external expression of this transfiguration, the representation of a man filled with the grace of the Holy Spirit. *Thus the icon is not a representation of the Deity, but an indication of the participation of a given person in Divine life.* It is a testimony of the concrete, practical knowledge of the sanctification of the human body.[42]

In this passage, one should note that Ouspensky includes several ways of describing deification, all of which we have seen previously. Deification is a "transfiguration" brought about by "the uncreated light of Divine Grace." (Notice here the influence of Palamas.) It is the "participation of a given person in Divine life," and the icon indicates that participation. Icons employ a set artistic style to convey those qualities that characterize people who have become most completely united to God, people who are farthest along the path of *theosis*. Thus the Orthodox believe that icons are images of the saints, depictions that reveal something of the process by which these believers became saints.

As mentioned earlier in this chapter, veneration of the saints is not limited to asking for their prayers. Saints also serve as examples to Orthodox faithful on earth. Ouspensky's statement above shows that one way this example is made available is through icons. Images depict the saints (the people who Orthodoxy claims have become sharers in divine life) in order that by venerating the icons, worshipers might profit from the example of others who have more completely succeeded in becoming united with God. Ouspensky describes the link between the saints and those who are presently undergoing *theosis*:

> The icon is regarded as one of the ways by means of which it is possible and necessary to strive to achieve the task set before mankind, to achieve likeness to the prototype, to embody in life what was manifested and transmitted by God-Man. With this significance, icons are placed everywhere as the revelation of the future sanctification of the world, of its coming transfiguration, as the pattern of its realisation and, finally, as the promulgation of grace and the presence in the world of holy objects, which sanctify.[43]

Icons thus remind worshipers of the future time when the entire world will be transfigured, united with God through deification. This function enables them to assist Orthodox faithful who are in that process themselves. One should notice that icons thus contribute to the future orientation of the Orthodox Church: they are part of the vision of the eschatological kingdom, a vision that the Church possesses now and which it gives to each believer so that the kingdom will be realized through *theosis*.

In Orthodox thought, icons do not facilitate deification simply by reminding worshipers of the godliness of deified saints. Ouspensky makes clear that the power of icons is greater than this: "The nature of holiness is to sanctify that which surrounds it; the deification of man is communicated to his surroundings."[44] Later he asserts, "Since the grace attained by the saints during their lives continues to dwell in their image, these images are placed everywhere for the sanctification of the world by the grace which belongs to them."[45] The idea that icons and relics of the saints possess a special power that can be communicated to people who touch them is at least as old as the fourth century and has been articulated by church fathers such as Basil the Great and Cyril of Jerusalem.[46] In fact, one should remember here the biblical roots of the concept of *theosis*. Moses was not merely the one to whom revelation was given, but also the one through whom revelation was communicated to others, as his face shone with the glory of divine light. In the same way, saints and their icons are channels through which the divine grace given to them is communicated to others. This understanding is consistent with the belief (discussed in chapter 6) that grace is the energies of God (the divine light) that can be communicated to a person. Icons, like the sacraments, are vehicles by which the Orthodox believe the Holy Spirit gives grace to people and deifies them.

The use of icons in worship, then, is closely linked to the veneration of saints as the means by which worshipers seek progress in *theosis*. Because saints are those beings who have most fully achieved union with God, Orthodox faithful stand and bow before icons of saints in order to commune with "the departed believers" and to ask for their prayers, in the hope that the faithful will be successfully united to the saints and to God. Moreover, the icons themselves are thought to portray the deification that the saints attained, and by observing the icons, kissing them, prostrating themselves before them, and lighting candles in front of them, faithful Orthodox worshipers believe they may receive the grace that the saints possessed. This role of icons in facilitating transformation adds to their role in safeguarding the truth of the incarnation. From the standpoint of the Orthodox, icons are an absolutely crucial aspect of Christian life. As a result, they play a role in Eastern worship that is perhaps second only to the Eucharist in importance.

Of course, the role of the saints and icons in Orthodox life is the most obvious way in which Eastern spirituality differs from that of Western Christianity (especially Western Protestantism). In this chapter, we have seen that the Orthodox attention to saints and icons is closely related to other Eastern distinctives previously discussed. The emphasis on salvation as a process, a journey (and the two-act understanding of humanity's vocation which produces it), the visual approach to reality, the emphasis on the Church as a whole rather than on individuals, and other aspects of Eastern thought all contribute to the prominence of saints and icons in worship.

In addition to these distinctives, one other difference between Eastern and Western perspectives that is closely related to the role of saints and icons is what could be called the emphasis on "delight" versus the stress on "utility." Westerners whose thought is governed by practical, utilitarian concerns are likely to ask whether a certain practice is necessary for Christian life; if the practice is not necessary, Westerners will perhaps reject it. The Eastern view of the world, in contrast, seeks to celebrate reality rather than to use it. Orthodox theologians argue that the sheer variety in our world indicates that God's approach to reality is one of delight, not merely usefulness. (Schmemann is said to have asked frequently, "Why the hippopotamus?") In light of this emphasis, the Orthodox would argue that while we do need each other and the saints as we progress toward the kingdom, the importance of saints and icons is not simply found in the question of how we use them. They are also a celebration of the world and of the life God has given the Church, a reflection of the delight that leads God to give himself to his Church abundantly.[47]

Chapter 8

Orthodoxy and the West:
Seeing through Each Other's Eyes

*W*hen Western Christians attempt to evaluate Eastern theology, we are likely to proceed by holding Orthodoxy up to our own standards. We look for a clearly defined locus of authority, a legal way of looking at salvation, an emphasis on substitutionary atonement, a stress on the state of grace (as Roman Catholics would say) or justification (as Protestants would say). Of course, for the most part we fail to find these emphases in Orthodoxy. As a result, our tendency is to reject Eastern theology out of hand. However, from what we have seen throughout parts 1 and 2 of this book, quick judgments do not do justice to the Orthodox vision of Christian life. In fact, such quick judgments harm us as well, since they prevent us from truly looking at our own traditions and asking whether we have something to learn from the East.

In contrast, a fairer way to proceed would be to deal with three major questions related to salvation (or as the Orthodox might prefer to say, three questions related to humanity's vocation), namely, "Who?" "What?" and "How?" First, who is the God who calls us, who saves us? Second, what is the nature of salvation/vocation? What does it mean to be saved or to fulfill the human vocation? Third, how are we saved? What is the means of salvation or of achieving humanity's vocation? Because of our history, Protestants (and to some degree, Roman Catholics as well) are concerned largely with the third of these questions, "How?" One could easily argue, though, that the first two questions are even more fundamental to Christian doctrine and life than the third. Is it not even more crucial to know *whom* we trust than to know what constitutes faith alone and what constitutes a work? Is it not even more central *what* salvation actually is than how one obtains it? In asking these rhetorical questions, my point is not at all to denigrate the "How?" question, but rather to help us see that we cannot simply assume the answers to the "Who?" and "What?" questions; we need to consider these with as much attention as we attend to the question "How?" In assessing the relation between the Eastern

Orthodox and Western Christian visions in this chapter, I organize my comments around these three questions.

The "Who" of Salvation: The Trinity and Christology

In chapter 4 we saw that Eastern Trinitarian doctrine seeks to avoid turning God into a mere philosophical idea, and that the primary method of doing so is to focus on the persons of the godhead, not simply on the abstract notion of God's essence or nature. Furthermore, we saw that this focus on the persons of the Trinity leads Eastern Orthodoxy to describe the incarnation as God the Son's taking humanity into his own person, not as the union of divine and human natures to make a person. The Orthodox way of describing the Trinity and Christ's person actually seems to correspond more closely to what most Western Christians believe than our own explanations.

In the West, we place most of our emphasis on the nature or essence of God, and we define this nature in terms of attributes or characteristics. Many of these attributes, such as omniscience and omnipresence, can easily turn into mere philosophical ideas, and we lose our emphasis on the personal character of God when describing him in this way. Moreover, one common way of dealing with the Trinity is to use physical analogies (such as the presence of water in solid, liquid, and gaseous phases), which further depersonalize our portrayal of God. The result is that our depiction of God sometimes sounds like a philosophical idea of a perfect, yet distant and somewhat impersonal, supreme being. When we talk about God in this way, we are far removed from the God of the Bible, the God who personally weeps and mourns over his people, who is filled with joy or sadness, who suffers with us and for us. What we say theologically about God does not square as well as it might with the personal God whom we actually know and in whom we believe.

In contrast, the Eastern emphasis on the threeness of God places Orthodoxy in a better position to talk about the communion at the heart of Christian faith. God does not just desire a relationship with us; he himself is a relationship. To be God is not just to have certain attributes, but is to be three divine persons who eternally share perfect fellowship with each other. In fact, the Orthodox interpret John's assertion that God is love (1 John 4:8, 16) to mean that God is a loving communion of three persons. They insist that the statement does not simply mean that God loves us, but that the persons of the Trinity love one another within the being of God. The first person of the Trinity is not one member of an undifferentiated triad; he is a Father to his beloved Son, in whom he delights, whom he has loved for all eternity (see Matt. 3:17; John 15:9, 17:21–24). In fact, this love between the Father and the Son is the basis for God's loving us—for his creating us initially and especially for his redeeming us through the incarnation and work of Christ.

Of course, emphasizing the threeness of God creates problems as well, and the greatest is the issue of how three separate persons can be the same God. Here we would do well to fall back onto the Western idea that Father, Son, and Spirit are the same being because they share identical attributes; they have a single nature. But even as we take this stance, our focus should lie not on the abstract idea of God's nature itself, but on the fact that the one God consists of three persons who alike possess that nature and who share perfect communion with one another. By taking a cue from the East and concentrating more on this triune fellowship, Westerners will be better able to explain the basis for our own emphasis on the fellowship we have with God. God gives us fellowship with himself on the basis of the communion he has within himself. This statement does not necessarily mean that we need to abandon the assertion that the Holy Spirit proceeds from the Father and the Son or that we must adopt all aspects of the Orthodox understanding of the Trinity. Regardless of how we answer the question of the *filioque,* we in the West have much to learn from Orthodox Trinitarian teaching. If we pay more attention to the interrelation of the persons within the godhead, our own Trinitarian theology can match up more precisely with the substance of our faith.

When one turns to Christology, the difference between what Western theology normally says and what Western Christians actually believe is quite pronounced, and here again listening to the Orthodox can prove beneficial. As I asserted in chapter 4, the Western idea that divine and human natures were combined into the person of Christ stems from our emphasis on the divine nature as if it were an entity in itself. The Orthodox correctly insist that the divine nature does not exist as an entity in itself; it could not have been united to humanity in Mary's womb. Pushing the Western idea to its logical conclusion leads to an implication that Christ's deity is simply the embodiment of the abstract idea of "divinity" in the concrete, individual man, Jesus. This may well be what a few Western thinkers mean by the deity of Christ, and some pantheistic or New Age thinkers may even mean this when they argue that Christ represented and embodied the divine perfectly. But the vast majority of Western Christians certainly do not mean this when speaking of the deity of Christ. What we mean, of course, is that the second person of the Trinity came down from heaven, became a man, and lived among us as a man, but what we say when we argue that divine and human natures were combined to make the person of Christ does not reflect well what we actually believe.

Instead, as we have seen, the Orthodox insist that the one person of Christ is not a product of the incarnation; his single person is the eternal person of God the Son. The incarnation was not a process of making a person out of two impersonal natures. Through the incarnation, God the Son added humanity to who he already was. He added human attributes and human experience to what he already possessed as God. He took a full human nature (including a human body, mind, and emotions) into his divine person, without thereby ceasing to be God or changing from who he already was. This Eastern language may sound very strange to us, but careful consideration should reveal that it is actually what conservative Christians of all stripes—Protestant, Roman Catholic, and Orthodox—actually believe about Christ. We insist that the man who taught in Jerusalem was the same one who existed before Abraham (as Jesus says of himself in John 8:58). We believe that the Word who was with the Father in the beginning dwelt among us in human flesh (as John 1:14 affirms). We believe that the one who was from Jewish lineage in human terms is also "God blessed forever" (as Paul declares in Rom. 9:5). None of these bold truths would be possible if the person of Christ came into existence by the combining of two natures into a person.

By listening to Orthodox theologians, we can learn to say what both Westerners and Orthodox believe. The Word became flesh. The eternal Son of God added a real, complete human nature to his own person while remaining who he always was. Christ's humanity came into existence and was added to his eternal divine person in Mary's womb, but his person is and has always been the second person of the Trinity, which is what we mean when we say that Christ is God and man, and which in fact is what the Orthodox say.

Of course, it should not be surprising that Western Christians have much to learn from the Orthodox regarding the way we explain the Trinity and the person of Christ. The Eastern Church focused most of its theological attention on these issues from the third through eighth centuries, at which time the Western Church was more concerned with issues of ecclesiology and anthropology. Somewhat ironically, the philosophical language Western Christians often use to talk about God and Christ is at odds with the emphasis on personal fellowship that we claim is one of our major distinctives, but this dichotomy is frequently the case. Orthodoxy is at its most biblical and most profound when explaining the Trinity and the person of Christ, and Western Christians would do well to listen to the East on these issues.

The "Who" of Salvation:
Apophaticism and the Mysteriousness of God

Just as the Orthodox way of understanding the Trinity and the person of Christ seeks to ensure that theology will not reduce God to a philosophical idea, so is the purpose of the Eastern apophatic approach to theology. As we saw in chapter 4, the Orthodox insist that God's essence is unknowable and that union with God in his energies does not involve rational or philosophical knowledge.

Westerners can certainly affirm the intent of this apophatic theology. There is a mystery in the oneness and threeness of God that we cannot understand. The way God could become a man through the incarnation and the way the Son could be separated from the Father during the crucifixion are beyond our comprehension. Although we resolutely affirm God's presence with believers through the Holy Spirit, the nature of this presence certainly defies explanation. We should remind ourselves of these and other mysterious aspects of our own doctrine, lest we be too quick to criticize the Orthodox emphasis on apophatic theology. Moreover, we should recognize that the Eastern emphasis on negative theology does not constitute a denial of the scriptural assertions that we can know God and that he wants us to know him.[1] Personal knowledge of God and union with him are a crucial part of Orthodox faith. Finally, although the terminology of the essence/energies distinction is not directly found in Scripture[2] and is foreign to Western theology, we can agree with the idea behind it: God cannot be contained by our attempts to describe him. Exhaustive rational knowledge of God is certainly impossible for finite beings, and rational knowledge does not always lead one to personal knowledge of God. Many people know a great deal about God without having any personal faith in him whatsoever.

On the other hand, the sharp distinction that the Orthodox draw between the essence and energies of God could lead to a crisis of confidence in God's character. If we insist that we can know nothing of God's inner life (of God as he exists in his communion between Father, Son, and Spirit), then can we really be confident that God's outer life (his energy by which he makes himself known to us) is consistent with his inner life? To state the question differently, can we really be confident that the way God has revealed himself to us is the way he really is in himself? In intention, apophaticism seeks to enable us to bow before the unknowable, mysterious God, so as to be united to him. But in actuality, I fear that sometimes this approach to Christian life leads people to see God not merely as unknowable, but also as distant, aloof, and unpredictable. The constant refrain of the Orthodox liturgy is, "Lord have mercy." Is this a confident prayer, or does the repetition of the prayer indicate that some—perhaps many—people have no confidence of God's mercy? (This question is not rhetorical.) Simply because God has shown himself to be merciful in the past does not necessarily mean he will be merciful now, unless mercy is an aspect of his inner being of which we can be assured. How often does a respectful awe of the God one knows turn into an unhealthy fear of an unknown Being because of a lack of confidence in God's character?

Some Russian Protestants say that Orthodoxy lacks confidence in God's mercy and that the driving force behind Orthodox spirituality is fear of God's punishment. Of course, Russian Protestants are hardly the most objective assessors of Russian Orthodoxy, and one should not give these comments more credence than they deserve. At the same time, one can fairly say that the essence/energies distinction at least opens the door to a lack of confidence in God's character. The best of Orthodox theologians, I am certain, do not walk through that door, but it seems all too easy for others to do so. Rather than asserting that God is beyond rational knowledge altogether, I would greatly prefer to say that he is beyond exhaustive comprehension. Even as we affirm that knowledge about God is not our goal, we should also recognize that to some degree, knowledge about God gives us the confidence in his character on which our personal communion with him is based. We do not need to flee knowledge of God in order to be united to him. On the contrary, the more we seek to understand God, the more we appreciate the God with whom we share fellowship, and the more we realize how far beyond our comprehension he is. Understood in this way, a cataphatic approach to theology can lead to both a confidence in God's character and to a reverent awe of how far beyond us he is. We cannot know God fully, but what we can know of him is sufficient to give us assurance that he will always act mercifully and lovingly toward us as we seek to know him personally.

The "What" of Salvation: Legal Status, Communion, and Union

In the introduction to this study and at several points in parts 1 and 2, I have referred to the legal lens through which Western theology views Christian life. Nowhere is this legal framework more clearly present than in Western (especially Protestant) depictions of the "what" of salvation. We have seen that most Westerners describe sin largely in terms of guilt, understand the atonement as Christ's taking the punishment for our sins upon himself, and see salvation as a condition of God's acceptance, a state of being declared "not guilty" although we are still sinners. Our juridical approach and our emphasis on states or conditions are quite apparent in our descriptions of what salvation is. In contrast, we have seen that Eastern Orthodoxy views the human vocation (and thus postfall salvation as well) in terms of communion with God, sharing in divine life, mystical union, seeing the light of divine grace. This emphasis, of course, is closely related to the Orthodox stress on the threeness of God and the communion between the persons of the Trinity. The "what" and the "who" of salvation are consistent with each other in Orthodox thought.

I believe that Western Christians can learn from the Orthodox understanding of the nature of salvation in two ways. First, the Orthodox stress on personal communion with God can serve to balance an excessively juridical way of looking at salvation in the West. While revivalism (Roman Catholic as well as Protestant) does see salvation in personal, relational terms, the dominant theological motifs (and in Roman Catholic and Protestant scholasticism, almost the only motifs) are legal in character. Salvation is the state in which one possesses the righteousness of Christ. While certainly part of the biblical picture of salvation, this legal righteousness is far from the only aspect. God's primary purposes toward humanity are not legal, but relational and filial: he longs to adopt us into his family, to make us his children. The Orthodox stress on the personal aspect of salvation can help call Western Christians back from an exclusively juridical understanding.

Second, the Orthodox understanding of the "what" of salvation can serve as a reminder that soteriology must grow directly out of Trinitarian doctrine and Christology. In the early Church, the controversies about the Trinity and the person of Christ were soteriological; mistakes in the way God was described were correctly believed to jeopardize the possibility of salvation. The close link between the Orthodox stress on the communion within the godhead and the communion that people are called to achieve through *theosis* preserves this connection between theology proper and soteriology. If we remember this connection, we can avoid dissociating salvation from the person of Christ and turning it into merely a set of goods (heaven, living forever, being sinless, and so on) that Christ procures for us but which have no direct link to Christ himself. In contrast to this minimalist understanding, salvation is not merely something that comes to us because of Christ; salvation *is* Christ. What is heaven? To see Christ face to face. What is forgiveness of sins? To be united through the Holy Spirit to the one who took our sins upon himself in order to remove our guilt. Salvation is to have eternal fellowship with the Trinity, just as God has eternal communion within himself. By paying attention to Orthodoxy's personal understanding of God and of salvation, we can avoid the distortions to which Western salvation doctrine is sometimes prone.

However, if Western Christianity has a tendency to underinterpret the "what" of salvation by reducing it to a state of forgiveness procured for the believer by Christ, Orthodoxy sometimes tends to overinterpret salvation and thereby to lose the very emphasis on personal communion with God that should be Orthodoxy's strength. In chapter 4, we saw that apophatic mysticism grows out of people's search for immediacy and intimacy with God, rather than merely for knowledge about God. On this point, Western Christians can certainly agree with the Orthodox: knowledge about God, considered by itself, is not our goal. As Orthodox theologians describe the union with God that they seek, they attempt to guard against a pantheistic interpretation of salvation/union as an impersonal absorption into God. Nevertheless, the Orthodox understanding of deification leans in this direction. As we have seen, Lossky asserts that in mystical union, one is no longer aware of the distinction between the subject (the theologian) and the object (God).[3] Such an assertion seems to imply that union with God, in Orthodoxy, is an absorption of the person into God's being in such a way that the believer's personality is lost. Even though Orthodoxy insists that we do not share in the essence of God, the idea of *theosis* can easily overstep its bounds and turn into an idea that we do not simply share in divine life, but actually become a part of God in some sense.

Such an absorptionist, impersonal idea of deification is not what Orthodoxy intends, and Eastern theologians take steps to avoid such an overinterpretation of salvation/union. However, speaking more of communion with God and less of union would be more biblical and also more consistent with the best of Orthodoxy's Trinitarian and christological thought. What Orthodoxy at its best means by mystical union is essentially communion with God, and by concentrating on this idea, the Orthodox could possibly avoid some of the dangers inherent in the idea of deification. In fact, the Eastern Church's greatest christological thinker, fifth-century theologian Cyril of Alexandria, took great pains to make clear that God does not share his own being or essence with us in any way at all, but that he does share with us the communion he has between the persons of the Trinity. Deification of human beings means our adoption as children of God and our sharing in the intimate fellowship that the Father and Son have with each other. Deification does not mean an absorption into God in which the believer loses personal identity.[4]

An excessive emphasis on either legal categories or mystical union can lead to distortions in one's portrayal of the "what" of salvation. Both East and West are well aware of the dangers to which the other's soteriology is prone, but we need also to be aware of the pitfalls in our own approaches. While juridical motifs are certainly appropriate, and the idea of mystical union does have a place, we would both do well to place most of our emphasis on communion with God, and indeed, on human participation in the fellowship and love that the persons of the Trinity share with one another. Jesus says, "As the Father has loved me, so have I loved you; abide in my love" (John 15:9). Our remaining in *this* love, the very love between the Father and the Son, is the heart of Christian life.

The "What" of Salvation: Condition versus Process

At the end of chapter 5, I asserted that a pivotal distinction between Western Christianity and Orthodoxy is the difference between what I call two-act and three-act understandings of vocation/salvation. If we grant that salvation is primarily communion with God, does salvation/vocation consist mainly of a *restoration* to the *condition* of fellowship with God given to humanity at creation, or does it consist more of a *process* of *elevation* to a higher sphere of divine life than humanity has ever known before? Of course, whether one adopts more of a two-act or a three-act understanding of salvation depends largely on how one understands humanity's original created condition and task.

The Orthodox understanding of humanity's original calling is based on a distinction between the image and likeness of God. The Hebrew word for "image" (*tselem*) is used thirty-three times in the Old Testament and in most cases denotes images of wood and stone (the idols of pagan worship). The word for "likeness" (*d'muth*) is used twenty-three times, usually in reference to patterns or figures. In two places, both words are used in the same verse (Gen. 1:26 and 5:3), so these verses are the most important ones for this discussion. Also significant is the use of "image" in Genesis 1:27, as compared with the use of "likeness" in Genesis 5:1.

In Genesis 1:26, God declares his intention to "make humankind in our image, according to our likeness." Nothing in this statement would necessarily lead one to conclude that a distinction should be made between the two words. Hebrew poetry frequently employs repetition of an idea using slightly different words, and while this passage is not poetic, it may still exhibit a similar use of synonyms to express one idea. One could also argue that the absence of "likeness" in the following verse is a further indication that the words are synonyms and that repeating both words in successive verses to convey the same idea is not necessary. Genesis 5:3 reads, "When Adam had lived one hundred thirty years, he became the father of a son in his likeness, according to his image, and named him Seth." To sustain an idea that Adam's likeness is a characteristic that Seth acquired only later in life is difficult indeed. A more natural approach is to take the verse as asserting that Adam's image and likeness are synonyms that both refer to qualities Seth inherited from his father. These two verses do not seem to make a distinction between "image" and "likeness."

More significant for this issue is the use of the two words in Genesis 1:27 and 5:1. As we have seen, Genesis 1:27 reads, "So God created humankind in his image, in the image of God he created them; male and female he created them." Genesis 5 traces the lineage from Adam to Noah and begins with a restatement of human creation. Verses 1 and 2 read, "When God created humankind, he made them in the likeness of God. Male and female he created them, and he blessed them." The language here is virtually identical to that of Genesis 1:27, except that the word "likeness" is substituted for "image." From this exchange of the two words, they certainly appear to be synonyms; both refer to those divine qualities with which God endowed people at creation. Even if one still seeks to assert that "image" and "likeness" refer to different qualities, both clearly are attributes given at creation. One cannot argue convincingly that "likeness" refers to qualities that humanity must acquire after creation.

However, the fact that the distinction between the words "image" and "likeness" is not exegetically defensible does not necessarily mean that the idea behind this distinction is wrong. Seeing humankind as called to achieve union with God, to be elevated with God's help to a higher sphere is still possible. Is this idea biblical? If an Orthodox theologian were to use this idea to argue that humanity had no fellowship with God at creation—that people were created merely with the call to aspire to union with God—then I believe one would have to respond that such an idea is not biblical. Genesis 1 and 2 provide some indication that humanity did have fellowship with God from the moment of creation. In Genesis 1:28–30, God's first recorded action toward people is to bless them and to speak directly to them, giving them the injunction to fill and subdue the earth. From Genesis 2:15–16 and 2:19–20, one learns of God's interaction with Adam through placing him in the garden and giving him a commandment, as well as bringing the animals to him to be named. Furthermore, the description of God's walking in the garden in Genesis 3:8 appears to indicate that this action was his customary practice but that Adam and Eve had not previously hidden from him. This interaction appears to imply a relationship between God and humanity from the beginning, even before people would have had the opportunity to aspire to union with God.

Official Orthodox theology does not argue that there was no communion between God and humanity at creation. People were children of God, but they were immature children, called to mature and grow into complete union with God. Moreover, none of the biblical evidence would lead one to believe that the human condition before the fall was a static one precluding the possibility of further growth and development. A plausible suggestion that the Orthodox make is that such growth in fellowship and divine life was a goal for humanity after creation, even though this communion was given to people at creation.

Are we then to conclude that the Western emphasis on humanity's created condition as a state of fellowship with God and the Eastern emphasis on humanity's vocation as a process of aspiring to deeper communion are both acceptable aspects of the same truth? To a certain degree, perhaps, we can affirm this conclusion, but a significant problem can result from the Orthodox emphasis on the immaturity of humanity as originally created. This emphasis makes showing that God is in no way responsible for evil a more difficult task.

As quoted in chapter 5, Zizioulas argues that the fall should be understood as *"revealing and actualizing the limitations and potential dangers inherent in creaturehood, if creation is left to itself."*[5] Of course, Zizioulas and other Eastern theologians stress the fact that sin is the result of human freedom, and one should remember that Orthodoxy has a robust view of that freedom. In this passage, Zizioulas's idea is that humanity's sin consisted of seeking its own way and therefore realizing the dangers of being created, rather than seeking the way leading to God. God did not intend for humanity to be left to itself but meant for people to aspire to divine life. Clearly, the intent of this understanding is to place the responsibility for sin and evil squarely on humanity's shoulders. The Orthodox explanation, however, does not actually succeed in absolving God of responsibility for evil. If limitation and even sin are inherent in the fact that people were created immature, then it is hard to avoid the conclusion (or at least the suspicion) that God created a sinful universe. Certainly Orthodox theologians will not draw this conclusion themselves, but I believe their understanding of humanity as originally created is particularly vulnerable to this charge.

In contrast, one can better affirm the biblical truth that God is not in any way responsible for evil by insisting that people were created in mature fellowship with God. (This approach does not have to mean perfect fellowship, nor must it exclude the possibility of growth in their understanding of and appreciation for the relationship they had with God.) If we assert that God created people with the opportunity to move either toward him or away from him, we do not as completely absolve God from responsibility for sin as we do if we say that God created them already in such mature fellowship, with every reason to remain there and to foster such communion. In the former case, sin consisted (at least in part) of staying where humanity was, of actualizing what was already inherent in creation, rather than moving toward God. In the latter case, sin consisted of willfully leaving a relationship that God had established, leaving a condition that God had set up in such a way that humanity would have every reason to stay and no genuine reason to leave.

One may certainly conclude, therefore, that humankind's original condition was not a static one and that there was room for a process of growth in communion with God. At the same time, faithfulness to the biblical picture of creation, and especially to the scriptural depiction of God's character, requires one to argue that humanity was created already in fellowship with God and that the fall was a drastic departure from that fellowship, not a failure to achieve a more complete union with God. This scenario implies what I call a three-act understanding of salvation, in which a very sharp distinction exists between the created and fallen conditions, rather than the two-act scheme (with its lesser distinction between the created and fallen states) that characterizes Orthodox thought.

The "How" of Salvation: Looking Forward versus Looking Back

As described in both the introduction to this book and chapter 6, Orthodox spirituality is largely forward-looking, whereas most Western spirituality is primarily backward-looking. Westerners see Christian life as a response of gratitude for something God has already done in adopting us as his children, in making us acceptable in his sight because of Christ's righteousness. In contrast, the Orthodox view Christian life mainly as the means by which God is doing and will do something in our lives, the means by which the Holy Spirit will lead us to fuller communion with God and participation in divine life. For Western Protestants, the key event of Christian life comes at the beginning, and God's justification of the sinner by grace through faith is the guarantee of the final sanctification and glorification that will take place on Christ's return. For the Orthodox, the journey toward deification (toward what Protestants would call sanctification and glorification) is the key event. The Eastern emphasis on *theosis* as a cooperative effort involving both divine and human action makes Easterners much less prone than Westerners to assert that the end result is something of which one can be confident from the beginning.

These differences in emphasis lead to an obvious question with respect to the "how" of salvation: Are human beings saved primarily through an instantaneous action of God to restore us to fellowship with himself, or through a synergistic process by which we gain union with him? This question hinges on the issue of how one interprets the beginning of Christian faith—especially how one interprets the idea of what Protestants call justification. Is it actually biblical to see justification as the decisive event in Christian life, the event by which God changes a sinner's status before him and relationship to him? Or, as the Orthodox charge, is this idea merely a product of the Western legal and positional emphasis? Are the Orthodox correct in arguing that instead, justification is simply the negative side of salvation, the removal of obstacles that had previously prevented the process of *theosis* from taking place?

The most extended biblical treatment of justification comes in Romans 1–5. Paul emphasizes that no one is able to be justified in God's sight by means of his or her own works (1:18–3:20) and asserts that this justification comes as a free gift through the redemption that Christ has brought about (3:21–31). Using Abraham and David as examples, Paul demonstrates that justification comes solely by faith, not by works (Rom. 4). Then in Romans 5, Paul declares, "Therefore, since we are justified by faith, we have peace with God through our Lord Jesus Christ, through whom we have obtained access to this grace in which we stand" (vv. 1–2). Clearly, in these chapters Paul writes of justification as an accomplished fact for people who trust in Christ, and he indicates that justification is more than simply removing obstacles to spiritual growth. Justification brings about peace with God, transforming people who had been enemies of God into his friends. Paul explains this idea more fully in Romans 5:9–11:

> Much more surely then, now that we have been justified by his blood, will we be saved through him from the wrath of God. For if while we were enemies, we were reconciled to God through the death of his Son, much more surely, having been reconciled, will we be saved by his life. But more than that, we even boast in God through our Lord Jesus Christ, through whom we have now received reconciliation.

These assertions show that justification is not simply a legal transaction, not simply "an appeal to an extrinsic justice," as Florovsky charges.[6] Rather, justification is also personal. We were enemies of God but have been reconciled to him. We who trust in Christ are now God's friends, and our relationship with him is secure enough that Paul can exclaim with confidence that we shall be saved from wrath through Christ. Justification is being declared righteous, but it is more than this as well. It is also God's acceptance of sinners into fellowship with him as though we were righteous.

While not obviating the need for believers to pursue sanctification, to become actually holy and righteous, this acceptance does imply that communion with God does not depend on one's completion of that process of sanctification. Paul's confident assertions about God's acceptance of believers come before he raises the question (in Rom. 6:1) of how Christians should live as a result of their justification. They come before, not after, his discussion of his struggles with sin and the solution to those struggles, life in the Spirit (Rom. 7–8). They come before the extended ethical discussions in Romans 12–15. These latter sections of the letter constitute Paul's discussion of sanctification, and human effort plays an important role. The decisive change takes place at the beginning of Christian life, and sanctification flows from the fact that God has already accepted a person as his child. Paul uses the word "justification" to refer to this decisive change. In using this word, he does not mean merely that salvation or sanctification is now possible for humanity because Christ has removed the enslavement to corruption that prevented us from undergoing *theosis* or sanctification. Paul means that God has radically and fundamentally changed our personal relationship with him; he has made us his children.

Although Romans offers the most extended New Testament treatment of the relation between the beginning of faith and the process of sanctification, this idea is not limited to Paul. Other writers do not use the phrase "justification by faith" in the way Paul does, and in fact, one may certainly find biblical warrant for using the word "justification" in the sense of actual righteousness (as James does in chap. 2, for example). Even when the words are not the same, though, the idea that Christian life flows from a decisive change that God has already brought about in the believer's relationship to him is present in the other New Testament writings. Peter's exhortation to holy living (1 Pet. 1:13–25) follows his praise to God for the new birth into a living hope and the imperishable inheritance in heaven that believers already possess (1 Pet. 1:3–12, especially vv. 3–5). John marvels at the greatness of the love God has lavished on us, that we might be called children of God. Only after affirming that believers are now children of God does he declare that people who hope in God seek to be pure, as God is pure (1 John 3:1–3). Jesus' words to the repentant thief on the cross show that this thief was immediately accepted into God's presence, even though he did not live to undergo any significant degree of sanctification (Luke 23:39–43).

Western Protestants (and to some degree, all Western Christians) believe that the biblical picture of Christian life is that of a transformed existence flowing from what God has done in justifying people, in accepting us as his children on the basis of Christ's incarnation and work. Christian life is not primarily a means to an end, but is the ongoing result of a change that God has already made in one's status before God, in one's relationship with God, and in one's inner nature. As we begin to trust in Christ, God accepts us into fellowship with himself, and then he calls us to a life of service, devotion, and growth in holiness. He does not call us to such a life so that he may accept us. If this order of acceptance followed by calling is reversed, then the resulting picture of Christian life is flawed and dangerous.

Does this mean, then, that a forward-looking spirituality is wrong or inappropriate? Not necessarily, as long as one looks forward to the kingdom of God with a confidence born out of looking back to what God has already accomplished in and for Christians. If we recognize that we are already God's children, already accepted and loved by the Father, already in communion with God, then we can look ahead with joy to the day when that communion will be perfected and we will be spotless and without blemish. But if we believe that we must achieve such perfection before God will accept us, then even if we know that God wants us to follow the path to union, even if we are assured that he will accompany us and help us along the road, it is unlikely that we will be able to walk the path of *theosis* with confidence. Only when the decisive event in Christian life is something God has done, not something we have yet to do with God's help, can uncertainty turn to confidence and terror to joy. Christian spirituality must first look back in order to look forward.

At its best, Orthodoxy sees the beginning of faith as a decisive change that God brings about in the believer. Especially noteworthy is Ware's assertion, previously quoted, that faith in Christ gives believers a living, personal relationship with God, a relationship that already contains the seeds of eternity.[7] But the strong emphasis that Orthodoxy places on the process of *theosis,* its dislike of the legal word "justification," and its two-act view of vocation/ salvation make it easy for Orthodoxy to lose this necessary emphasis on the beginning of faith.

At the same time, Westerners (especially Western Protestants) need to remember that emphasis on the beginning of faith can lead to the misunderstanding that sanctification, growth in holiness, and other aspects of Christian life are unnecessary. The more strongly one emphasizes the beginning of faith, and the more closely one associates the presence of real faith with a "once-for-all" external sign (such as being baptized or responding to an evangelistic invitation), the more likely one is to give the impression that such a personal decision for Christ is the beginning and end of Christian life. People could hear us as saying, "Raise your hand today to accept Christ (or be baptized today), and you will be saved regardless of what you do subsequently, regardless of whether you continue to believe or to follow Christ." Obviously, we do not actually mean that. We care deeply about the progress of Christian life; our hope is certainly that everyone who makes any sort of decision for Christ will become a vibrant follower of the Lord. Sometimes, though, our strong emphasis on the beginning of faith prevents us from adequately emphasizing that true faith will lead to a genuinely changed life. In such cases, we should not be surprised that people have the impression that our message is a shallow one, a message of easy pseudo-forgiveness that does not require people to take up a cross or to seek a changed life in humility and reverence for God.

When one describes the "how" of salvation, therefore, two things are crucial: the order of events and the balance with which they are presented. Orthodoxy is prone to underemphasize God's acceptance of believers at the beginning of faith to such a degree that Orthodoxy is in danger of reversing the order: growth in *theosis* leads to God's acceptance, rather than flowing from it. A greater emphasis on what I call a three-act scheme of salvation, stressing the actuality of humanity's communion with God at creation and at the beginning of faith, can help avoid this danger. On the other hand, some expressions of Western thought so strongly emphasize the beginning of faith that they lose the balance that comes from stressing both God's acceptance and his call to holiness. In this case, we need to assert that any faith which does not lead to a lifetime of following Christ faithfully is not true faith in Christ.

In this chapter I have attempted not simply to critique those aspects of the Orthodox vision that differ from Western thought, but to explain the heart of Christian theology in terms of three fundamental questions related to salvation: "Who?" "What?" and "How?" In the process, we have seen several areas in which Western Christians would do well to listen to the Orthodox, other areas in which both Western and Orthodox emphases are appropriate but need to be balanced in order to avoid distortion, and still other areas in which Orthodox theology is prone to dangers that Western thought is better able to avoid.

If I may summarize the suggestions I have made in somewhat simplified form, the most consistent and biblical way of viewing the "who," "what," and "how" of salvation would be to hold to a strongly personal view of the Trinity, a view of the incarnation as God the Son's taking humanity into his own person, and a view of salvation in which the priority rests with God's action of creating people in communion with himself and then through redemption restoring people to that communion which we had lost (a three-act understanding of salvation). This view allows all of Christian life to revolve around the personal relationships within the Trinity and sees both creation and redemption largely in terms of human participation in that fellowship. Furthermore, this view links the priority of God the Son in Christ's person with the priority of God's action at the beginning of salvation.

If this view, which incorporates elements of Orthodox Trinitarian doctrine and Christology and elements of Western thought about the structure of salvation, is really the most biblical picture, then both Western and Eastern theology contain significant internal tensions or fault lines, although they lie in different places. Eastern theology properly preserves the priority of God the Son in Christ's person but inconsistently views salvation in terms that are too symmetrical (that is, in terms that give too much emphasis to the human action in salvation). Orthodoxy's idea of salvation largely as a cooperative process and its lack of emphasis on the beginning of faith (its two-act salvation scheme) consort ill with its brilliant Christology.[8] Conversely, Western Augustinian and Reformed theology properly retains the priority of divine action in initiating salvation by making the believer acceptable to God, while inconsistently viewing the incarnation too symmetrically (as a union of divine and human natures to make the person of Christ). In contrast to both of these views, a more biblical and more consistent approach would be to argue that God the Son took humanity into his own person so that he could accomplish for us something we could not do at all.

Throughout this chapter, I have sought to make clear that some Orthodox theologians are aware of the problems I have enumerated. In its best expressions, Orthodoxy does not blur the line between the Creator and creatures in its understanding of human participation in divine life, nor does Orthodoxy deny that human beings were in fellowship with God at creation. Orthodoxy does not deny that believers have communion with God and are acceptable in his sight from the beginning of faith. Given the fact that Orthodoxy at its best avoids these problems, one might wonder why they are presented as problems at all. The reason is that potential problems which are successfully avoided at the most nuanced levels of theological expression often resurface in dangerous ways in the more popular expressions of spirituality. In order to show how some of the emphases in Orthodox thought turn into dangerous distortions at the popular level, I now turn from the renaissance strand of Orthodoxy to its more traditional or popular expressions.

PART III   The Orthodox Vision
and Its Distortions

Chapter 9

Popular Orthodoxy

When people become Christians, their attitudes, beliefs, and values obviously do not change all at once, nor in fact do they ever completely change. Christian life is in part a process of developing the mind of Christ, of bringing one's convictions more and more into line with the truth of Scripture. What is true of individuals is also true of societies. When cultural groups or nations become Christian, they do not immediately abandon their pre-Christian ways of looking at the world. Rather, to some degree they see Christianity through the lenses of their own cultures. Throughout parts 1 and 2 of this work, I have sought to generalize about the different cultural lenses through which Easterners and Westerners approach Christian life. Sometimes extrabiblical influences help a group to see certain aspects of Christian truth more clearly. (We should remember that not all non-Christian beliefs and values are wrong.) We have seen that such extrabiblical influences are very much a part of our own Western approach to Scripture, and we should not assume that Orthodoxy is wrong simply because it sounds different from what we say.

At the same time, extrabiblical influences often do more than provide a helpful lens through which to view Scripture and Christian life. Frequently, they introduce significant distortions into the way that group views the Bible and understands its teaching. Christianity is a faith for all the world and therefore can be heard and understood in the midst of all the world's cultures, but it does not coincide completely with the mindset of any single culture. In every case, when people become Christians, they must adopt a new worldview, a new way of looking at themselves and their lives. Christianity demands change, and an adherence to the cultural thought patterns of one's people often constitutes a failure to grasp and to live by the radical newness of the gospel. In such cases, interpreting Christianity too much in light of one's culture constitutes incomplete conversion, the pouring of new wine into old wineskins.

Such incomplete conversion is obviously more common in the popular expressions of Christianity than in the mature, more carefully considered expressions. Our concern as Christians is also not with theology for its own sake, but primarily with the spiritual condition of men and women. Thus, we must ask not simply what a given form of Christianity intends in its best expressions, but also what typical practitioners of that faith believe and intend. Orthodoxy at its best, while problematic in some ways, has much to commend it as a profound expression of Christian truth, but how similar is the practice of typical Orthodox people, both in the East and West, to the Christianity of Lossky, Zizioulas, and Ware?

A number of Eastern theologians believe that a great gap exists between the mature and popular expressions of Orthodoxy. Alexander Schmemann writes that in its earliest days, Russian Orthodoxy displayed a ritualistic piety that was an outward veneer masking the paganism which lay just beneath the surface. He continues,

> Its [Christianity's] external elements—the divine service, the ritual—were easily accepted; it charmed the people and won their hearts; but there was the danger that they would not see, or even try to see, the meaning or *Logos* behind these externals, without which the Christian rite would in fact become pagan in becoming an end in itself. The soul of the people continued to feed upon the old natural religious experiences and images.[1]

Furthermore, Florovsky argues that this paganized form of Christianity later began to be regarded as the Orthodox norm. He explains that during the seventeenth and eighteenth centuries, Russian theological education began to be Westernized, resulting in a split between theology and faith. This tragic divorce led to a situation in which "the faith of the old nanny, or of the illiterate churchgoer, was considered as the model and most authentic type [of Christianity]." Florovsky insists that this sector of peasants has retained many uncertain and pagan beliefs.[2]

Although Schmemann and Florovsky have Russian Orthodoxy specifically in view when they make these assertions, the same sort of paganism beneath a Christian veneer is also present in popular Orthodoxy outside of Russia, in both East and West. This chapter considers three ways in which popular Orthodox practice sometimes deviates from the more mature vision of the faith considered in part 2 of this work.

Grace and Power in Popular Orthodoxy

Mature Orthodox thought understands grace as God's energies, which are communicated to people and which enable us to see the divine light, to become partakers of the divine nature. These energies are God's divine life outside of his essence, that is, the communion between the persons of the Trinity as that communion expresses itself in love toward the world. As a result, God's gift of grace to people is not simply the gift of power or assistance in Christian life, nor merely the gift of forgiveness, but rather the gift of God himself to people. By grace we participate in the communion between the Father, Son, and Spirit; we share in divine life. God shares this grace with Christians through the life of the Church, especially through the Eucharist and the icons. Icons (and relics as well) contain the grace that enabled the saints to be united to God, and through the icons Orthodox worshipers can be transformed.

However, in popular Orthodoxy, the idea of grace as God's energies often degenerates into the mere notion of spiritual power. Instead of using icons and relics as a way of participating in God's own life by communing with him and with other believers (saints), Orthodox people are often prone to see the physical objects as a means of gaining the power they need to live the Christian life. This idea often declines further into the notion that icons and relics have power in themselves and can thus help people gain what they need or want for life in this world. Schmemann argues that in the earliest centuries of the Church, the relics of martyrs were treated with veneration, but no evidence survives to indicate that believers regarded these relics as possessing any power in themselves or that they thought any supernatural result could be gained by touching them. During the fourth century, though, after the Christianization of the empire, the emphasis shifted. He explains, "The remains of the saint, and later even articles belonging to him or having once touched his body, came to be regarded as sacred objects having the effects of communicating their power to those who touched them."[3]

Similarly, Lossky writes that in Orthodoxy, there are many stories of the "apparition of an icon," that is, a miraculous event by which a previously unknown icon is discovered and becomes notable as a source of grace. As an example, Lossky mentions that in 1579 the Mother of God appeared several times in dreams to a young girl living in Kazan (the capital of Tatarstan in central Russia), instructing her to point out to Church leaders the place where an icon of the Mother of God was buried. When the Church leaders did not believe the girl, she and her mother dug up the icon themselves. The icon distinguished itself by various miracles and was carried into battle before the troops who liberated Moscow from the Poles in 1612 and who fought Napoleon in 1812. The Icon of the Mother of God of Kazan is one of the most famous, and believed to be one of the most powerful, icons in the world today.[4] In fact, popular Orthodoxy contains many stories of icons that have performed miracles such as weeping and sweating drops of blood. These icons are regarded as being especially powerful and are the frequent objects of religious pilgrimages.

Once the theological role of icons and relics as emblems of the incarnation and of God's communion with the world has been replaced with the idea that such material objects contain power in themselves, Orthodox people can easily lose sight of the distinction between venerating icons and worshiping God alone. Rather than being means to union with God, the icons can become the means by which people's attention is distracted from God to the physical objects themselves. These objects then become the focus of people's worship, as they seek the power for their lives that they believe the icons can bring. Russian historian George Fedotov asserts,

> In the ancient Russian Church the divine is felt to dwell not above, in heaven, but right there present in the shrine in all the holy objects that fill it, in icons, crosses, relics, in the chalice and the golden book of the Gospels, in all these things that are kissed and worshiped. The complete incarnation of the spiritual in the material is one of the essential tendencies of the Russian religious mind.[5]

He goes on to write that the Church thus becomes not a place of assembly for the celebration of the Eucharist, "but rather a treasure chest, a shrine for holy things which embody the presence of God." As a result, Fedotov contends, the religious attention that has been directed toward the Eucharist is focused on icons instead.[6]

This kind of attention to icons and relics as sources of divine power, and even as objects of worship, virtually contradicts the Orthodox vision of the Church and of Christian worship and life. The Eucharist is no longer the focal point of worship, the idea of the communion of saints has been lost, and the issue is merely one of power, not participation in God's life. This version of popular Orthodoxy well fits Schmemann's description of a pagan substance lurking below the surface of a Christian veneer, which is far from the vision of Christianity presented in part 2. A closely related question revolves around the role of the saints in popular Orthodoxy.

The Saints as Mediators in Popular Orthodoxy

The Orthodox attention to saints is intended to show the communion between all Christians (living and departed) and to guide Orthodox faithful toward union with God. The saints are saints because of their relationship to Christ, and the veneration of saints is thus a means of honoring Christ, not a detraction from worship of the Trinity alone. However, just as in the case of icons, so also with veneration of saints, some strands of popular Orthodoxy have long held a different emphasis than has mature Eastern theology.

Schmemann asserts that in the fourth century (at the same time that relics began to be seen as having power in themselves) the respect paid to the saints began to change in character. He writes,

> Originally the invocation of the departed was rooted in the faith in the "communion of saints"—prayers were addressed to any departed person and not especially to martyrs. In the new life of the Church the communion of saints in Christ (their prayers for one another and their bond of love) was not destroyed by death, since in Christ no one was dead, all were alive. But a very substantial change took place when this invocation of the departed was narrowed down and began to be addressed only to a particular category of the departed. From the fourth century onward there appeared in the Church first a practical and unnoticed but later a carefully worked out theological concept of the saints as special intercessors before God, as intermediaries between men and God.[7]

From this passage it is clear that at least for Schmemann, the critical issue is not whether departed believers are invoked in prayer, but whether a given class of departed believers is given special status. If no such special status is given (as he argues was the case in the earliest Church), then one may see prayer to the saints as a means of expressing the truth that in Christ all believers are alive, none are dead. But the elevation of martyrs (and later other saints) to a higher status made it virtually inevitable that these would be given greater honor, which in turn made it likely that they would be seen as mediators between God and humanity.

A notable example of how easily this change can happen comes when Bulgakov writes, "We are conscious, at one time, both of the immediate nearness and dearness of Christ and of the presence of our Lord and Judge. It is naturally necessary to hide ourselves in awe before the Judge of all, and here we take our refuge beneath the protection of the Virgin and the Saints."[8] This statement obviously does not represent official Orthodox doctrine regarding the saints. However, it is striking that Bulgakov, an important Russian theologian, could advocate a view that the saints are mediators who deflect God's wrath away from those who hide beneath them. If Bulgakov can adopt such a position, then many Orthodox laypeople will likely also fail to regard the saints simply as intercessors and will begin to view them as mediators. In fact, as Schmemann makes clear, this shift has occurred and still happens frequently among the many Orthodox who are faithful but who lack the theological sophistication to distinguish intercession from mediation or veneration from worship. In spite of the careful distinctions that theologically mature Orthodoxy makes, many people (including some priests) tend to see the saints as being much more accessible than God and therefore more able to offer help, power, and protection.

In fact, Fedotov charges that in the case of Russian Orthodoxy, Christian saints often inherited the mythological traditions of pagan deities worshiped in pre-Christian Russia. Elijah absorbed the traditions related to Perun, the god of thunder. St. Blasius (the protector of cattle) replaced Volos, the god of cattle. Fedotov argues that such absorption of beliefs about a pagan deity into the veneration of a Christian saint was especially pronounced in the case of Mary, who was seen in Russia in connection with the pagan goddess of birth, Rozhanitsy. Fedotov writes that Mary was believed to be the "Giver of life to all creatures, and in that dignity she rightly succeeded to the modest and nameless, somewhat shadowy Rozhanitsy."[9] Fedotov points out that Russian Christianity seemed to involve much more syncretism with paganism than did Byzantine Greek Orthodoxy, since the cult of Mary was and is much more developed in Russia than elsewhere.[10]

As in the case of attention to icons as objects containing power in themselves, so also in the view that the saints are mediators and even deities, we have moved very far from what Eastern theology at its best intends. Perhaps such distortions are not as widespread in popular Orthodoxy as Westerners might think, but these distortions are doubtless present among some people. There is a pronounced tendency to move from viewing saints and icons in terms of the community of believers (and thus seeing them in their connection to Christ) toward seeing them as separate objects of worship from Christ. If Schmemann is correct, this tendency has been present for most of Eastern Christendom's history, even though it flies directly in the face of the mature Orthodox vision.

Popular Attitudes Concerning the Church

As we have seen, distortions in the popular understanding of saints and icons have plagued Orthodoxy since at least the time of Constantine in the early fourth century, but the third significant difference between official and popular Orthodoxy has become prominent only much more recently. From the time of the split between the Eastern and Western Churches until the Reformation, Eastern Christendom had relatively little contact with the Western Church. The Orthodox renaissance that has produced the mature expression of Eastern theology was itself a product, in part, of increasing contact between Orthodox scholars and Western thought. To some degree, contact with the West helped to prod Orthodoxy into reevaluating its own tradition and recapturing the best of that tradition. Because of this reevaluation, mature Orthodox thought in its renaissance expression has generally been at least cordial (and sometimes favorable) toward Protestantism and Roman Catholicism.

However, the increasing contact between East and West has led many within popular Orthodoxy in the opposite direction, as they have adopted a generally triumphalistic attitude toward other branches of Christendom. Early in 1999, when Hilarion Alfeyev (external affairs officer for the Moscow Patriarchate of the Russian Orthodox Church) was giving a lecture at Cambridge, he was asked by one of the faculty members whether the Orthodox believe that non-Orthodox Christians can be saved. Alfeyev replied that the official position of the Russian Church is that salvation is present among Christians in other confessions, although the Orthodox do not try to delineate which aspects of the true Church are and are not present in those confessions. However, he said, in popular Russian Orthodoxy the idea is that the sacraments of other confessions are not valid, and therefore no one in those confessions can be saved.[11]

Alfeyev's explanation of the reason Orthodox people typically say that no members of other Christian confessions can be saved is significant. Salvation hinges on the sacraments, on one's relation to the sacramental organism that is the Church. While mature Orthodox theology sees the Church in direct connection to its head (Christ) and as the vehicle through which the Holy Spirit works to make people participants in divine life, popular Orthodoxy is much more prone to view the Church apart from Christ. In this case, the Church becomes the replacement for the centrality of Christ, and participation in the Church's sacraments and ceremonies replaces one's own commitment to Christ and longing for divine life. As an Orthodox theological student once put it while talking to me (in a quotation cited earlier in this book), "The difference between your faith and ours is that yours is a personal faith, but ours is an idea of the Church." In its best expressions, Orthodoxy does not at all deny the importance of personal faith; we have seen that it places more emphasis on personal communion than most of Western Christendom does. But in popular Orthodoxy, it is all too easy for the idea of the Church to replace a direct focus on God, on Christ. As in the case of saints and icons, what was intended to lead us to Christ tends to become a replacement for Christ in the popular Orthodox mind.

When this happens, people tend to think that being a member of the Orthodox Church is more significant than having a genuine desire to follow Christ. When reading popular Russian Orthodox propaganda against Protestantism, one has the impression that the writers are concerned as much that their audience not affiliate with any other group as they are that the people in question genuinely aspire to divine life through Orthodoxy. For example, Russian

Orthodox deacon Andrei Kouraev concludes his book *Does It Really Matter How We Believe?* with twelve rules for obtaining religious security. Some of these are reasonable enough, such as his reminder that "not everything which is from above is from God" and his advice that one ask a foreign Christian worker what group he or she represents.[12] Others are more revealing, such as his encouragement that people who are far from any sort of Christian faith decide not to associate with non-Orthodox groups. Kouraev writes, "Try to say in your heart, 'If there should come a time when I need to turn to God and to faith, I would want to pray as an Orthodox person, but I would not want to become a member of some sect.'"[13] Most striking is the advice which Kouraev offers after he concludes his twelve rules:

> If you want to know what attitude the Christian preacher who confronts you takes toward Orthodoxy, there is one very simple means of obliging him to make an honest acknowledgment of his confessional position. Ask him to cross himself. And ask him to kiss an icon of the Mother of God. If he refuses, it means that he represents one of the innumerable anti-Orthodox Protestant fellowships.[14]

Here the mention of crossing oneself and kissing an icon of Mary indicates that Kouraev's concern is not just with the foreigner's attitude toward the Orthodox form of spirituality, with the question of whether that person tolerates Orthodox worship forms or is hostile to them. Rather, his concern is that the foreigner be willing to take part in that form of spirituality. If one is not so willing, then Kouraev believes that person to be anti-Orthodox and sincerely hopes that a Russian, even a nonreligious Russian, will have nothing to do with such a person.

Kouraev's work makes clear that he is *not* content for Russians to retain only a nominal association with Orthodoxy, but he also believes that being a committed member of another Christian group is worse than being a nominal, but inactive, Orthodox affiliate. Such an attitude is widespread in Orthodoxy, and this attitude often degenerates into the view that if one is simply associated with Orthodoxy, however loosely, then one is "safe." Such an attitude toward the role of the Church, an attitude at once nominal and triumphalistic, is present in Orthodoxy in the West as well as in the East. Internet chat groups (some of whose participants have more zeal for Orthodoxy than they have knowledge about it) are commonly peppered with questions to others such as, "You seem to have a great deal of spiritual sensitivity. Why don't you join the true Church?" New converts to Orthodoxy from Protestantism or even from Roman Catholicism often cite the desire to join the one true Church as their major reason for changing confessions. The presence of such an attitude in the West indicates that this triumphalistic view of the Church in popular Orthodoxy does not arise simply in places where Orthodoxy is the majority faith. This attitude can arise whenever Orthodoxy's strong emphasis on the Church is dissociated from its proper link to Christ himself and to the path toward participation in divine life.

In light of such disturbing distortions of Eastern Christian teaching and life, one must ask how widespread such ideas are in popular Orthodoxy. As urgent as this question is, answering it in general terms is almost impossible. One needs to live and work among a particular group of Orthodox people in a given location in order to gain an understanding of how much (if any) their spirituality deviates from official teaching. One could guess that distortions are much more likely to be widespread in rural areas than in urban ones, because communication and easy access to Orthodox teaching in the cities might make for a better-educated laity. Similarly, one could guess that popular Orthodoxy in the West is less prone to these mistakes than Orthodoxy in the East. Where Orthodoxy is a relatively new phenomenon, it will more likely be heard in a form that is free of the pagan accretions from its earlier history which still cling to popular Orthodoxy in rural Russia and elsewhere. Similarly, outside the formerly Communist world, a more intellectually rigorous form of Orthodoxy is likely to flourish even among the laypeople, since in those places there has never been a time when the "faith of the old nanny" was the major form of Orthodoxy.

However prevalent such attitudes may be, the fact that these distortions of mature Orthodox teaching exist at all stands as a significant challenge to Eastern Christendom. Eastern Europe emerged from its years of Communist domination hungry for spiritual water for its parched soul, whereas the West became increasingly post-Christian during the twentieth century. If Orthodoxy is to nourish the Eastern soul and make a positive contribution to revival in the West, it needs to be honest about the misconceptions and distortions that have marred its teaching. It must be willing to work painstakingly to remind people that neither the Church nor spiritual power are ends in themselves, but rather they are means to the greater goal of union with God. Orthodoxy needs to care more for the spiritual state of the people of Russia, Greece, Romania, and others, than for the simple maintenance of its own supremacy to other confessions in those regions. Perhaps Orthodoxy needs to be less triumphalistic and more willing to value the contributions that other Christian confessions can make to the spiritual life of its people. Most of all, Orthodoxy must be dedicated to teaching the communion between God and humanity that lies at the heart of its vision.

While distortions in the popular Orthodox understanding of saints, icons, and the Church itself certainly constitute a challenge to Eastern Christendom, a Western Christian (especially a Protestant) might also ask whether these constitute an indictment of Orthodox theology. Does the fact that such distortions have arisen indicate the presence of a fundamental weakness within the Orthodox vision, even in its best expressions? More specifically, do these distortions not point to a dangerous overemphasis in Orthodoxy on God's mediated action, rather than his direct action? Protestants might be tempted to conclude that the very emphasis on the Church, sacraments, and other visible signs invites problems by predisposing people to concentrate on the signs themselves, rather than on the reality of participating in divine life. We might well ask whether Orthodoxy can even avoid the distortions discussed in this chapter, given what we would call its excessive emphasis on sacraments and saints.

When we raise such questions, however, we need to remember that the idea of a "direct" action of God is slippery. Faith comes by hearing, and hearing by the word of Christ (Rom. 10:17), but is it really any more a direct action of God when he works through proclamation in sermons or the personal witness of believers to bring people to Christ than when he works through the liturgy's proclamation of Christ? Furthermore, we need to recognize that Westerners, especially revivalistic Protestants, are also prone to place more emphasis on signs of faith than on the reality they signify. Revivalism as a movement understandably hungers for discernible indications that people are coming to faith in Christ, and we often place more emphasis on the external indications than we do on whether faith is actually present (or more important, whether that faith is actually directed toward Christ alone). We believe that people are saved by not trusting in themselves, their Church, ceremonies, works, and so on, but solely by trusting in Christ for forgiveness of sins, communion with God, and eternal life. Often, though, the means by which we encourage people to express such trust turn into actions by which people could take confidence in themselves. One might say, "I am saved because *I* have asked Christ into my heart, because *I* have prayed to receive Christ, because *I* have committed my life to Christ as an act of the will, or even because *I* have been baptized." Such signs as these certainly may indicate a genuine faith in Christ alone, but our focus on such signs can displace our attention from Christ himself to the actions themselves. In this case, we find that revivalism, like Orthodoxy, is guilty of unwittingly allowing something that was designed to point toward Christ to direct some people's attention away from Christ. Rejecting Orthodoxy out of hand because its forms can sometimes distract people from Christ is no more justified than their dismissing us because our forms may sometimes do the same thing.

Nevertheless, even if popular Orthodox distortions of official teaching do not constitute an indictment of Orthodoxy as a whole, they do pose important questions for official Orthodox leaders. How aware are Orthodox leaders of the distortions to which their emphasis on the Church, saints, and icons is prone? Do they naively assume that typical Orthodox people understand their teaching? Do they turn a blind eye toward the distortions taking place? Do they show a genuine concern for the souls of their people, a concern that exhibits itself in continual attempts to explain their teaching, to foster people's movement toward Christ through the Church? The Orthodox may claim that many of the problems come from the ignorance fostered by Communist domination and the hindrances to teaching that it imposed on the Church. While true enough, at least in Eastern Europe, this assertion cannot now be an excuse for a lack of vigilance. To some degree, whether we are willing to say that Orthodoxy in any given place is genuinely preaching the gospel will depend on whether we see that Orthodox leaders in that place are working to imbue people with the best and most biblical expression of their faith, to correct the disastrous distortions that often spring up in popular Orthodoxy. Surely Orthodox leaders themselves will grant that popular distortions of their faith are a challenge. Whether we Westerners will also see such distortions as an indictment will depend on what we see the Orthodox leadership doing to correct them.

Chapter 10

Orthodoxy and Nationalism

*R*eligious nationalism is essentially a confusion of people's religious sensibilities with their nationalistic interests, and it manifests itself in the belief that a particular nation or ethnic group, as a whole, is closer to God than other nations (or, in extreme form, the belief that one's own nation alone is the beneficiary of God's favor). This belief frequently leads people to make ironclad distinctions between their own nation as "good" and others as "evil" and renders them unable to distinguish between religious and nationalistic concerns. Nationalism is certainly not a specifically Orthodox phenomenon, nor by any means an exclusively Eastern malaise. Rather, this outlook has been present just as strongly in the West (in both Protestant and Roman Catholic countries) in the last five hundred years as it has in the East. In fact, some observers argue that nationalism in the East is actually a reflection of nationalism in the West, an attempt on the part of Eastern nations to imitate their Western neighbors.[1]

Nationalism in Eastern Europe (usually in historically Orthodox lands) has been prominent in the last decade or so. Throughout the twentieth century, the Soviet regime sought to contain the various nationalisms within its empire, but by the late 1980s, these proved to be too volatile to keep bottled up. Throughout Eastern Europe and the Soviet Union, religious nationalism was closely tied to the movement of the nations and republics for independence, as religious and political rhetoric were combined in the momentum leading to revolution. Of course, the ongoing conflict in the Balkans has been tinged with an overtly religious nationalism. From an outsider's point of view, Serbs, Croats, and Bosnian Muslims are all of one race (they speak the same language), and yet their different religious histories as Orthodox, Roman Catholics, and Muslims have determined their own senses of national heritage. The resurgence of openness to religion in Eastern Europe in the last decade of the century has had a strongly nationalistic flavor to it. Both Orthodoxy and Roman Catholicism have been tied to the national identity of the newly free nations that emerged from the Eastern bloc. In spite of the national and religious enthusiasm of these peoples, however, the link between Orthodoxy and nationalism represents a significant distortion of Eastern theology.

The Rise of Nationalism

In general, one may say that a society is ripe for the rise of nationalism whenever it has both a strong national identity (usually with a fair degree of ethnic uniformity among its people) and a fairly uniform religious makeup. What often holds nationalism in check is a strong supranational identity, usually the result of belonging to a more universal empire. During the Western Middle Ages and the Byzantine period in the East, nationalism was (to some degree) held in check by the larger political and social units. Eastern Christians saw themselves as being a part of the Byzantine Empire (sometimes called the Byzantine Commonwealth), an entity that was Orthodox by allegiance and that included people of several different national identities. In the same way, the so-called Holy Roman Empire in the West held the allegiance of people from many nations. As these empires began to break down in the late Middle Ages, people's allegiance began to shift more toward the newly emerging nations, paving the way for the rise of religious nationalism.

In the West, that nationalism was closely tied to the age of exploration, conquest, and colonialism from the late fifteenth century through the middle of the twentieth century. Roman Catholic nations (most notably Spain and Portugal) and newly Protestant nations (the Netherlands, England, and later the United States) sought to expand their power worldwide, and part of what fueled this quest for expansion was the religious desire to see Christianity of a particular stripe (Anglican, Dutch Reformed, Spanish Roman Catholic, and so on) become triumphant. This religious nationalism was part of the driving force behind the building of the Portuguese and Spanish empires in the sixteenth century, behind British colonialism in the nineteenth and early twentieth centuries, and behind America's sense of "Manifest Destiny" in the nineteenth century.

In the East, the rise of nationalism as the Byzantine Empire unraveled followed a somewhat similar course, but in order to understand this Eastern nationalism, we need to take a brief look at the way Orthodoxy is structured. Unlike Roman Catholicism, which is organized into a hierarchy whose locus of power and authority is centralized, the Chalcedonian Orthodox Churches are organized into local bodies. We saw in chapter 2 that because of Orthodoxy's belief that the Eucharist is the celebration that makes believers into the

Church, its emphasis lies on the preservation of local eucharistic assemblies. Orthodoxy affirms a priority of honor among the different local groups, but not a priority of power or authority. (Of course, this approach is in keeping with Orthodoxy's lack of emphasis on juridical categories.)

The most honored sees are the four ancient patriarchates that were centers of Eastern Christianity in the early Church: Constantinople, Alexandria, Antioch, and Jerusalem. Just below these in priority are groups that are called "autocephalous" ("self-headed" or self-governing), followed by churches that are autonomous but have not yet received full autocephalous status. The final group includes ecclesiastical provinces in the Orthodox disperson (that is, regions not historically associated with Orthodoxy), each of which is under the jurisdiction of one of the autocephalous Churches.[2] Even though the autocephalous Churches are understood as local groups, eight of them (Russia, Romania, Serbia, Greece, Bulgaria, Georgia, Cyprus, and Albania) coincide closely with ethnic and national boundaries and include the majority of the people in the ethnic group. Within a given one of these autocephalous Churches (or even within a smaller group), the belief frequently arises that the nation or ethnic group stands in a special relationship to God. This organizational structure has historically made Orthodoxy somewhat more prone to the development of nationalism than Roman Catholicism, with its centralized structure, has been. In fact, part of what made the Reformation possible was the rise of a strong nationalistic sentiment in Germany in the late fifteenth century, which helped people to throw off the shackles of Latin language and submission to "foreign" Roman control. If the movement could arise in the West despite the centralization of the Roman Church, nationalism could certainly arise in the East (with its less centralized churches) as well.

In spite of the organization of Orthodoxy into groups that often coincide with national and ethnic boundaries, Eastern Christendom's emphasis on the wholeness and unity (*sobornost*) of the Church would seem to have precluded the rise of religious nationalism. Schmemann explains how such nationalism could arise within Orthodoxy. During the early period of Byzantium, he writes, the empire and the Church were closely allied. This alliance was not nationalistic, because the empire was seen as a universal one that incorporated many groups of people within the fold of Christian Hellenism. However, as the empire eroded during the Middle Ages (particularly after Charlemagne led the resurgence of the Western Holy Roman Empire in the early ninth century), the universal dimension of this alliance began to be lost (as mentioned at the beginning of this section). The idea thus changed into one of Greek nationalism and the desire to preserve the Greek nature of the Church, rather than the universal Church of the earlier period.[3]

At the same time, the other Eastern Churches that had begun as part of the Byzantine Empire (particularly Serbia, Bulgaria, and Russia) began to assert their independence from Constantinople and to understand their heritage as Slavic, rather than simply Byzantine Greek. (The fact that they had been encouraged from the beginning to use their own languages, rather than Greek, for worship and preaching contributed to this sense of nationalism.) The atmosphere created by the breakdown of the empire provided the spark for an increasingly nationalistic understanding of Orthodoxy. In this atmosphere, the idea began to arise in the East that each nation stands before God on its own.[4] After the fall of Constantinople to the Turks in 1453, nationalism began to flourish as a way of preserving the conquered people's identity in the face of the foreign (and hostile) ruling regime of the Turks.[5] Subsequently, nationalistic sentiment in various nations of the Christian East began to be exacerbated as those nations watched the growing power (and the growing nationalism) of the Western nations from the seventeenth through the nineteenth centuries.

Religious Nationalism and Official Orthodoxy

Religious nationalism is not a product of official Orthodox doctrine regarding the Church. Lossky asserts that in the face of the catholicity, the wholeness of the Church, the very notion of a national church is erroneous.[6] Meyendorff calls religious nationalism "that bane of modern Orthodoxy,"[7] and Schmemann is even more direct when he asserts that religious nationalism is essentially a heresy about the Church, since it views people as divided into "one's own" and "the aliens" and prevents catholicity.[8] One should remember that in Orthodoxy, the *sobornost* of the Church is centered around the celebration of the Eucharist and is viewed eschatologically. The Church is the gathered community of the faithful in a single place for the purpose of reflecting the future age when division and imperfection will be overcome, when all creation will be united to God. Because of this community, any national divisions (or, for that matter, any divisions at all) are inappropriate within the Church. In fact, the problem of nationalism becomes most obvious, and most directly opposed to official Orthodox theology, when separate ethnic Orthodox Churches (Russian, Greek, Romanian, and so on) are formed in the same city, as often happens in the West.

Zernov and Meyendorff both comment on the tragic results of nationalism within Orthodoxy. Zernov writes that in the last five hundred years the Church has been so closely associated with nationalism that people have confined

Orthodoxy to their own ethnic group and have become indifferent to the religious condition of the rest of the world.[9] Meyendorff asserts, "Instead of the Church making a legitimate use of cultural pluralism in order to make its message heard and better understood, the various nationalisms are making use of the Church in order to achieve their own goals."[10] These national commitments, he writes, "constitute real cover for *de facto* separatism. They inhibit the missionary spirit, and hide the universal nature of the Church."[11] Similarly, O'Callaghan points out: "It is clearly not enough to be Orthodox by birth or inheritance. The church cannot be limited to a function of one's ethnic heritage."[12] Many people and groups within popular Orthodoxy (and, for that matter, popular Roman Catholicism or Protestantism) are guilty of limiting the Church to a function of ethnicity.

The Fuel for Nationalism

In any given area, popular nationalistic sentiment is usually fueled by well-known legends that have a significant impact on the national or regional psyche. For example, while I was working in what was then Soviet Georgia, virtually everyone who knew I was a Christian told me the historically reliable account of the introduction of Christianity into the trans-Caucasus in the early 300s. With this account, however, I was also treated to numerous stories about the "facts" that the apostles Andrew and Simon the Zealot preached the gospel in Georgia during the first century, that the garment which Christ wore to the crucifixion (and for which the soldiers cast lots) later made its way to Georgia and was buried at Mtskheta (the site of the country's first monastery), and that the Virgin Mary was the spiritual protector of Georgia, granting that country a unique relationship to God.

Armenia, like Georgia, has its share of legends about the early history of Christianity in the region. According to one such legend, at the end of the third century Christ descended from heaven to appear to Gregory the Illuminator (the historical founder of Christianity in Armenia), in order to show him the place where the first church in Armenia should be built. The building was erected on the site allegedly shown to Gregory and was completed in 303. According to tradition, the apostles Thaddeus and Bartholomew brought Christianity to Armenia between A.D. 35 and 60, and one popular myth even asserts that Armenian was the language spoken by all the world's people before God confused human speech at the tower of Babel.

While working in Ukraine, I have come across similar legends. The most popular one contends that the apostle Andrew journeyed to Ukraine to bless the hills on which the city of Kiev would later be built. While there, Andrew erected a cross and predicted that a great Christian city would be built on that site. Today, St. Andrew's Cathedral stands on the site where the apostle allegedly placed the cross. A second legend (with perhaps more historical foundation than the first) holds that several of the delegates at the Council of Nicaea (in 325) had been proclaiming Christianity in southern Ukraine before they came to the council. Other legends assert that the patron saint of Kiev is none other than the archangel Michael and that St. Sophia's Cathedral (the oldest in Kiev) was actually built by God the Father at the request of the Virgin Mary shortly after the creation of the world.

Westerners working in other areas of Eastern Europe or the former Soviet Union will doubtless hear many similar legends, some of which (like the belief that Andrew preached in Georgia and traveled to Ukraine) may have historical substance behind them, and others that are obviously fanciful. Generally, such legends seek to trace the beginnings of Christianity in the region to the apostles themselves or to ascribe special importance to their land through events believed to have taken place there early in human history. The myths serve to imbue the popular consciousness in a given region with the belief that that nation is uniquely important to God, uniquely privileged in comparison with other nations. As a result, the myths can lead people to believe that everyone in that country is automatically a Christian, simply by virtue of belonging to the nation most favored by God. While I worked in Georgia, many people assured me that all Georgians were Christians, and one young woman went as far as to say, "Christianity is in their [the Georgians'] blood, and the Bible is in their genes. Even if someone never learns anything about Christ, he is still a Christian."

Russian Nationalism

Of all the nations in Eastern Europe and the former Soviet Union, the one that may have the strongest nationalistic sentiment and probably has the most unique reasons for it is Russia. Furthermore, Russian Orthodoxy comprises half of Eastern Christendom, claiming more than 70 million adherents. Russian nationalism is thus a major force throughout the Orthodox world.

A legend connected with the beginning of Orthodoxy in ancient Rus (the kingdom comprising what is today Ukraine and European Russia) is indicative of one of the major sources of national pride in Russia. After Prince Vladimir of Kiev converted to Christianity toward the end of the tenth century (he was baptized in 988), he allegedly sent emissaries to both Rome and

Constantinople to study the Western and Eastern forms of Christianity. According to the legend, the people sent to Constantinople were so enthralled by the beauty of the ritual conducted in the Cathedral of Holy Wisdom that they reported, "We knew not whether we were on earth or in heaven." Based on this report, the legend affirms, Vladimir chose Eastern Christianity over Western for himself and his people. However much historical truth may reside in this legend, it is indisputable that from the beginning, "The love of beauty has been one of the chief characteristics of Russian Christians."[13] The beauty of the spoken and sung Slavonic liturgy and the aesthetics of Russian Church architecture and especially Russian iconography are a major focal point for Russian national identity.

In addition, and probably more important, the Russian sense of national identity and destiny is furthered by the idea of Moscow as the third Rome. Because of the alliance between the Byzantine Empire and the Church, Easterners had long regarded the imperial capital (first Rome and then Constantinople) as the center and hub of Christianity. After the fall of Constantinople to the Turks in 1453, Eastern Christendom was left without a focal point. Meanwhile, the Mongol forces that had controlled Russia for more than two hundred years were gradually being forced back across the Urals and out of Europe, and Moscow itself (which by this time had replaced Kiev as the capital of Russia) was freed from Mongol control the same year the Turks captured Constantinople. As a result, Moscow was suddenly the only patriarchal city in Eastern Christendom that was not under the domination of a Muslim regime. (Alexandria, Antioch, and Jerusalem had long been under Muslim control, and now Constantinople had joined them.) As a result, many in Russia quickly adopted the view that the future of Eastern Christendom lay in the hands of Russia, and thus Moscow was the new center of Christianity.

The idea of Moscow as the center of Christianity is expressed most dramatically in a letter written in 1532 by a Russian monk named Philothey to Basil III, grand prince of Moscow. Philothey declares,

> The Church of the old Rome fell for its heresy; the gates of the second Rome, Constantinople, were hewn down by the axes of the infidel Turks, but the Church of Moscow, the new Rome, shines brighter than the sun over the whole universe. Thou art the ecumenical sovereign, thou shouldst hold the reins of government in awe of God; fear Him who has committed them to thee. Two Romes have fallen, but the third stands fast; a fourth there cannot be. Thy Christian Kingdom shall not be given to any other ruler.[14]

This letter reflects the popular Russian view that Moscow is not simply the center of the largest branch of Orthodoxy, but is the divinely ordained focal point for all of Christendom and thus can never fail to be the hub of Christianity.[15]

Such a sentiment understandably brings with it a sense of unique vocation and the idea that the Russian people stand in God's special favor. This attitude persisted in popular Orthodoxy even after the Communist takeover. Many Russians regarded the struggle between the Communists and the Russian Orthodox Church as the climactic battle between good and evil and thus as a further indication of the Russian Church's privileged position before God.

Religious nationalism constitutes a serious distortion of Orthodox faith and life. Like the popular understandings of the saints, icons, and the Church, religious nationalism draws people's attention away from Christ himself. Like the problems presented in the previous chapter, nationalism constitutes a great challenge to mature Orthodoxy. As a result, Westerners are prone to regard the prominent presence of nationalism within Orthodoxy as an indictment of Eastern Christian thought, a reason for rejecting Orthodoxy altogether. Before we are too quick to turn a problem into an indictment, however, we need to remember two things.

First, religious nationalism is not simply a distortion of Orthodox theology; it is a direct contradiction of it. The Orthodox insistence on the Church as the locus of grace can easily lead to the idea that grace is simply a power that the icons and sacraments transmit to people, as shown in the previous chapter. In those cases, one could argue that the seeds of the popular misunderstanding are present in the official theology. In the case of nationalism, no such seeds are latent in the mature expression of Orthodox theology. As Schmemann reminds us, nationalism is an ecclesiological heresy, a violation of the unity that lies at the heart of the Orthodox vision of the Church and Christian life.

Second, Orthodoxy is hardly the only form of Christianity that has produced (or at least failed to temper) nationalistic sentiment. Western Christianity is more closely intertwined with nationalism than we might want to admit. I have mentioned above that nationalism was, in part, what made the German Reformation possible, and we should never forget how closely religious and ethnic identity were linked in Hitler's regime. Religion and nationalism are painfully intertwined in the conflict in Northern Ireland, and I have known more than a few English people who have little interest in Christianity at all, but whose attitudes toward Roman Catholics betray the most blatant form of Anglican religious nationalism. Nationalism of a Protestant variety is especially common in the United States, where religion plays a large role in our national folklore. American Protestantism has produced such gems of nationalistic civil religion as *The Great American Hymnbook* and a myriad of sermons that mixed Cold War rhetoric with the interpretation of biblical prophecy. No one who has ever witnessed a Fourth of July service in an American church can be too confident that we have avoided considering ourselves to be a nation in a unique relationship with God. Of course, such sentiments are no more a part of Western theology at its best than they are of mature Orthodox theology. Still, the intertwining of the religious and the national is a danger to which all forms of Christianity in all countries are prone, and against which all need to guard appropriately.

As a result, we as Western Christians need to pay attention not simply to the fact that nationalism is present within Orthodoxy, but also to what Orthodox leaders are doing to correct the problem. Are Church leaders actually fostering nationalistic sentiment through unwarranted or inaccurate antiforeign rhetoric? Are they simply doing nothing and allowing people to think that their nation is uniquely in God's favor, regardless of whether people turn to Christ in faith or not? Are leaders allowing the Church to become a pawn in political power struggles within the country? Or are they seeking to speak biblically to the nation about its responsibilities before God and to individuals about their need to become followers of Christ, not simply participants in a reductionistic, flag-waving civil religion? The way Orthodoxy responds to the dragons in its midst will determine how we as Western Christians will ultimately assess Eastern theology. At the same time, we need to ask all of these questions not merely of Orthodox Christian leaders, but also of ourselves. Nationalism is a danger against which Christians of all stripes need to guard carefully.

Conclusion

Single Vision?

*I*n this book, we have seen much about Eastern Orthodox theology with which Western Christians can agree, and indeed, much from which we need to learn. The Eastern way of describing the Trinity as a fellowship of persons helps to avoid the pitfalls inherent in the typical Western philosophical approach. The Orthodox explanation of the incarnation as the Son's taking humanity into his own person expresses more clearly what most Western Christians believe than our own explanation does. The classic emphasis on the atonement as a victory over sin and death provides a valuable corrective to the exclusive emphasis on the atonement's juridical and substitutionary aspects, an overemphasis to which Westerners are often prone. When properly understood, the Eastern concept of *theosis* or transformation is an appropriate way of describing sanctification, as well as a reminder (much needed in some Western circles) that salvation results in a change of life, not merely a change of status before God.

Moreover, it should be clear that Orthodoxy is not simply an eclectic mixture of Christian and pagan elements, as some charge. Some aspects of popular Orthodoxy (such as the typical belief that icons possess spiritual power in themselves) contradict mature theology, but similar distortions certainly exist in popular Western Christianity as well. Far from being an inconsistent mixture of competing elements, Eastern theology in its mature form presents a remarkably unified vision of the Christian faith. This theology begins with a view of creation in which human beings were given the task of attaining union with God, a task at which they failed. From this starting point, Orthodoxy elaborates its understanding of the human vocation (and thus salvation), the Church, the sacraments, and worship in relation to the idea of *theosis*. The result is a vision that is systematic and internally coherent.

Nevertheless, on one of the central issues of Christianity, the nature and means of salvation, much Orthodox thought wanders from the message that

Western Christians (especially Protestants) claim to find in Scripture. Westerners believe that the Eastern view of salvation as a journey from this world to eternity fails to emphasize adequately that a person becomes acceptable to God and an adopted child at the inception of faith, rather than after a period of sanctification. Moreover, Orthodoxy insists that *theosis* occurs predominantly by means of the Church (especially through the sacraments, the prayers of the saints, and the veneration of icons), an emphasis that seems to overstep the role many Westerners believe Scripture assigns to the Church. In light of Orthodoxy's unbroken tradition from the heirs of the apostles down to the present, Westerners may be puzzled that Eastern Christendom could arrive at such an understanding of one of Scripture's most crucial teachings. Some Protestants, noting the relative infrequency with which Orthodox theologians refer directly to Scripture, might be tempted to argue that the Eastern doctrine of salvation is the result of a simple failure to attend to the biblical message. As inviting as this explanation may be, it is not accurate. The reading of Scripture plays a major role in the daily and yearly cycles of Eastern Church life. Furthermore, the Orthodox adhere to tradition because they are convinced that this tradition is the life of the Church, a life to which Christendom testifies through many complementary forms. Eastern theologians refer to the fathers as well as to Scripture because they believe that both the Bible and the writings of the early Church bear truthful witness to the common life of tradition. They listen to the fathers because the fathers listened to Scripture.

It is much more likely that the differences between the Western and Eastern Christian visions derive from the varying perspectives that the Western and Eastern minds bring to Scripture. Throughout this work, I have attempted to expose such differences and to explain the way they influence our varying understandings of Christian faith. Of course, to speak of "Western" and "Eastern" mindsets or ways of viewing reality is an oversimplification, since myriads of variations exist from place to place in either East or West. The Russian view of the world is not the same as the Georgian, nor is the German mindset the same as the English. Nevertheless, the general ways of viewing reality inherited from the Greek and Latin minds have persisted within Christendom, even as smaller subdivisions have arisen as well. Americans are certainly more individualistic in outlook than Scots are, but both generally reflect the character of the Latin mind and its emphasis on the individual to some degree. Similarly, Russians may have a more finely developed aesthetic sense than Romanians, but both reflect the Greek love of beauty and a visual approach to the world. As a result, my simplified way of describing cultural influences is certainly not as precise as one might like, yet it is accurate in a general way. To a large degree, Eastern Christians view the faith through the lens of a common cultural inheritance, which differs substantially from the Western inheritance. This raises the question of how we are to evaluate these different cultural lenses. What are we to make of the double vision that has led the Christian Church into two distinctive ways of viewing its faith?

Is Culture Neutral?

A natural way of evaluating this double vision is to assert that both Eastern and Western mindsets are culturally appropriate in their own contexts and that the different theological emphases which they produce are complementary. The argument is frequently made that the allegedly distorted emphases of Orthodoxy are not actually distortions at all. They simply appear as distortions to people who view Scripture from a Western perspective. One could argue that the Bible emphasizes justification no more strongly than it emphasizes deification/transformation and that the emphasis which Westerners and Easterners place on these ideas has to do simply with their different cultural understandings of reality. If this argument is true, one could view both Eastern and Western theology as completely appropriate expressions of biblical truth in their own contexts. In that case, the gospel should be expressed in terms of justification in a Western setting, and in terms of partaking of divine life in an Eastern setting, which would obviate the need to try to compare the perspectives and choose between the various ideas. To use current theological terminology, each way of expressing salvation is contextualized and is acceptable in its context.

Many people who study the way Christianity is expressed in various cultural settings insist that no single vision of Christian life should be promoted. Instead, many visions, each growing out of and applying to a given cultural context, should be recognized. People argue that the different visions of Christian life that have arisen in Orthodoxy and Western Christendom are simply two large-scale examples of what should also be taking place on a smaller scale in all of the world's cultures. To a certain degree, of course, this outlook is true. Virtually all Christians would agree with the importance of translating the Bible into all of the world's languages and proclaiming Christ to all people in ways they can understand. These tasks of translation and explanation involve recognizing the mindset and thought patterns of a given culture and speaking to that mindset. For Christianity to have a somewhat different look and feel in different cultures is perfectly legitimate and necessary. Just as we do not require identical worship styles throughout the world, so also we should not require the expression of Christian truth to take identical forms everywhere.

When one admits, however, that Christianity should take somewhat different forms in different cultures, this admission does not mean that culture itself is necessarily neutral. Christianity should not simply accommodate its message to different cultures in an uncritical way; it must also judge those cultures. As Christians we cannot simply assume that any culture is a biblically based culture, although we frequently make such a mistaken assumption about our own culture without realizing it. Instead, recognizing what our cultural inheritances are and submitting these inheritances to the judgment of Scripture is important. This task of evaluating the cultural perspectives that a group or nation brings to Scripture can almost never be successfully carried out in isolation. A lens is not something at which one looks; it is something through which one looks. As a result, we often fail to see that our cultural lenses are present at all, and we are often unable to identify our cultural perspectives specifically so as to evaluate them. We usually do not see our own lenses until we begin to look at Christian faith through other eyes. As a result, by now the reader probably realizes that this book's purpose has been not simply to help Western Christians to understand *Orthodoxy,* but also to help us see *ourselves* more clearly by borrowing the lenses with which the East views Christian life.

Our cultural perspectives (such as our legal approach to reality in the West) have helped us to understand some aspects of biblical truth very well, but these same perspectives have hindered us from seeing other parts of the whole. To make this claim is to say that Christian theology should not stop with contextualization; moving from double vision (or a myriad of visions) toward single vision is important. Emphasizing those aspects of biblical teaching that are most congenial to one's own culture and neglecting other aspects of scriptural truth is simply not enough. Christianity transforms lives and societies, partly by challenging and stretching our cultural assumptions. Only by continually evaluating whether these assumptions are actually consistent with the message and emphases of the Bible can we move beyond a purely culture-bound understanding of Scripture and approach its full message more closely. Furthermore, only through this kind of evaluation can we determine the degree to which a given culture is biblical, and thus, the degree to which that culture's expression of Christian teaching is appropriate. Only in this way can we move from double vision toward single vision, toward a more complete and accurate expression of Christian truth.

Therefore, when we look at the cultural lenses that East and West bring to Scripture and Christian life, we need first to resist our natural urge to claim that Orthodoxy is wrong simply because it does not wear our glasses. A nonlegal approach to reality is not wrong simply because we Westerners adopt a legal perspective. On the other hand, we should also resist the temptation to say that different cultural perspectives are necessarily acceptable. Culture is not neutral (at least not in all cases), and we cannot assume that all lenses for looking at Scripture are valid just because some group wears them.

Another Look at Eastern and Western Cultural Lenses

Some of the cultural perspectives discussed in this book seem to be genuinely complementary and to provide valuable correctives to each other. A legal view of Christianity certainly does capture part of what Scripture means by salvation but is inadequate and dangerous in isolation. A legal lens needs to be balanced with a personal and relational perspective. Similarly, an individual orientation highlights the responsibility of each person to turn to Christ himself or herself, but is sadly distorted without a corresponding stress on the corporate body of Christ. In these cases, East and West each need to heed the perspective of the other, to use the other's lenses to move past its own cultural understanding of Scripture toward a fuller expression of truth.

However, of the cultural perspectives discussed, the most haunting one to me is the difference between a text-based and an image-based approach to meaning. Ugolnik argues that the Western emphasis on wrestling meaning from a text and the Eastern search for meaning in the relation of images are both cultural inheritances, and his assumption is that they are equally valid ways of looking at the faith in their own contexts.[1] That these are cultural inheritances is indisputable, but whether they are neutral inheritances appears open to question. The world of ancient Israel was every bit as image-oriented as modern Russia, and in fact, one could argue that ancient Israel was far more image-oriented. (Russia is one of the world's most literate societies and perhaps the society that contains the most vociferous readers in the world.) Yet in that image-oriented world of the ancient Near East, God chose to speak not through images, not in the most seemingly appropriate way, but through a text, a word.

Of course, the Orthodox are quick to point out in response that the Old Testament was not the final or the highest revelation of God. God's supreme revelation was through the incarnation, through the visible image of the invisible God, which of course is true. But it is also true that the three passages in the New Testament referring to Christ as the image or representation of God all come in the context of discussions of preaching or speaking. In 2 Corinthians 4:4, Paul declares that unbelievers are blinded "to keep them from seeing the light of the gospel of the glory of Christ, who is the image of God." Here the strongly visual imagery of the passage is sandwiched between references to Paul's preaching ministry. The reason people should be able to understand is that Paul is stating the truth plainly (v. 2) and is preaching not himself, but Christ Jesus the Lord (v. 5). Similarly, when Paul calls Christ "the image of the invisible God" in Colossians 1:15 and then follows this assertion with a statement of Christ's work in creation and redemption, he concludes the section by writing that this is "the gospel that you *heard,* which has been proclaimed to every creature under heaven" (v. 23, my emphasis). Finally, when Hebrews 1:3 declares that the Son is "the reflection of God's glory and the exact imprint of God's very being," the overall point is that God has now spoken not just through prophets, but through his Son (vv. 1–2). The implication of these passages seems to be that the way we are to come into contact with Christ, the image of God, is primarily through preaching, through words, not through images.

Of course, I do not want to pretend that these passages can be interpreted only in this way, because one could argue that visual representations do proclaim and preach truth. Nor do I want to give the impression that quoting three passages will resolve the issue or to imply that we should reject visual means of proclaiming the gospel altogether. Nonetheless, the primary way God communicates, in both the Old and New Testaments, appears to be through word, through texts and proclamation. Of course, the content of the proclamation is a person, Jesus Christ, not simply words. But the medium of the proclamation seems to be primarily preaching and writing, rather than visual images. Why would God communicate this way? Would it not have been more appropriate in the ancient Near East to focus on the visual? Was God establishing a pattern that in all cultures, the central means of making the message of Christ known should be that of proclaiming the Word, not representing the Word visually? I do not ask these questions rhetorically. Instead, I offer them as an indication of the sort of reflection that Christians need to undertake if we seek not only to reflect our cultures in our presentations of Christian truth, but also to allow Scripture to judge and to determine our expressions of the gospel.

Toward a Single Vision of Christianity

We have seen that Eastern Orthodoxy raises many questions for Western Christians. Most readers of this book are probably concerned mainly with the question of how we are to evaluate Orthodoxy, what we are to make of the Orthodox family on our street or the Eastern Europeans with whom we come into contact. I pray that the pages of this book would provide some guidance as readers bring the unfamiliar Eastern vision into focus. Whether or not you come to the same conclusions as I do, you now have at your disposal a more accurate understanding of Orthodoxy from which to draw your conclusions. I pray also that this work would be useful to people who minister among ethnic Easterners who do not yet know Christ, that it will help you proclaim Christ to them in ways that will be most biblical, comprehensible, and compelling to the Eastern mind.

However, I have tried to make clear that Orthodoxy does not just pose ministry-related questions to us. Instead, the primary question that Orthodoxy brings to our attention is the more pressing one of what it means to be scriptural. Many Westerners (especially conservative Western Protestants) who have had little contact with Christians from other parts of the world are apt to assume that our terminology, our way of expressing truth, is *the* biblical form of Christianity, the only way one can faithfully proclaim Christ. (A dozen years ago this was certainly my assumption.) When we do not hear our emphases expressed in the same way we proclaim them, we are tempted to assume that we are not hearing genuine, scriptural Christianity. Contact with committed Christians from different cultures almost invariably leads us to realize that we always come to Scripture with some preconceived ideas of what it means. We always see the Bible through the lenses of our own culture, our own strand of Christianity.

To be fully biblical, then, requires that we not be content to view our faith through our own lenses. A fully biblical approach demands that we also look at the lenses themselves, that we make the cultural matrix through which we view the Bible a part of our investigation. To do this almost invariably requires that we look at Christianity through other eyes as well as through our own, but we must also judge the emphases and perspectives of all cultures, including our own (especially our own!) from the perspective of Scripture. We need not only to look at Scripture through eyes other than our own, but also to look at ourselves through the eyes of Scripture. This task cannot be fully accomplished in a year, or a lifetime, or a millennium. It is the unfinished task of Christians and of the entire Church to develop the mind of Christ, to move closer to a fully biblical expression of faith and practice. We have the truth when we have the Son, Jesus Christ. To learn to see more clearly and to express whom and what we have in the most appropriate and biblical way requires that we patiently and humbly allow Scripture to judge our own understandings of Scripture. As we do so, we will know and appreciate more fully whom we have, and thus we will become more and more who we already are in Christ.

Appendix A

Recommended Reading

Part 1: Some suggestions for people
with no prior experience reading Orthodox sources:

These books are listed in the order in which I recommend that a person read
them.

Ugolnik, Anthony. *The Illuminating Icon*. Grand Rapids, Mich.: Eerdmans, 1989.

> Anthony Ugolnik (born in 1944) is a second-generation Russian-American who has been a lifelong Russian Orthodox, but who fought for the United States in Vietnam and now teaches English literature at Franklin and Marshall College in Pennsylvania. As a result, he understands both East and West very well and is in an excellent position to explain them to each other. This book is extremely helpful in understanding the differing mindsets that Westerners and Easterners bring to Christian faith.

Ware, Kallistos. *The Orthodox Way*. Rev. edition. Crestwood, N.Y.: St. Vladimir's Seminary Press, 1995.

> Ware (born in 1934) is an Englishman who converted to Orthodoxy from Protestantism in 1958 and has since become a monk and bishop, as well as a lecturer at Oxford on Eastern theology and liturgy. In this very readable book, he offers a clear description of the journey from this world to the kingdom of God that constitutes the heart of Orthodox spirituality. Ware treats Orthodoxy in such a way that a typical Westerner can begin to understand it and to compare it to his or her own tradition.

The Divine Liturgy of Saint John Chrysostom. Brookline, Mass.: Holy Cross Orthodox Press, 1985.

> The liturgy is, of course, the expression of Orthodox tradition that has

the greatest influence on faithful Orthodox laypeople. This edition includes the Greek text and a modern English translation on parallel pages. In addition to the text of the liturgy itself, the book contains the order of worship for several special services, as well as the Scripture readings for particular days.

Ouspensky, Leonid, and Vladimir Lossky. *The Meaning of Icons*. Rev. edition. Trans. G. E. H. Palmer and E. Kadloubovsky. Crestwood, N.Y.: St. Vladimir's Seminary Press, 1982.

Ouspensky (1902–1987) and Lossky (1903–1958) were both members of the Parisian community that was the mainstay of twentieth-century Russian Orthodox thought after the Bolshevik Revolution forced most of the intelligentsia out of Russia. In this beautifully illustrated book, they offer a very readable defense of icons, as well as a theologically developed explanation of their significance in the life of the Orthodox Church. For a Western reader who has difficulty seeing icons as anything but idols, this book is a needed corrective, providing an excellent statement of the theologically mature Eastern approach to icons.

Meyendorff, John. *Catholicity and the Church*. Crestwood, N.Y.: St. Vladimir's Seminary Press, 1983.

Meyendorff (1926–1992) was also a part of the Parisian community and was educated at the theological institute of St. Sergius, a major center of Russian Orthodox thought and scholarship since its founding in 1925. After he immigrated to America, he became professor of Church history and patristics at St. Vladimir's Russian Orthodox Seminary in New York, where he later served as dean. Meyendorff gives a good introduction to the Orthodox understanding of the Church, including a significant discussion of the Church as the action of the Holy Spirit and as *sobornost*. He also explains the historical basis for the organization and structure of the Orthodox Church.

Schmemann, Alexander. *For the Life of the World: Sacraments and Orthodoxy*. Crestwood, N.Y.: St. Vladimir's Seminary Press, 1973.

Schmemann (1921–1983), like Meyendorff, was educated at St. Sergius's in Paris and later taught liturgical theology at St. Vladimir's in New York. He explains clearly the sacramental nature of the Church by means of a thorough discussion of the Eucharist and briefer discussions of the other sacraments. His major theme is the joy to which the Church is called, a joy most fully realized in the Eucharist.

*Part 2: Some suggestions for further
reading in modern Orthodox sources:*

Arseniev, Nicolas. *Mysticism and the Eastern Church.* Trans. Arthur Chambers. Oxford: Mowbray, 1979.

Florovsky, Georges. *Collected Works.* Vol. 1, *Bible, Church, Tradition: An Eastern Orthodox View.* Belmont, Mass.: Nordland, 1972.

_____. *Collected Works.* Vol. 2, *Christianity and Culture.* Belmont, Mass.: Nordland, 1974.

_____. *Collected Works.* Vol. 3, *Creation and Redemption.* Belmont, Mass.: Nordland, 1976.

Lossky, Vladimir. *The Mystical Theology of the Eastern Church.* Crestwood, N.Y.: St. Vladimir's Seminary Press, 1976.

_____. *In the Image and Likeness of God.* Ed. John H. Erickson. Crestwood, N.Y.: St. Vladimir's Seminary Press, 1974.

_____. *Orthodox Theology: An Introduction.* Trans. Ian and Ihita Kasarcodi-Watson. Crestwood, N.Y.: St. Vladimir's Seminary Press, 1978.

Meyendorff, John. *The Orthodox Church: Its Past and Its Role in the World Today.* Trans. John Chapin. New York: Pantheon, 1962.

_____. *Living Tradition: Orthodox Witness in the Contemporary World.* Crestwood, N.Y.: St. Vladimir's Seminary Press, 1978.

Schmemann, Alexander. *The Historical Road of Eastern Orthodoxy.* Trans. Lydia W. Kesich. New York: Holt, Rinehart & Winston, 1963.

_____. *Of Water and the Spirit: A Liturgical Study of Baptism.* Crestwood, N.Y.: St. Vladimir's Seminary Press, 1974.

_____. *Church, World, Mission: Reflections on Orthodoxy in the West.* Crestwood, N.Y.: St. Vladimir's Seminary Press, 1979.

_____. *The Eucharist: Sacrament of the Kingdom.* Trans. Paul Kachur. Crestwood, N.Y.: St. Vladimir's Seminary Press, 1988.

Ware, Kallistos. *The Orthodox Church.* Rev. edition. Hammondsworth, Middlesex, England: Penguin, 1997.

Zernov, Nicolas. *Eastern Christendom: A Study of the Origin and Development of the Eastern Orthodox Church.* London: Weidenfeld and Nicolson, 1961.

Zizioulas, John D. *Being as Communion: Studies in Personhood and the Church.* Crestwood, N.Y.: St. Vladimir's Seminary Press, 1985.

Part 3: Some suggestions for reading in
patristic sources (in chronological order):

The standard collections of patristic writings in English are the late nineteenth-century series Ante-Nicene Fathers (ANF), Nicene and Post-Nicene Fathers, First Series (NPNF [1]), and Nicene and Post-Nicene Fathers, Second Series (NPNF [2]). These collections have been reprinted by several different publishers and are readily available in North American and British libraries. Because these translations are somewhat archaic and difficult to read, I list newer translations of the patristic writings as well as these standard editions.

Ignatius of Antioch. *Epistles.* In *The Apostolic Fathers.* Trans. J. B. Lightfoot and J. R. Harmer. Ed. Michael Holmes, 79–118. Grand Rapids, Mich.: Baker, 1989. (Also in ANF, vol. 1, 45–96.)

Irenaeus of Lyons. *Against Heresies.* ANF, vol. 1, 315–567.

Origen: On First Principles. Trans. G. W. Butterworth. Gloucester, Mass.: Peter Smith, 1973. (Also in ANF, vol. 4, 239–382.)

_____. *Against Celsus.* ANF, vol. 4, 395–669.

Athanasius: Contra Gentes and De Incarnatione. Ed. and trans. Robert Thomson. Oxford: Clarendon, 1971. (Also in NPNF [2], vol. 4, 4–67.)

Faith Gives Fullness to Reasoning: The Five Theological Orations of Gregory of Nazianzen. Ed. Frederick Norris. Trans. Lionel Wickham. Supplements to Vigiliae Christianae 13. Leiden: E. J. Brill, 1991. (Also in NPNF [2], vol. 7, 280–328.)

Gregory of Nyssa. *That There Are Not Three Gods.* In *The Trinitarian Controversy.* Ed. William Rusch. Sources of Early Christian Thought, 149–161. Philadelphia: Fortress, 1980. (Also in NPNF [2], vol. 5, 331–336.)

_____. *Sermon on the Sixth Beatitude.* In *Theological Anthropology.* Ed. J. Patout Burns. Sources of Early Christian Thought, 29–38. Philadelphia: Fortress, 1981.

St. Basil the Great: On the Holy Spirit. Trans. David Anderson. Crestwood, N.Y.: St. Vladimir's Seminary Press, 1980. (Also in NPNF [2], vol. 8, 1–50.)

Pseudo-Dionysius: The Complete Works. Classics of Western Spirituality. New York: Paulist, 1987.

Maximus Confessor: Selected Writings. Classics of Western Spirituality. New York: Paulist, 1985.

Gregory Palamas: The Triads. Classics of Western Spirituality. New York: Paulist, 1983.

In addition to the writings of the fathers themselves, one may also want to examine the documents connected with the seven ecumenical councils. An extensive collection of documents related to the councils is presented in NPNF [2], vol. 7. In addition, brief excerpts from the decrees and creeds of the councils may be found in (among other places) the following works:

Bettenson, Henry, and Chris Maunder, eds. *Documents of the Christian Church.* 3d ed. Oxford: University Press, 1999.

Leith, John H., ed. *Creeds of the Churches: A Reader in Christian Doctrine from the Bible to the Present.* 3d ed. Atlanta: John Knox, 1982.

Suggestions for Christian Workers in the East

As I wrote in the preface, I have sought throughout this book to address a general Western Christian audience, to write for people who have come into contact with Orthodoxy in the West as well as for those who live and work in the East. In this appendix, I will turn my attention specifically to Western Protestant Christian workers ministering in predominantly Orthodox countries, although what I write here should also interest other people. I think the suggestions I offer could be useful for Christians who are involved in ministries to ethnic Easterners living in the West, and perhaps even to Western Christians with good friends who are practicing (or merely culturally) Orthodox.

My suggestions in this appendix are gleaned from several sources: first, my personal contact with Orthodox people (in Georgia, Ukraine, America, and England) and my years of teaching Russian and Ukrainian Protestants who work among Orthodox people; second, the criticisms that Easterners (both Orthodox and Protestant) make of Western Christians working in the former Soviet Union; third, my reading of Orthodox theology and my reflection on the way that theology is likely to impact the mindsets of typical Orthodox people. As I have explained my understanding of Orthodoxy to my Georgian, Russian, and Ukrainian students, I have asked them how much of the official theology has filtered down to them and to other people with whom they come into contact, and which aspects of Orthodoxy have made the deepest impression on the general populace. While most of my examples come from the former Soviet Union, I hope that my suggestions will be relevant for other parts of Eastern Europe as well.

As a result, this appendix is based much more on what could be called "anecdotal evidence" than the text of the book proper. I am admittedly on much shakier ground here than when I sought to explain what the best of Orthodox theology teaches, and even on less stable ground than I was in chapters 9 and 10 when I described popular Orthodoxy. I offer this appendix as a set of suggestions, not a list of rules for Christian workers. I invite critique from readers who have found that the ideas I present here are inadequate, unhelpful, or insufficient. In spite of these qualifiers, I think this book would be incomplete without such suggestions, and I offer them in the hope that they will help the advance of God's kingdom in Eastern Europe and the former Soviet Union. My thoughts are presented in three major categories: ideas concerning preparation and strategy, suggestions dealing with what I call the "public presence" of Westerners in a given area, and ideas for talking about Christianity in an Orthodox environment.

The 1990s saw a remarkable increase in dialogue between Eastern Orthodox and evangelical Protestant leaders. Much of that discussion concerned questions that I treat briefly in this appendix. People who would like to read more can find a very useful guide to this new discussion in an article written by Bradley Nassif (professor at the Antiochian House of Studies) entitled "Eastern Orthodoxy and Evangelicalism: The Status of an Emerging Global Dialogue" (*Scottish Bulletin of Evangelical Theology,* spring 2000, pp. 21–55). This article contains an extensive bibliography of evangelical and Orthodox contributions to the dialogue.[1]

Preparation: Attitudes and Understanding[2]

Perhaps the most important way Westerners can prepare for work in Eastern Europe is to ask some direct questions about our own attitudes and goals. Are we going to the East to build Christ's kingdom or simply to expand our denomination or group? Do we overtly or subconsciously believe that true faith is to be found only among Protestants? Do we believe that only a style of Christianity that looks like that of the revivalistic English-speaking world can be biblical? I recently read a magazine article by a Christian who has an evangelistic ministry to Greek immigrants in a certain Western country. The author clearly believed that a Greek must necessarily leave Orthodoxy in order to find Christ. I have also known Western Protestants in Russia who have seen people come to Christ, have spent years discipling them, and then have been devastated when those young disciples ultimately chose to be part of the Orthodox Church.

If I have accomplished anything in this book, I hope I have succeeded in showing that the words "Orthodox" and "non-Christian" are not synonyms. Popular Orthodoxy has serious problems that often obscure the message of Christ. Many people who have an affiliation with Orthodoxy are not genuine

Christians, and even worse, some of these people are convinced that they are genuine Christians simply because they are from an Orthodox country. Perhaps God will be pleased to grant Western Christians the joy of helping such people come to know Christ truly. Some of these people may find their home in Protestant or Roman Catholic churches. But Orthodoxy at its best does preach Christ, can nourish the souls of people, and can provide a place for believers to grow. We should not consider it necessarily a tragedy if people with whom we work go to or remain in Orthodox communions.

Thus I suggest that we take a larger view of God's action to build his kingdom than many of us are accustomed to taking. Without minimizing the significance of our differences with the Orthodox, and certainly without ignoring the dangerous distortions of the gospel that are present in popular Orthodoxy, we can still recognize that God does not work merely through Protestantism; he can and does also work through the Orthodox Church. Furthermore, if God's purpose is to work through Orthodoxy, his desire is not that all genuine Christians leave that Church. Rather, Easterners who gain exposure to the best of Western Christianity through contact with Protestant Christian workers might be the very ones who help to bring about a revitalization of popular Orthodoxy. Western Christian activity in the East could result not only in the advance of indigenous Protestantism, but also in the renewal of Orthodoxy in Eastern Europe. We should be open to the possibility that God may choose to use our work in this fashion, and we should resolve to seek the advancement of Christ's kingdom by whatever means God might choose.

A second way Westerners can prepare for ministry in Eastern Europe is to learn as much as we can about the religion, the culture, and the artistic and literary heritage of the region where we will work. Of course, such an education is important for ministers working in any part of the world, but especially for Protestants working in the East, for two reasons. First, most (but by no means all) Protestant Christian workers come from rather countercultural backgrounds: we think that too much involvement in the art and literature of our society constitutes "worldliness" and is therefore to be avoided. As a result, we are often far too quick to dismiss—in ways that give offense to natives of those countries—the great cultural heritages of Eastern European nations. In fact, Western Christians' cavalier dismissal of Russian culture leads to some of the angrier reactions of Russians toward us.

Another reason to learn the cultural heritage of Eastern Europe is that much of this heritage is Christian, at least in the general sense of that word. In the case of Russia, for example, much well-known cultural material can be very helpful in pointing people toward the gospel. Early fifteenth-century iconographer Andrei Rublev was an artistic genius and was doubtless a sincere worshiper of Christ, and we can acknowledge these facts even though we may not agree that icons are an appropriate part of Christian worship. Nineteenth-century author Fyodor Dostoevsky was one of the world's greatest novelists and was also a man of deep spiritual insight, and we can acknowledge these characteristics in spite of the fact that his novels include elements of popular Orthodox piety with which we disagree. Orthodox spirituality has had an immense, positive influence on the culture of Russia and other Eastern countries, and this influence has meant that many Eastern European non-Christians are closer to Christ than are most Western unbelievers. We should be grateful for this fact, even though we do not believe the influence of Orthodoxy has been completely good. If we feel obliged to reject something altogether whenever it does not completely agree with our theological views (or worse yet, simply because we are ignorant of it), we give needless offense and even erect barriers in people's minds that make it harder for them to hear the gospel we seek to bring to them.

As Western Christian workers, we need to do our homework. We need to learn Orthodoxy and its influence on the life of the people with whom we work, and we need to be willing to express an appreciation for the ways in which that influence has been positive, even as we admit that we do not agree with it completely. We need to be familiar with the cultural expressions that have shaped the minds and hearts of the people, so that we can begin to understand and identify with them. Of course, I hardly need to make this suggestion to the reader, since you would probably not have reached this part of the book if you had not realized the importance of understanding Orthodoxy. The influence of the writings of Orthodox theologians on the people is less direct than the influence of the country's artists, poets, novelists, and playwrights.These expressions of culture can give us our most transparent window into the soul of the people with whom we work.

The Public Presence of Western Christians in the East

In the late 1980s and early 1990s, there was an unprecedented openness to the West on the part of Eastern Europeans. As people sought to disentangle themselves from the ties of atheistic socialism, they readily embraced all things Western: religions, economic policies, and consumerism. But by the middle of the 1990s, that brief infatuation had largely ended, and an angry and confused anti-Western sentiment became more prominent. Part of the reason for this dramatic change in attitude was that Easterners found themselves bewildered by the array of religious ideas that found their way into their countries in the aftermath of communism's fall. While many of these religions actually came from Asia, the perception was often that they were Western, and especially American. The tendency has therefore been to label all "new religions" (that is, religions or denominations that have not had a long history in Eastern Europe) as Western imports and to reject them out of hand. In the process, Easterners have experienced even greater difficulty in telling the difference between Protestant Christian groups and "Christian" cults or even religions that have no connection to Christianity. In addition to this antipathy toward non-Orthodox groups in general, the mid- and late-1990s have also seen a growing suspicion of any groups that appear secretive about their beliefs and practices. Great scares have resulted from the Japanese suicide cult (which has more members in Siberia than in Japan) and by the Ukrainian White Brothers (which people often forget is an indigenous movement, not a foreign one). As a result, any somewhat secretive Protestant group is likely to be equated with such cults.

As a result of Eastern Europeans' fear of secrecy and their confusion of Protestantism with cults, missionaries must be publicly open about who we are and what we are doing. One of the first things I recommend to my Russian and Ukrainian Protestant students is that they contact the Orthodox leaders in the area where they will be working. Such a step is even more important for Westerners, who not only have the "disadvantage" of not being Orthodox, but also have the handicap of being foreigners. Assuming that Western Christians will be in close contact with indigenous Protestants in the area, perhaps those leaders can arrange meetings with Orthodox leaders. If (as often happens) a lot of aversion exists on the part of the indigenous Protestants to such an idea, we may do well to suggest to them that a meeting with the local Orthodox priest would be mutually beneficial.

The most obvious benefit to be gained from contact with the local priest is that it will give missionaries the opportunity to learn that priest's vision of Orthodoxy. If he is extremely nationalistic in his understanding, he will likely refuse to meet with foreigners at all. If his attitude toward the Church is triumphalistic, he may even refuse to talk to indigenous Protestants. But if he is willing to have regular contact, we can learn whether he has a biblical focus on the beginning of faith as well as on the journey to union with God. We can learn what his understanding of saints and icons is and what he is doing to educate the people about them. Learning these things can give us a good idea of how much, if any, we will be able to work together with the Orthodox in that location. If, as is likely, the local leadership does not have enough sympathy with our emphases for any religious cooperation to be possible, charitable work together may still be possible. However, sometimes

priests themselves are sympathetic with our concerns and greater cooperation is possible. At the least, if we take the initiative to make contact with
Orthodox leaders, we demonstrate that we do not completely and disre-
spectfully reject something that is deeply important to many of the people
with whom we work.

Another result of local contact is that we can have some feel for what the
people with whom we interact are receiving from Orthodoxy, or what they
will receive if they opt for an Orthodox Church rather than a Protestant one.
Will people be pointed toward faith in Christ? Or will they merely hear a message of allegiance to the Church or to their national religious heritage? If we
know what strand of Orthodox thought the local leadership represents, we can
glimpse the people's spiritual condition. Furthermore, if we see people come
to Christ who then want to affiliate with Orthodoxy rather than Protestantism,
we will have some idea of how well or poorly the local Orthodox church will
feed them spiritually.

A second important question related to the public presence of Westerners
is the degree to which we should identify ourselves confessionally. Most
Protestant Christian workers, especially in the early 1990s, had the impression that we might not receive a hearing from people at all if we admitted that
we were not Orthodox, and so it was very common to attempt some sort of
evasion when the question was inevitably asked, "Are you Orthodox?" For
example, in Georgia in 1990, my general response was to say that I had not
come to talk about Orthodoxy, Roman Catholicism, or Protestantism; I had
come to talk about Christ and what the Bible said about him. Such ambiguity
seemed to satisfy people at that time but is unlikely to be effective now. Eastern Europeans are now all too painfully aware of the variety of religious
groups flocking to their lands, and they are likely to assume that we are from
the most radical of the secretive cults if we are unwilling to identify ourselves.
On the other hand, some of the ignorant prejudice toward Protestants that
characterized the landscape a decade ago is breaking down. For example, if
Eastern Europeans ever did believe that Baptists were all forerunners of the
antichrist, corrupters of children, and American spies (as Father Archil, advi-
sor to Georgian Orthodox Catholicos Iliya II, charged in 1990), they are less
likely to believe this now.

As a result, I suggest that Westerners now be more forthright about our
identity, as long as we also make clear that our focus is not anti-Orthodox, but
pro-Christ. If we are working with indigenous national Protestant groups, our
identification with these groups (which are genuinely Russian, Romanian,
and so on, and have been present in the country for a long period) should not
foster undue prejudice against us. In one sense, our obligation is to make such

disclosures, simply for the sake of honesty. In addition, our identification with a long-standing indigenous group will help to alleviate people's fears that we represent one of the "new" cults about which they have been hearing the worst possible horror stories. We can and should be honest about the distinctiveness of our own vision of Christian life, while still emphasizing that we are not trying to pull people out of their culture, nor are we completely opposed to Orthodoxy.

Discussing Christianity in an Orthodox Environment

The suggestions made thus far in this appendix have been general (and perhaps obvious), and they pertain to virtually all Christians working in Eastern Europe. At this point, I would like to address specifically people engaged in evangelistic ministries in Eastern Europe or among ethnic Easterners living in the West. I would like to concentrate on our presentation of three cardinal tenets of Protestant Christianity, ideas that we believe to be central to biblical faith: the authority of Scripture alone, the substitutionary atonement, and justification by faith. The reader may have noticed the absence of these tenets in the assessment of Orthodoxy in chapter 8, because I believed it would be unfair to evaluate Orthodoxy using purely Western categories. However, Protestant Christian workers believe that the ideas behind these phrases are fundamental biblical truths, and they certainly should be a part of our teaching. The following pages represent an attempt to suggest ways we can translate our fundamental ideas into terms that Easterners can understand. The Orthodox emphases discussed in this book are likely to influence the way typical Eastern Europeans understand these spiritual ideas and hear the message of Christ as Western Protestants proclaim it. I envision situations in which Western Christians (or the indigenous Protestant students whom we help to equip) preach the gospel publicly or discuss Christianity privately with unbelievers. However, much of what I suggest will also pertain to conversations with Orthodox people who are genuine believers but whose understanding of Christian life is (we believe) incomplete because of its basis in an unbalanced or distorted strand of Orthodoxy.

Before I offer these suggestions, however, I should mention that Christian workers must take Orthodoxy into consideration even when talking to people who are avowedly secular, because of the depth of Orthodox roots in Eastern Europe and the former Soviet Union. Slavic Christianity traces its documented history to the work of Cyril and Methodius in Moravia (modern Slovakia) in the mid-800s, and in some regions, such as Georgia and Armenia, the roots go back as far as the beginning of the fourth century. For a millennium or more, the Eastern form of Christianity has shaped the culture and thought patterns of these peoples. Thus, whether a person is Orthodox or not, Orthodox thought and tradition will likely color his or her concept of Christianity and ability to grasp spiritual ideas.

The Unique Authority of Scripture

In this book, the first (and to a Protestant, perhaps the most fundamental) difference between Western Protestantism and Orthodoxy was the Orthodox idea of tradition, rather than Scripture alone, as the source of theology. Because of the centrality of *sola Scriptura* to Protestantism, we are particularly prone to make this difference a major issue in itself. However, Orthodoxy does not neglect Scripture. The liturgical life of the Church is, as Ware has asserted, a vast meditation on Scripture.[3] Nevertheless, even in cases when Orthodox theology's attention to witnesses besides Scripture does lead it astray from biblical truth, little is accomplished by insisting on the authority of the Bible alone in Christian life. Such an insistence will be flatly incomprehensible to people who are unused to thinking in terms of juridical authority.

Instead, a better approach is to follow an Eastern style in the evaluation of issues on which we think Orthodoxy has departed from Scripture. Eastern theology holds that a particular witness is true if it is accepted as being consistent with other witnesses to the Church's life. No Orthodox person would deny that Scripture is one of the main witnesses (if not *the* main witness) to this life. Accordingly, even from an Eastern perspective, we have the right to compare other expressions of tradition with the expression that we know the best, the Bible. If we are willing to join our Eastern friends in looking carefully at other Orthodox sources in comparison to the witness of Scripture, we will demonstrate our own allegiance to Scripture in a way they can comprehend. Moreover, we will also show a willingness to take the ideas of Orthodoxy seriously, rather than dismissing them *a priori* because we believe they are founded on nonauthoritative sources instead of on the Bible.

The Substitutionary Atonement

Another prominent aspect of Western Christian thought is our emphasis on Christ's death in our place, as he took on himself the punishment we deserved for our sins. As we prepare to discuss the work of Christ with Eastern Europeans, we need to remember two things. First, substitution is not the only aspect of Christ's atoning work as described in the New Testament, even though we are convinced it is the most prominent emphasis. We saw in chapter 6 that the classic idea of victory over death and the devil comes directly from Hebrews 2:14 and is also present in passages such as 1 Corinthians 15:54–57 and Colossians 2:13–15. As we teach about the work of Christ, we should emphasize this aspect of the atonement as well as the substitutionary aspect.

Second, when talking about Christ's substitution of himself for us, we need to explain this concept in a way that avoids the distortions to which Orthodoxy correctly objects. When we speak with people from an Orthodox background about the necessity for God to punish sins or about Christ's suffering the Father's wrath toward our sins, they might interpret our words as if we are depicting the Father as only a God of justice, not a God of love. Furthermore, we might sound as if we are pitting the Son against the Father when we speak of the necessity of satisfying the Father's wrath toward sin. Accordingly, Christian workers must be careful to emphasize that the necessity for punishment stems not from God's hatred of us, but from the vastness of his holiness. We need to assert that Christ's paying the penalty for our sins genuinely constituted God's suffering *himself* (the unity of the godhead is important here: the Son is the same God as the Father), and that the motive for such suffering was unquestionably his love for us.

Furthermore, we must not give the impression that we believe the atonement exempts Christians from *all* suffering. Orthodoxy regards such an idea as the bedrock of Western "easy believism" and caricatures our faith as implying, "Christ has borne my cross so that I can go to heaven without having to bear a cross myself." We do not mean this, but it is all too easy for the Orthodox to hear us as saying this. Thus we need to stress that believers are not exempt from suffering in this world and that Christ is our companion in the suffering that we undergo. At the same time, we will never suffer God's wrath, because Christ has taken that wrath, that punishment, on himself in our place. By acknowledging the valid insights of the classic view of the atonement and by correcting potential Orthodox misconceptions about the Western view, Western Christian workers can help ensure that Eastern Europeans will hear the message of the atonement accurately.

Justification by Faith

When we approach justification by faith, we come to what Protestants are convinced is the heart of the gospel. As shown in chapters 5 and 6, the Orthodox emphasis on human vocation and on life as a journey to the kingdom (the two-act salvation scheme) tends toward an idea that people are saved only at the end of the process of *theosis*. Mature Orthodox theology does not promulgate such a view but stresses that we become God's children at the beginning of faith, and therefore that Christian life is in part a response to what God has already done in saving us. The best of Orthodoxy does agree with our emphasis on justification by faith, although Eastern theologians do not use that phrase to express the idea. However there are two things which make it difficult for people from Orthodox backgrounds to hear us accurately when we talk about justification. First, when we describe justification using legal definitions, when we speak of a change in our status before God or of imputed righteousness, people who do not possess our Western legal mindset typically have a hard time understanding us. Second, Easterners who are well-versed in Orthodox polemics will have heard that justification by faith is a Protestant idea and therefore a heresy. If we use the phrase "justification by faith," we will sometimes accomplish nothing except ending the conversation, and perhaps ending our friendship with the person to whom we are talking.

Therefore, as we discuss this crucial issue, we need to remember that the phrase "justification by faith" occurs only in Romans and Galatians, whereas the idea that the phrase signifies is expressed in other ways in the rest of the New Testament books. We can use other words to convey to Easterners this crucial idea, and the best vocabulary to use might be that of acceptance. Does God's acceptance of people as his children come at the beginning of faith? Do we as believers begin to share in fellowship with the Trinity from the beginning? Or does this acceptance (as well as the communion that flows from it) await the completion of sanctification, the accomplishment of union with God? As we have seen, mature Orthodoxy answers these questions with the emphatic assertion, "At the beginning." But Orthodoxy's stress on life as a journey often leads people toward the idea that God accepts us only at the completion of that journey. If people have only a vague understanding of Orthodox doctrine, they are likely to have a sense that they need to perfect themselves in order to have communion with God. For many people who are only loosely affiliated with Orthodoxy, this idea may take the form of nothing stronger than a sense that receiving the Eucharist and pursuing good works are desirable things to do. But for others (especially nonbelievers with a strong spiritual hunger), the emphasis on salvation as *theosis* can lead to a great deal of guilt and frustration over their seeming inability to perfect themselves enough to gain union and fellowship with God.

What such people need to hear more than anything else is that God is ready to accept them into fellowship with himself, even though they are not perfect and will not be perfect until the end of the age. God's acceptance does not need to wait until the completion of a long process of sanctification or deification. Instead, through his Son Jesus Christ, God has already accomplished all that he requires in order to accept people. A person needs simply to be united to Christ by faith in order to begin experiencing now the joy of fellowship with him. This acceptance, which begins at the inception of faith, is the basis for pursuing a life of Christ-likeness. I have known Eastern Europeans who had a tremendous spiritual sensitivity but whose distorted understanding of Orthodoxy led them to despair that they were not succeeding at gaining union with God. Their lives were dramatically changed almost instantaneously when I simply explained that God was ready to accept them now, on the basis of Christ's person and work.

As we proclaim the message of God's free acceptance of people who trust in Christ, the misunderstanding that such acceptance comes only at the end of Christian life is not the only one that we need to address. In light of the strong link between religion and nationalism in the minds of many Eastern Europeans, we also need to emphasize that God's acceptance accompanies personal faith in Christ, not citizenship in a nation that has uniquely received God's favor. When we encounter the sentiments associated with religious nationalism, we need to recognize that downplaying the national consciousness of the people with whom we work is neither necessary nor productive. To do so would communicate only that we do not care about something that is deeply important to them. Instead, we can affirm that the national hopes and dreams of a people are important to God.

At the same time, we must make clear that some of the conclusions drawn from nationalistic sentiment are wrong. Perhaps an appropriate way to make this point is to emphasize that while a nation's dreams are important to God, he does not care for any single country alone. God taught this lesson to Jonah, as the prophet sought to restrict God's love only to Israel. In contrast to Jonah, God loved even the people of Nineveh (the capital of Israel's most hated enemy, Assyria) and wanted them to turn to him. Because God's love extends to all nations, no people group stands in such a unique relation to him that it is the main beneficiary of God's favor. By emphasizing the universality of God's love, perhaps we can begin to jar people out of spiritual complacency based on their national heritage, so that they can recognize their own need to turn to Christ in faith.

As Christian workers we can bring this message of God's acceptance to Eastern Europe. In order to make sure that the message is genuinely heard, we need to correct both the idea that such acceptance awaits the completion of sanctification and the belief that acceptance comes automatically to people of a certain nation. The more carefully and sensitively we tailor our presentation of this message to an Eastern European audience, the more likely people will be to hear what Christ really means when he says, "Come to me, all you that are weary and are carrying heavy burdens, and I will give you rest" (Matt. 11:28).

Appendix C

The Structure and Organization of Orthodoxy

Overall Structure

Unlike the Roman Catholic Church, the Chalcedonian Orthodox Churches are organized into local bodies. Some of these groups are given greater honor than others because of antiquity, size, or importance, but those groups that have more honor do not thereby have greater power than others. Schmemann explains how the Church can be organized into a hierarchy without subordination of certain groups to others:

> The absence of "jurisdictional" subordination of one church to another, of one bishop to another, does not mean absence of hierarchy and order. This order in the early canonical tradition is maintained by the various levels of *primacies,* i.e. episcopal and ecclesiastical centers or focuses of unity. But primacy is not a "jurisdictional" principle. If according to the famous Apostolic Canon 34, the bishops everywhere must know the *first* among them, the same canon "refers" this primacy to the Holy Trinity which has "order" but certainly no "subordination." The function of primacy is to express the unity of all, to be its organ and mouthpiece.[1]

Therefore, just as the bishops express the unity of the Church without subordinating the laypeople to themselves, so also the more honored churches express the unity of the entire Church, but neither they nor their bishops stand above other churches or bishops. As Schmemann mentions, this understanding of hierarchy is rooted in the order of the Trinity, in which the Father holds first place as the source of the godhead and unifying principle, but the Son and the Spirit are not subordinate to him.

In this understanding, the primacy of honor among Orthodox groups falls to the four ancient patriarchates that were centers of Eastern Christianity in the early Church: Constantinople, Alexandria, Antioch, and Jerusalem. Beyond these are groups that are called "autocephalous" (self-governing), all of which

179

are national groups except for the monastery on Mount Sinai. Next in priority are the Churches that are autonomous but have not yet been given full auto-cephalous status. Then come ecclesiastical provinces in the Orthodox *diaspora* (generally composed of immigrants living outside of historically Orthodox areas), each of which is under the jurisdiction of one of the autocephalous Churches. The overall organization looks something like the following:[2]

Ancient Patriarchates	Autocephalous Churches	Autonomous Churches
Constantinople	Russia	Czech Republic/Slovakia
Alexandria	Romania	Finland
Antioch	Serbia	China
Jerusalem	Greece	Japan
	Bulgaria	
	Georgia	
	Cyprus	
	Poland	
	Albania	
	Sinai Monastery	

In spite of the insistence that no group has authority over another group, significant jurisdictional struggles still take place within Orthodoxy. Several groups are officially under the jurisdiction of one of the autocephalous Churches but claim autonomous status for themselves. These groups include the Ukrainian Autonomous Orthodox Church and the Macedonian Orthodox Church.

Orthodox Clergy

The Orthodox divide their ordained clergy into two groups: major orders and minor orders. The major orders are bishop, priest, and deacon. The minor orders are subdeacon and reader. There are two classes of priests, "white" or married priests, who are usually in charge of parishes, and "black" or unmarried monastic priests, who are eligible to become bishops. No one may marry after he has been ordained to a major order, so if a man aspiring to the ministry wishes to marry, he must do so before he is even made a deacon. He must thus decide ahead of time whether he wants ultimately to become a white or black priest. If a white priest's wife dies, he cannot remarry.

Orthodoxy employs a number of titles to refer to its clergy, and unfortunately, the use of such titles is not entirely consistent. The following chart explains the meaning of each title as the Greek Church and the Russian Church use the term.[3]

Title	Greek Usage	Russian Usage
Patriarch	The head of certain auto-cephalous churches	Same
Metropolitan	A title of honor given to an eminent bishop	The bishop of a capital city or an autocephalous Church
Archbishop	The bishop of a capital city or an autocephalous Church	A title of honor given to an eminent bishop
Archimandrite	A title of honor given to an eminent priest-monk	Same
Higumenos	The abbot of a monastery	A title of honor that could be given to any priest-monk
Archpriest	A title of honor equal to Archimandrite but given to a nonmonastic priest	Same
Protopope	Same as Archimandrite	Same
Hieromonk	A priest-monk	Same
Hierodeacon	A monk who is a deacon	Same
Archdeacon	A title of honor given to an eminent hierodeacon	Same
Protodeacon	A title of honor given to a nonmonastic deacon	Same

The Orthodox Liturgical Calendar

Chapter 3 of this book described the major feasts of the Orthodox liturgical year. This appendix lists the feasts in tabular form for ease of reference. The date listed first is the date on which the feast is held in regions that use the Gregorian calendar. The second is the date (according to the Gregorian calendar) on which the feast is held in regions (mainly Jerusalem, Russia, and Serbia) that use the Julian calendar.

Name of Feast	Date	Description of Feast
Nativity of the Mother of God	Sept. 8 (Sept. 21)	Beginning of Christian year through celebration of the birth of the one who bore Jesus
Exaltation of the Cross	Sept. 14 (Sept. 27)	Celebration of important historical events related to the cross
Presentation of Mary in the Temple	Nov. 21 (Dec. 4)	Celebration of Mary's complete devotion to God and readiness for her vocation
Christmas	Dec. 25 (Jan. 7)	Celebration of the incarnation
Theophany	Jan. 6 (Jan. 19)	Celebration of the baptism of Christ
Meeting of our Lord	Feb. 2 (Feb. 15)	Celebration of Mary and Joseph's presentation of Jesus in the temple

Name of Feast	Date	Description of Feast
Annunciation	Mar. 25 (Apr. 7)	Celebration of Gabriel's announcement to Mary that she would bear the Messiah
Palm Sunday	Sunday before Easter	Celebration of public presentation of Christ as King of the Jews
Easter	See below*	The central feast of the Christian year; celebration of Christ's resurrection
Ascension	40 days after Easter	Celebration of the completion of Christ's work as he returns to the Father and the Spirit
Pentecost	50 days after Easter	Celebration of the birth of the Church through the gift of the Holy Spirit
Transfiguration	Aug. 6 (Aug. 19)	Celebration of the revelation of Christ's divine glory to the apostles
Dormition of the Mother of God	Aug. 15 (Aug. 28)	Celebration of Mary's death and of her resurrection three days later

*The dates of Easter for the Eastern and Western churches sometimes coincide, but they often vary by one, four, or five weeks.

Notes

INTRODUCTION—DOUBLE VISION

1. For excellent introductory historical surveys of Eastern Orthodox history, see Kallistos Ware, *The Orthodox Church*. rev. ed. (Hammondsworth, Middlesex, England: Penguin, 1997); and Alexander Schmemann, *The Historical Road of Eastern Orthodoxy,* trans. Lydia W. Kesich (New York: Holt, Rinehart & Winston, 1963). For a more advanced history, see Nicolas Zernov, *Eastern Christendom: A Study of the Origin and Development of the Eastern Orthodox Church* (London: Weidenfeld and Nicolson, 1961).

2. In this book, I will write very little about typical Protestant/Roman Catholic issues, such as whether the apocryphal/deuterocanonical books belong in the Old Testament, whether the bread and wine of communion actually become the body and blood of Christ, whether water baptism itself conveys forgiveness of sins, or even whether salvation is purely by faith or by works as well.

3. Russian theologian Alexander Schmemann uses the phrase "theological renaissance" to describe the flowering of Orthodox theology in the twentieth century, and Nicolas Zernov has made the phrase the title of one of his books. See Schmemann, *Church, World, Mission: Reflections on Orthodoxy in the West* (Crestwood, N.Y.: St. Vladimir's Seminary Press, 1979), 15. See also Zernov, *The Russian Religious Renaissance of the Twentieth Century* (London: Darton, Longman & Todd, 1963).

4. The adjective "patristic" and the corresponding noun "patristics" come from the Latin word for "father" and refer to the fathers of the Church who have been most influential in shaping Christian life and doctrine. Many of these church fathers lived during the first eight centuries of the Christian era, but Orthodoxy regards some people from later periods, and even contemporary figures, as being fathers.

5. Many Orthodox writers express this idea using the Greek word *theosis* or its English equivalent "deification," and I return to this word in chapter 5.

6. When I use the words "conservative," "moderate," and "radical" in this paragraph, I am referring to the degree to which the various groups distanced themselves from the Medieval Roman Catholic Church.

CHAPTER 1—AUTHORITY VERSUS LIFE

1. As contemporary Russian theologian John Meyendorff declares, "This lack in Orthodox ecclesiology of a clearly defined, precise, and permanent criterion of Truth besides God Himself, Christ, and the Holy Spirit, is certainly one of the major contrasts between Orthodoxy

185

and all classical Western ecclesiologies" (John Meyendorff, *Living Tradition: Orthodox Witness in the Contemporary World* [Crestwood, N.Y.: St. Vladimir's Seminary Press, 1978], 20).

2. There were seven councils from the early period of the Church, as well as several other major councils since the rupture between East and West, which Orthodoxy regards as bearing normative doctrinal status. I will discuss these councils briefly in chapter 3.

3. John D. Zizioulas, *Being as Communion: Studies in Personhood and the Church* (Crestwood, N.Y.: St. Vladimir's Seminary Press, 1985), 242 (emphasis his).

4. Ware, *The Orthodox Church*, 253 (emphasis his).

5. Georges Florovsky, *Collected Works*, vol. 1, *Bible, Church, Tradition: An Eastern Orthodox View* (Belmont, Mass.: Nordland, 1972), 96 (emphasis his).

6. I should point out here that Eastern Christianity is not nearly as united as some of its adherents would like us to believe. Orthodoxy is plagued by deep divisions and significant power struggles, just as much of Western Christianity is.

7. Quoted in Zernov, *Eastern Christendom*, 187.

8. Zernov, *Eastern Christendom*, 231.

9. Nicolas Arseniev, *Mysticism and the Eastern Church*, trans. Arthur Chambers (Oxford: Mowbray, 1979), 60.

10. Archimandrite Chrysostomos, *Contemporary Eastern Orthodox Thought: The Traditionalist Voice* (Belmont, Mass.: Büchervertriebsanstalt, 1982), 104.

11. Maximos Aghiorgoussis, "The Dogmatic Tradition of the Orthodox Church," in *A Companion to the Greek Orthodox Church*, ed. Fotios K. Litsas (New York: Greek Orthodox Diocese of North and South America, 1984), 151–52.

12. Vladimir Lossky, *In the Image and Likeness of God*, ed. John H. Erickson (Crestwood, N.Y.: St. Vladimir's Seminary Press, 1974), 143–44.

13. Sergei Nikolaevich Bulgakov, *The Orthodox Church* (London: Centenary, 1935), 21.

14. Ibid., 28.

15. Ibid., 30.

16. Ware, *The Orthodox Church*, 199 (emphasis his).

17. Florovsky, *Bible, Church, Tradition*, 74–75.

18. Meyendorff, *Living Tradition*, 14.

19. Schmemann, *The Historical Road of Eastern Orthodoxy*, 43.

20. Meyendorff, *Living Tradition*, 16.

21. Georges Florovsky, *Collected Works*, vol. 6, *Ways of Russian Theology, Part Two*, trans. Robert L. Nichols (Vaduz, Germany: Büchervertriebsanstalt, 1987), 304.

22. Florovsky, *Bible, Church, Tradition*, 103.

23. Schmemann, *Church, World, Mission*, 7.

24. Ibid., 84 (emphasis his).

25. Leonid Ouspensky and Vladimir Lossky, *The Meaning of Icons*, rev. ed., trans. G. E. H. Palmer and E. Kadloubovsky (Crestwood, N.Y.: St. Vladimir's Seminary Press, 1982), 15 (emphasis his).

26. The words "eschatology" and "eschatological" come from the Greek word *eschaton* (whose plural is *eschata*), which means "the end." These words all refer to the consummation of history in the events surrounding the return of Christ and the fulfillment of God's kingdom.

27. Zizioulas, *Being as Communion*, 173–76.

28. Ibid., 180–81 (emphasis his).

CHAPTER 2—TRADITION AND THE CHURCH

1. Bulgakov, *The Orthodox Church*, 11.

2. John Meyendorff, *Catholicity and the Church* (Crestwood, N.Y.: St. Vladimir's Seminary Press, 1983), 10.

3. See, e.g., Vladimir Lossky, *The Mystical Theology of the Eastern Church* (Crestwood, N.Y.: St. Vladimir's Seminary Press, 1976), 186.

4. Lossky, *The Mystical Theology of the Eastern Church,* 156–57 (emphasis his).

5. Maximos Aghiorgoussis, "Orthodox Soteriology," in *Salvation in Christ: A Lutheran-Orthodox Dialogue,* ed. John Meyendorff and Robert Tobias (Minneapolis: Augsburg Fortress, 1992), 51–52.

6. Florovsky, *Bible, Church, Tradition,* 39 (emphasis his).

7. Ibid., 41–42.

8. Alexander Schmemann, *Of Water and the Spirit: A Liturgical Study of Baptism* (Crestwood, N.Y.: St. Vladimir's Seminary Press, 1974), 16–17.

9. Zernov, *Eastern Christendom,* 230.

10. Anthony Ugolnik, *The Illuminating Icon* (Grand Rapids: Eerdmans, 1989), 88.

11. John Meyendorff, *The Orthodox Church: Its Past and Its Role in the World Today,* trans. John Chapin (New York: Pantheon, 1962), 212 (emphasis his).

12. Bulgakov, *The Orthodox Church,* 131.

13. The seven Roman Catholic sacraments are baptism, confirmation (chrismation), the Eucharist (the Mass), penance, marriage, holy orders, and extreme unction. Of course, most Protestants regard only baptism and the Eucharist as sacraments, and some prefer to call these "ordinances," rather than sacraments.

14. Schmemann, *Of Water and the Spirit,* 41.

15. Zizioulas, *Being as Communion,* 149 (emphasis his).

16. Alexander Schmemann, *Introduction to Liturgical Theology,* trans. Asheleigh E. Moorhouse (Leighton Buzzard, England: Faith Press, 1966), 20 (emphasis his).

17. Schmemann, *Introduction to Liturgical Theology,* 63.

18. Nicolas Afanasiev, "The Church Which Presides in Love," in *The Primacy of Peter* (Leighton Buzzard, England: Faith Press, 1963), 74–75.

19. Zizioulas, *Being as Communion,* 148 (emphasis his).

20. Afanasiev, in *The Primacy of Peter,* 75 (emphasis his).

21. John Meyendorff, "St. Peter in Byzantine Theology," in *The Primacy of Peter,* 27.

22. If a person who has previously been baptized in a Christian church converts to Orthodoxy, he or she is usually simply chrismated, rather than being rebaptized. However, some Orthodox groups, such as the Russian Orthodox Church in Exile, do rebaptize such people.

23. John Meyendorff, "Humanity: 'Old' and 'New'—Anthropological Considerations," in *Salvation in Christ: A Lutheran-Orthodox Dialogue,* 64.

24. Alexander Schmemann, *For the Life of the World: Sacraments and Orthodoxy* (Crestwood, N.Y.: St. Vladimir's Seminary Press, 1973), 78 (emphasis his).

25. Under Roman Catholic influence, the Russian Church of the seventeenth century introduced an absolution formula into the prayer the priest uses when hearing confession. Even though this prayer's use is discouraged on theological grounds, it is still common.

26. Schmemann, *For the Life of the World,* 79 (emphasis his).

27. See Zizioulas, *Being as Communion,* 168.

28. For information about the organization of Orthodoxy and the relation between the bishops and other classes of clergy, see appendix C.

29. Meyendorff, *Catholicity and the Church,* 53–54.

30. Georges Florovsky, *Collected Works,* vol. 3, *Creation and Redemption* (Belmont, Mass.: Nordland, 1976), 191.

31. Schmemann, *The Historical Road of Eastern Orthodoxy,* 30–31. Here Schmemann quotes Ignatius of Antioch, *Epistle to the Ephesians* 6 and *Epistle to the Magnesians* 7.

32. Bulgakov, *The Orthodox Church,* 68.

33. Zizioulas, *Being as Communion,* 135–36.

34. Ibid., 238.

35. A diocese is the city or region over which a bishop is the head.

36. Zizioulas, *Being as Communion,* 168 (emphasis his).

37. Meyendorff, in *The Primacy of Peter,* 25.

38. Afanasiev, in *The Primacy of Peter,* 81.

39. Florovsky, *Bible, Church, Tradition,* 45.

40. Of course, no one can dispute that historically, many of the councils were characterized by political maneuvering and by the attempts of some factions to control others, rather than by a united witness to the truth. In the Orthodox mind, this reality simply underscores the fact that no council is authoritative in advance. Regardless of how ordered or tumultuous, how united or fractured a given council was, that council's decision is not considered to be an expression of tradition until all the eucharistic communities of the Church have accepted it.

41. Ware, *The Orthodox Church,* 252–54.

CHAPTER 3—TRADITION AND ITS EXPRESSIONS

1. Aghiorgoussis, in *A Companion to the Greek Orthodox Church,* 150.

2. *The Festal Menaion,* trans. Mother Mary and Archimandrite Kallistos Ware (London: Faber & Faber, 1977), 16.

3. Ware, *The Orthodox Church,* 200.

4. Ibid. I should note that there is slight variation among Orthodox translations regarding which apocryphal books are included in the Old Testament. The Slavonic Bible includes the books I have listed, whereas Byzantine Greek editions omit 2 Esdras but include 4 Maccabees as an appendix.

5. The most famous of the monks who followed this pattern was Simeon the Stylite (ca. 390–459), a Syrian who spent most of his life alone atop a pillar, from which place he engaged in prayer and intercession, carried out correspondence related to the political and doctrinal controversies of his time, and received pilgrims and admirers. Although the popular image of Simeon (and of the rest of the anchoritic monks) is that they completely abandoned the world, in many cases this was not true at all. They remained engaged with the world from their places of personal withdrawal.

6. As I discuss the major aspects of Orthodox theology in part 2, I will make reference to the writings of many of the church fathers I have mentioned in this section. Readers who would like to consult these writings themselves may find English translations of them listed in appendix A: Recommended Reading.

7. Translations of the Creeds of Nicaea and Constantinople may be found in *Creeds of the Churches,* ed. John Leith, 3d ed. (Atlanta: John Knox, 1982), 30–31, 33.

8. See Leith, ed., *Creeds of the Churches,* 35–36.

9. Ibid., 46–50.

10. Ibid., 51–53.

11. The Orthodox generally regard this as a christological council, since icons are images of the incarnation, representations of the fact that God the Son has become visible as a man.

12. Leith, ed., *Creeds of the Churches,* 54–56.

13. Appendix A includes further information about where to locate English translations of documents related to the ecumenical councils.

14. These ten days are Christmas Eve, St. Basil's Day (January 1), the eve of Theophany (January 5), the first five Sundays in Lent, Holy (Maundy) Thursday, and Holy Saturday (the day before Easter).

15. Ware, *The Orthodox Church*, 280.

16. See, e.g., *The Divine Liturgy of St. John Chrysostom* (Brookline, Mass.: Holy Cross Orthodox Press, 1985), 4, 16.

17. At this point, an explanation of the Orthodox calendar may be helpful. Both Eastern and Western Churches used the Julian calendar until the time of Pope Gregory XIII in the sixteenth century. Gregory introduced a new calendar (the Gregorian) in order to correct the increasing differences between the Julian calendar and astronomical time. The Eastern Church rejected this new calendar. However, in 1923, a number of Orthodox groups voted to adopt the Gregorian calendar in the case of the fixed feasts, while still using the Julian calendar to calculate the date of Easter and the other holidays related to it. So the current situation finds some Orthodox autocephalous churches (Constantinople, Alexandria, Antioch, Greece, Cyprus, Romania, Poland, and Bulgaria) celebrating the feasts according to the Gregorian calendar and others (Jerusalem, Russia, Serbia) according to the Julian calendar. At present the Julian calendar is thirteen days behind the Gregorian. Throughout this book, I will first list the date on which each feast or fast is observed by those Orthodox groups that use the Gregorian calendar, and then the Gregorian date on which the holiday is celebrated by those who use the Julian calendar. This calendrical discrepancy is also the reason Easter usually falls on a different date in the West and East. Easter comes on the first Sunday after the full moon which follows the vernal equinox (March 21). However, March 21 according to the Julian calendar is April 3 by the Gregorian calendar, and in addition, Orthodox regulations stipulate that Easter must follow the Jewish celebration of Passover. So in any given year, Orthodox Easter can either come on the same day as Western Easter, or it can follow Western Easter by one, four, or five weeks, depending on the various combinations of the factors used to calculate the date.

18. The information in the preceding three paragraphs comes primarily from *The Festal Menaion*, 41–64.

19. Lewis Patsavos, "The Calendar of the Orthodox Church," in *A Companion to the Greek Orthodox Church*, 81.

20. Leonid Ouspensky, *Theology of the Icon*, vol. 1 (Crestwood, N.Y.: St. Vladimir's Seminary Press, 1978), 10.

21. Aghiorgoussis, in *A Companion to the Greek Orthodox Church*, 155.

22. Ouspensky and Lossky, *The Meaning of Icons*, 60.

23. *Tchin* is an old Slavonic word that translates the Greek word *taxis*. It refers to order or rank, and in particular, to the order of clergy in a liturgical procession. In this context, the word implies the proper order of the universe, as all creatures submit to and worship Christ.

24. Ouspensky and Lossky, *The Meaning of Icons*, 67–68.

CHAPTER 4—GOD AS DARKNESS; GOD AS THREE

1. Eastern Christendom is divided into Chalcedonian and non-Chalcedonian groups. The former (those who accepted the formula propounded by the Council of Chalcedon in 451) include all the Orthodox groups in Eastern Europe and the former Soviet Union except the Armenian Apostolic Church. The non-Chalcedonian groups (who rejected the Council of Chalcedon) are found primarily in the Middle East and North Africa. As we shall see, the difference between these groups is not one of actual faith; it is a disagreement about whether Chalcedon adequately expressed that faith through its formula "one person in two natures."

2. Andrew Louth, *The Origins of the Christian Mystical Tradition: From Plato to Denys* (Oxford: Clarendon, 1981), xv (emphasis his).

3. Lossky, *The Mystical Theology of the Eastern Church,* 28.

4. Zernov, *Eastern Christendom,* 236.

5. Hieromonk Auxentios, contributing to *Contemporary Eastern Orthodox Thought: The Traditionalist Voice,* 3.

6. In making this point about the roots of Orthodox apophaticism in the Sinai revelation, I am indebted to Alexander Golitzin, who kindly gave me a copy of a paper he read at Brown University in November 1993, entitled "Liturgy and Mysticism: The Experience of God." Part of this paper was subsequently published in *Pro Ecclesia* 8.1 (1999): 159–86, but unfortunately the portion of the paper on which I am relying here has been published only in a Romanian translation.

7. See Gregory of Nyssa, *Oration* 28.1–5, Pseudo-Dionysius, *Mystical Theology* 1, and Maximus the Confessor, *Chapters on Knowledge* 1.83.

8. Zizioulas, *Being as Communion,* 90 (emphasis his).

9. Vladimir Lossky, *Orthodox Theology: An Introduction* (Crestwood, N.Y.: St. Vladimir's Seminary Press, 1978), 24.

10. Zizioulas, *Being as Communion,* 92 (emphasis his).

11. Ware, *The Orthodox Way,* rev. ed. (Crestwood, N.Y.: St. Vladimir's Seminary Press, 1995), 15.

12. Schmemann, *For the Life of the World,* 32 (emphasis his).

13. See Gregory Palamas, *Triads,* especially 2.3.37, 3.2.7, and 3.3.10.

14. John Meyendorff, introduction to *Gregory Palamas: The Triads,* ed. John Meyendorff, trans. Nicholas Gendle, Classics of Western Spirituality (New York: Paulist, 1983), 14. Within this quotation, Meyendorff is himself quoting Lossky, *The Mystical Theology of the Eastern Church,* 43.

15. Aghiorgoussis, in *A Companion to the Greek Orthodox Church,* 157 (emphasis his).

16. Ware, *The Orthodox Way,* 22.

17. Lossky, *The Mystical Theology of the Eastern Church,* 80.

18. The most comprehensive statement of Cappadocian Trinitarian theology comes in Gregory of Nazianzus's *Orations on the Trinity.* See also Basil's *On the Holy Spirit* and Gregory of Nyssa's *That There Are Not Three Gods.*

19. See Augustine, *On the Trinity* 4.8, 9.1, for classic Western statements of Trinitarian doctrine.

20. Auxentios, in *Contemporary Eastern Orthodox Thought,* 5.

21. Lossky, *In the Image and Likeness of God,* 89.

22. Zizioulas, *Being as Communion,* 40–41.

23. The political controversy had two major elements. First, there was a struggle over whether the pope had the right to intervene in the appointment or deposition of a bishop of Constantinople. Second, there was a struggle for the ecclesiastical allegiance of the Bulgarian tribes, which had recently converted to Christianity. The issue of the *filioque* itself was not so much the source of the controversy as it was the ammunition with which Rome and Constantinople did battle.

24. This split is usually dated at 1054, although it would be more accurate to say that it was a gradual process extending from the rise of Charlemagne as Holy Roman Emperor in 800 to the sacking and burning of Constantinople by Latin crusaders in 1204. The other major issue in the dispute was the power and authority of the Roman pope.

25. Some Westerners argue that Jesus' statement in John 16:7, "If I go, I will send him [the

Counselor] to you," implies that the Holy Spirit proceeds from the Son as well as the Spirit. However, the Orthodox correctly respond that this assertion is referring to the post-Pentecost work of the Holy Spirit, not to the source of his being. In terms of his eternal existence, they argue, the Spirit proceeds from the Father alone, but both the Father and Son commission the Spirit for his temporal work in the world.

26. Lossky, *The Mystical Theology of the Eastern Church*, 8.

27. Ibid., 62–64.

28. For an excellent discussion of the issues at stake in the Eastern and Western understandings of the Trinity, see Ware's *The Orthodox Church*, 211–18.

29. See Ware, *The Orthodox Way*, 27.

30. John Meyendorff, *Christ in Eastern Christian Thought*, rev. ed. (Crestwood, N.Y.: St. Vladimir's Seminary Press, 1975), 213.

31. See Leith, ed., *Creeds of the Churches*, 35–36.

32. See Gregory of Nazianzus, *Epistle* 101.32.

33. It may be difficult for an English-speaking Christian to imagine how the words "nature" and "person" could be used in a similar sense. But for most of the third through fifth centuries, there was a great deal of confusion regarding the relations between the Greek words *ousia, physis, hypostasis,* and *prosopon.* The first of these clearly referred to the duality of Christ (he had both divine and human essences), and the fourth clearly referred to his unity (he appeared before people as a single entity). The question was whether *physis* and *hypostasis* should be used to refer to Christ's unity or his duality. At Chalcedon it was decided that *physis,* like *ousia,* should refer to the separate divine and human elements in Christ and that *hypostasis,* like *prosopon,* should refer to his unity of personal subject. But many theologians still used *physis* in the older sense of personal subject, thus creating confusion and making it almost impossible for the non-Chalcedonians and the Chalcedonians to see that they held the same faith.

34. Readers who are interested in the technicalities of this issue may consult *Greek Orthodox Theological Review* 10, no. 2 (1964–65). The entire number is devoted to christological discussion between Chalcedonian and non-Chalcedonian Orthodox theologians. Especially helpful is John Romanides' preface on 7–8. The discussions included in that number were preliminary talks that led eventually to a full healing of the split in the 1990s.

35. Georges Florovsky, *Collected Works,* vol. 8, *The Byzantine Fathers of the Fifth Century,* trans. Raymond Miller et al. (Vaduz, Germany: Büchervertriebsanstalt, 1987), 279 (emphasis his).

36. In my forthcoming book *Grace and Christology in the Early Church,* I argue that the belief that God the Son added humanity to his own person was the consensus of the entire Church, both Eastern and Western. If this contention is correct, then the typical modern Western way of describing the incarnation was a later development, perhaps not emerging until after the Enlightenment.

CHAPTER 5—HUMANITY: CREATION, VOCATION, AND FALL

1. See Irenaeus, *Against Heresies* 4.37–38.

2. See Pseudo-Dionysius, *The Celestial Hierarchy* 3.3.

3. Lossky, *The Mystical Theology of the Eastern Church,* 97.

4. Ibid., 99.

5. Panagiotes K. Chrestou, *Partakers of God* (Brookline, Mass.: Holy Cross Orthodox Press, 1984), 19–20.

6. Lossky, *The Mystical Theology of the Eastern Church,* 126.

7. Meyendorff correctly points out that this was not a patristic consensus. Many of the church fathers (most notably Athanasius and Cyril of Alexandria) saw "image" and "likeness" as synonyms. See *Christ in Eastern Christian Thought*, 114. Contrast Origen, *On First Principles* 3.6.1, with Athanasius, *On the Incarnation of the Word* 11.

8. Chrestou, *Partakers of God*, 20–21.

9. Ouspensky, *Theology of the Icon*, vol. 1, 185.

10. Ware, *The Orthodox Way*, 51 (emphasis his).

11. Aghiorgoussis, in *A Companion to the Greek Orthodox Church*, 160 (emphasis his).

12. Lossky, *Orthodox Theology*, 71–72.

13. Meyendorff, *Christ in Eastern Christian Thought*, 211.

14. Meyendorff, *Catholicity and the Church*, 73 (emphasis his).

15. Lossky, *The Mystical Theology of the Eastern Church*, 69–70.

16. Ibid., 87.

17. For my understanding of the link between the transfiguration and the revelation of divine glory on Mount Sinai, I am again indebted to the portion of Alexander Golitzin's paper "Liturgy and Mysticism" that has been published only in Romanian.

18. See Palamas, *Triads* 1.3.21, 3.1.15.

19. For an excellent discussion of the patristic treatment of the transfiguration, see John McGuckin, *The Transfiguration of Christ in Scripture and Tradition*, Studies in the Bible and Early Christianity 9 (Lewiston, N.Y.: Edwin Mellen Press, 1986).

20. Ouspensky, *Theology of the Icon*, vol. 1, 185.

21. Ware, *The Orthodox Way*, 59.

22. Archimandrite Christophoros Stavropoulos, *Partakers of Divine Nature*, trans. Stanley Harakas (Minneapolis: Light & Life Publishing, 1976), 18.

23. Florovsky, *Bible, Church, Tradition*, 115.

24. Florovsky, *Creation and Redemption*, 240.

25. Meyendorff, *Catholicity and the Church*, 21.

26. Zizioulas, *Being as Communion*, 49–50.

27. Auxentios, in *Contemporary Eastern Orthodox Thought*, 8.

28. Aghiorgoussis, in *A Companion to the Greek Orthodox Church*, 160–61. Cf. Maximus the Confessor, *Commentary on the Our Father* 5; *The Church's Mystagogy* 23–24.

29. Auxentios, in *Contemporary Eastern Orthodox Thought*, 8.

30. Lossky, *The Mystical Theology of the Eastern Church*, 133.

31. Aghiorgoussis, in *A Companion to the Greek Orthodox Church*, 161.

32. Zizioulas, *Being as Communion*, 101–2 (emphasis his).

33. Zernov, *Eastern Christendom*, 266.

34. Auxentios, in *Contemporary Eastern Orthodox Thought*, 9.

35. Schmemann, *For the Life of the World*, 18.

36. Ware, *The Orthodox Way*, 62.

37. Lossky, *The Mystical Theology of the Eastern Church*, 135.

38. Meyendorff, *Catholicity and the Church*, 72.

CHAPTER 6—SALVATION: THE PATH OF *THEOSIS*

1. Lossky, *The Mystical Theology of the Eastern Church*, 135–36 (emphasis his).

2. Some extreme forms of this view argue that the ransom was paid to the devil, and much of the opposition to the classic view of the atonement is directed against this idea. But more mature expressions of the classic view argue that one should not push the ransom image of Matthew 20:28 too far, and that it is inappropriate to ask the question, To whom is the ransom

paid? The point is that Christ forfeited his life for the sake of those whose lives were owed, those who were under the power of death. In the early Church, Origen and Gregory of Nyssa argued that the ransom was paid to the devil, and Gregory of Nazianzus and John of Damascus insisted that one should not speculate about the question, To whom was it paid? See Origen, *Commentary on Matthew* 16.8; Gregory of Nyssa, *Catechetical Oration* 26; Gregory of Nazianzus, *Oration* 45.22; and John of Damascus, *The Orthodox Faith* 3.27.

3.   *The Divine Liturgy of Saint John Chrysostom,* 170–71.

4.   *The Divine Liturgy of the Holy Orthodox Catholic Apostolic Graeco-Russian Church,* trans. P. Kuvochinksy (London: Cope & Fenwick, 1909), 32–33.

5.   Lossky, *Orthodox Theology,* 92.

6.   Ibid., 110.

7.   Ibid., 111.

8.   Ibid., 113–14.

9.   Lossky, *In the Image and Likeness of God,* 99–101. Contrast Anselm, *Why God Became Man* 2.19, with Athanasius, *On the Incarnation of the Word* 8–9.

10.   Florovsky, *Creation and Redemption,* 102–3.

11.   Ibid., 104.

12.   Bulgakov, *The Orthodox Church,* 126.

13.   Ware, *The Orthodox Way,* 82 (emphasis his).

14.   Ibid., 69–70.

15.   Ibid., 70–71.

16.   Meyendorff, *Catholicity and the Church,* 21.

17.   Florovsky, *Creation and Redemption,* 163.

18.   Lossky, *In the Image and Likeness of God,* 97.

19.   Lossky, *Orthodox Theology,* 75.

20.   A strong belief in God's impassibility may lead some people to balk at the statement that God descends to the ultimate limit of our fallen human condition. Orthodoxy insists that since the person of Christ was that of God the Son, it was God the Son who suffered and died. He died as a man, in his human nature, but nevertheless, the second person of the Trinity was the one to whom that death happened.

21.   Here one should remember that the arrangement of icons within an Orthodox church building is designed to convey the same idea: God descended to humanity through the prophets and the incarnation, and people ascend to God through deification.

22.   Athanasius, *On the Incarnation of the Word,* 54.

23.   Soteriology is the study of the doctrine of salvation. The Greek word *soteria* means "salvation."

24.   Aghiorgoussis, in *Salvation in Christ,* 56–57.

25.   Lossky, *In the Image and Likeness of God,* 109.

26.   Stavropoulos, *Partakers of Divine Nature,* 29.

27.   Schmemann, *Of Water and the Spirit,* 79 (emphasis his).

28.   Ibid., 80 (emphasis his).

29.   Ouspensky, *Theology of the Icon,* vol. 1, 215.

30.   Lossky, *The Mystical Theology of the Eastern Church,* 162–63.

31.   Ibid., 172.

32.   Florovsky, *Bible, Church, Tradition,* 37.

33.   Aghiorgoussis, in *Salvation in Christ,* 51.

34.   Stavropoulos, *Partakers of Divine Nature,* 32.

35.   Ibid., 37–38.

36. Meyendorff, *Catholicity and the Church*, 28.
37. Bulgakov, *The Orthodox Church*, 56.
38. Stavropoulos, *Partakers of Divine Nature*, 33 (emphasis his).
39. Lossky, *The Mystical Theology of the Eastern Church*, 180.
40. Ware, *The Orthodox Way*, 105–6. This threefold way of looking at Christian life comes from Origen, Evagrius (a late fourth-century Egyptian monk and staunch follower of Origen's teaching), and Maximus the Confessor. See Origen, *Against Celsus* 4.16, 6.68. See also Maximus, *Commentary on the Our Father* 5; *Chapters on Knowledge* 1.16, 1.53–55, 1.97, 2.9, 2.13.
41. Bulgakov, *The Orthodox Church*, 127.
42. Lossky, *Orthodox Theology*, 73 (emphasis his).
43. Georges Florovsky, *Collected Works*, vol. 10: *The Byzantine Ascetic and Spiritual Fathers*, trans. Raymond Miller et al. (Vaduz, Germany: Büchervertriebsanstalt, 1987), 31.
44. Paul O'Callaghan, *An Eastern Orthodox Response to Evangelical Claims* (Minneapolis: Light & Life Publishing, 1984), 24.
45. Zernov, *Eastern Christendom*, 235.
46. Bulgakov, *The Orthodox Church*, 208–9.
47. Aghiorgoussis, in *Salvation in Christ*, 48–49.
48. Florovsky, *The Byzantine Ascetic and Spiritual Fathers*, 30.
49. Schmemann, *Introduction to Liturgical Theology*, 84.
50. Ware, *The Orthodox Way*, 133.

CHAPTER 7—SALVATION AND THE COMMUNION OF SAINTS

1. Ugolnik, *The Illuminating Icon*, 115.
2. Bulgakov, *The Orthodox Church*, 143.
3. See Gregory of Nazianzus, *Oration* 18.37, and Basil, *Homilies*, 19, 23.
4. George Bebis, "The Saints of the Orthodox Church," in *A Companion to the Greek Orthodox Church*, 86. O'Callaghan makes the same point in *An Eastern Orthodox Response to Evangelical Claims*, 9–11.
5. Schmemann, *Introduction to Liturgical Theology*, 144.
6. Bebis, in *A Companion to the Greek Orthodox Church*, 85.
7. Zernov, *Eastern Christendom*, 233.
8. Bulgakov, *The Orthodox Church*, 141.
9. Florovsky, *Creation and Redemption*, 205.
10. Bulgakov, *The Orthodox Church*, 137.
11. Lossky, *In the Image and Likeness of God*, 199.
12. E.g. *The Divine Liturgy of Saint John Chrysostom*, 4, 16.
13. Ibid., 23.
14. Ibid., 33.
15. Florovsky, *Creation and Redemption*, 184.
16. Bulgakov, *The Orthodox Church*, 138. Ware explains further in *The Orthodox Way*, 77, when he argues that the Roman Catholic doctrine of the immaculate conception of Mary is not so much wrong as it is superfluous. Since the Orthodox do not accept the Augustinian understanding of original sin as guilt inherited through sexual conception, they have no need to argue that Mary was immaculately conceived.
17. Lossky, *The Mystical Theology of the Eastern Church*, 140–41.
18. *The Festal Menaion*, 51.
19. Ibid., 63–64.
20. Lossky, *In the Image and Likeness of God*, 208.

21. Ouspensky and Lossky, *The Meaning of Icons,* 76.

22. Ibid., 213.

23. Bulgakov, *The Orthodox Church,* 139.

24. Florovsky, *Creation and Redemption,* 173. One of the arguments put forth at the Council of Ephesus in 431 was that if Mary was not, strictly speaking, the bearer of God (as Nestorius claimed), then Christ was not, strictly speaking, God.

25. Schmemann, *The Historical Road of Eastern Orthodoxy,* 193.

26. Bulgakov, *The Orthodox Church,* 138 (emphasis his).

27. Peter Gillquist, who headed a group of American Protestants in a well-known conversion to Orthodoxy in the late 1970s, writes: "In an overreaction against Rome, Protestantism has seriously ignored Mary. The Orthodox Church, on the other hand, has carefully maintained the biblical injunction to call her blessed, while making the Holy Trinity the sole object of Christian worship" (Peter Gillquist, *Making America Orthodox* [Brookline, Mass.: Holy Cross Orthodox Press, 1984], 13).

28. In fact, Orthodox worship involves all of the senses: especially vision, hearing, and smell, but also taste and touch.

29. Ugolnik, *The Illuminating Icon,* 52.

30. Ouspensky and Lossky, *The Meaning of Icons,* 26.

31. Schmemann, *The Historical Road of Eastern Orthodoxy,* 98.

32. Ouspensky, *Theology of the Icon,* vol. 1, 150.

33. Ibid., 168.

34. Ibid., 51–52.

35. Ware, *The Orthodox Church,* 33.

36. Ugolnik, *The Illuminating Icon,* 45.

37. Florovsky, *Creation and Redemption,* 210.

38. Ouspensky, *Theology of the Icon,* vol. 1, 58.

39. Ouspensky and Lossky, *The Meaning of Icons,* 31–32.

40. Ibid., 34.

41. Nicolas Zernov, *The Russians and their Church* (New York: The MacMillan Company, 1945), 107.

42. Ouspensky and Lossky, *The Meaning of Icons,* 36 (emphasis theirs).

43. Ibid., 43–44.

44. Ouspensky, *Theology of the Icon,* vol. 1, 219.

45. Ibid., 228.

46. See Basil, *Epistle* 252. Both Bebis (in *A Companion to the Greek Orthodox Church,* 87–88) and Schmemann (in *Introduction to Liturgical Theology,* 144) make this historical point in defense of this idea.

47. The difference between an approach characterized by use and one characterized by delight was pointed out to me in a letter by John Jillions, director of the Institute for Orthodox Christian Studies in Cambridge, England.

CHAPTER 8—ORTHODOXY AND THE WEST: SEEING THROUGH EACH OTHER'S EYES

1. That God does want us to know him is clear from numerous biblical passages. Jeremiah announces the coming New Covenant by declaring, "'They shall all know me, from the least of them to the greatest,' says the LORD" (Jer. 31:34). Knowledge of God constitutes one of the major themes of John's Gospel, as shown, for instance, by his statement that the incarnate Word has made the Father known (John 1:18) and his inclusion of Jesus' declaration during

his high priestly prayer, "This is eternal life, that they may know you, the only true God, and Jesus Christ whom you have sent" (John 17:3). And Paul claims, "I regard everything as loss because of the surpassing value of knowing Christ Jesus my Lord" (Phil. 3:8).

2. The Orthodox find support for the idea of God's revealing himself to us in his energies in passages such as Romans 1:20, in which Paul asserts that God's invisible qualities, his power and deity, have been made known through the things that he has made. These invisible qualities, the Orthodox argue, are the energies of God.

3. Lossky, *The Mystical Theology of the Eastern Church*, 28.

4. In chapters 3 and 4 of my forthcoming book *Grace and Christology in the Early Church*, I offer a technical discussion of the way Cyril uses theological terminology to make this point clear.

5. Zizioulas, *Being as Communion*, 101–2 (emphasis his).

6. Florovsky, *The Byzantine Ascetic and Spiritual Fathers*, 30.

7. Ware, *The Orthodox Way*, 133.

8. Two of the Greek fathers most revered for their Trinitarian and christological thought, Athanasius and Cyril of Alexandria, both held to something more like a three-act scheme of salvation than modern Orthodoxy does. For the details, see chapters 1 and 3 of my forthcoming book *Grace and Christology in the Early Church*.

CHAPTER 9—POPULAR ORTHODOXY

1. Schmemann, *The Historical Road of Eastern Orthodoxy*, 300–301.

2. Georges Florovsky, *Collected Works*, vol. 4, *Aspects of Church History* (Belmont, Mass.: Nordland Publishing Company, 1975), 188–89.

3. Schmemann, *Introduction to Liturgical Theology*, 144. See Chrysostom, *Homily on St. Ignatius* 6.

4. Ouspensky and Lossky, *The Meaning of Icons*, 88.

5. George Fedotov, *The Russian Religious Mind*, vol. 2, *The Middle Ages, The Thirteenth to the Fifteenth Centuries* (Cambridge, Mass.: Harvard University Press, 1966), 355–56.

6. Ibid., 356–57.

7. Schmemann, *Introduction to Liturgical Theology*, 144.

8. Bulgakov, *The Orthodox Church*, 142.

9. George Fedotov, *The Russian Religious Mind*, vol. 1, *Kievan Christianity, The Tenth to the Thirteenth Centuries* (Cambridge, Mass.: Harvard University Press, 1946), 361.

10. Fedotov, *Kievan Christianity*, 362.

11. Alfeyev's comments came during the discussion following his lecture, "The Russian Orthodox Church's Interaction with the World Council of Churches," delivered on 3 March 1999.

12. Andrei Kouraev, *Vsyo li ravno kak verit'? Sbornik statei po sravnitelnomy bogosloviyu (Does It Really Matter How We Believe? A Handbook of Articles on Comparative Theology)* (Klin: Brotherhood of St. Tikhon Press, 1994), 169–70. The translations of Kouraev's work in this paragraph are my own.

13. Ibid.

14. Ibid., 172–73.

CHAPTER 10—ORTHODOXY AND NATIONALISM

1. While reviewing a previous draft of this book, Alexander Golitzin pointed out to me his conviction that Eastern nationalism is actually a reflection of the West, and my discussion in this chapter is on several points indebted to Golitzin's correspondence with me.

2. See appendix C for more information about the organization of Orthodoxy.

3. Schmemann, *Church, World, Mission,* 98.

4. Fedotov, *Kievan Christianity,* 405.

5. Meyendorff, *The Orthodox Church,* 90. We shall see later in this chapter that the fall of Constantinople was a pivotal event in the growth of specifically Russian nationalism.

6. Lossky, *In the Image and Likeness of God,* 184.

7. Meyendorff, *The Orthodox Church,* 90.

8. Schmemann, "The Idea of Primacy in Orthodox Ecclesiology," in *The Primacy of Peter,* 54.

9. Zernov, *Eastern Christendom,* 173–74.

10. Meyendorff, *Catholicity and the Church,* 139.

11. Ibid., 140.

12. O'Callaghan, *An Eastern Orthodox Response to Evangelical Claims,* 34.

13. Zernov, *Eastern Christendom,* 112.

14. Cited in Zernov, *Eastern Christendom,* 140.

15. I have occasionally heard Russians insist that a special kind of spiritual force field surrounds the world and that this field is most intense over Moscow. Such stories can be seen as an odd way of expressing the conviction that Moscow forms the hub and center of the Christian world.

CONCLUSION—SINGLE VISION?

1. Ugolnik, *The Illuminating Icon,* 52.

APPENDIX B—SUGGESTIONS FOR CHRISTIAN WORKERS IN THE EAST

1. See also Bradley Nassif, "New Dimensions in Eastern Orthodox Theology," in *New Dimensions in Evangelical Thought: Essays in Honor of Millard J. Erickson,* ed. David Dockery, 92–117 (Downers Grove, Ill.: InterVarsity Press, 1998). In this article, Nassif offers helpful suggestions for evangelicals who want to begin studying Eastern Orthodoxy.

2. The ideas behind my two suggestions in this section are developed more fully in my article, "Orthodox Supremacy in Russia: Is There a Place for Evangelicalism?" in *God in Russia: The Challenge of Freedom,* ed. Sharon Linzey and Ken Kaisch (Lanham, Md.: University Press of America, 1999), 288–314.

3. *The Festal Menaion,* 16.

APPENDIX C—THE STRUCTURE AND ORGANIZATION OF ORTHODOXY

1. Schmemann, *Church, World, Mission,* 91–92 (emphasis his).

2. Summarized from Ware, *The Orthodox Church,* 4–7.

3. Taken from Ware, *The Orthodox Church,* 1st ed., 299–300. (This section has been removed from the latest edition.)

Select Bibliography

Arpee, Leon. *A History of Armenian Christianity: From the Beginning to Our Own Time.* Princeton, N.J.: University Press, 1946.

Arseniev, Nicolas. *Mysticism and the Eastern Church.* Trans. Arthur Chambers. Oxford: Mowbray, 1979.

Bulgakov, Sergei. *The Orthodox Church.* London: Centenary, 1935.

Callian, Carnegie Samuel. *Icon and Pulpit: The Protestant-Orthodox Encounter.* Philadelphia: Westminster, 1968.

Chirovsky, Nicolas L., ed. *The Millennium of Ukrainian Christianity.* New York: Philosophical Library, 1988.

Chrestou, Panagiotes K. *Partakers of God.* Brookline, Mass.: Holy Cross Orthodox Press, 1984.

Chrysostomos, Archimandrite. *Contemporary Eastern Orthodox Thought: The Traditionalist Voice.* Belmont, Mass.: Büchervertriebsanstalt, 1982.

The Divine Liturgy of the Holy Orthodox Catholic Apostolic Graeco-Russian Church. Trans. P. Kuvochinsky. London: Cope & Fenwick, 1909.

The Divine Liturgy of Saint John Chrysostom. Brookline, Mass.: Holy Cross Orthodox Press, 1985.

Fairbairn, Donald. "Not Just 'How' but Also 'Who': What Evangelicals Can Learn from the Orthodox." *Evangel* 17, no. 1 (spring 1999): 10–13.

_____. "Orthodox Supremacy in Russia: Is There a Place for Evangelicalism?" In *God in Russia: The Challenge of Freedom.* Ed. Sharon Linzey and Ken Kaisch, 288–314. Lanham, Md.: University Press of America, 1999.

_____. "Eastern Orthodox Mystical Theology." In *Mysticism East & West: Christian Studies in Mysticism.* Paternoster, forthcoming.

_____. *Grace and Christology in the Early Church.* Oxford Early Christian Studies. Oxford: University Press, forthcoming.

Fedotov, George. *The Russian Religious Mind.* Vol. 1, *Kievan Christianity, The Tenth to the Thirteenth Centuries.* Cambridge, Mass.: Harvard University Press, 1946.

_____. *The Russian Religious Mind.* Vol. 2, *The Middle Ages, The Thirteenth to the Fifteenth Centuries.* Cambridge, Mass.: Harvard University Press, 1966.

The Festal Menaion. Trans. Mother Mary & Archimandrite Kallistos Ware. London: Faber & Faber, 1977.

Florovsky, Georges. *Collected Works.* Vol. 1, *Bible, Church, Tradition: An Eastern Orthodox View.* Belmont, Mass.: Nordland, 1972.

_____. *Collected Works*. Vol. 2, *Christianity and Culture*. Belmont, Mass.: Nordland, 1974.

_____. *Collected Works*. Vol. 3, *Creation and Redemption*. Belmont, Mass.: Nordland, 1976.

_____. *Collected Works*. Vol. 4, *Aspects of Church History*. Belmont, Mass.: Nordland, 1975.

_____. *Collected Works*. Vol. 5, *Ways of Russian Theology, Part 1*. Belmont, Mass.: Nordland, 1979.

_____. *Collected Works*. Vol. 6, *Ways of Russian Theology, Part 2*. Trans. Robert L. Nichols. Vaduz, Germany: Büchervertriebsanstalt, 1987.

_____. *Collected Works*. Vol. 7, *The Eastern Fathers of the Fourth Century*. Trans. Catherine Edmunds. Vaduz, Germany: Büchervertriebsanstalt, 1987.

_____. *Collected Works*. Vol. 8, *The Byzantine Fathers of the Fifth Century*. Trans. Raymond Miller et al. Vaduz, Germany: Büchervertriebsanstalt, 1987.

_____. *Collected Works*. Vol. 9, *The Byzantine Fathers of the Sixth to Eighth Centuries*. Trans. Raymond Miller et al. Vaduz, Germany: Büchervertriebsanstalt, 1987.

_____. *Collected Works*. Vol. 10, *The Byzantine Ascetic and Spiritual Fathers*. Trans. Raymond Miller et al. Vaduz, Germany: Büchervertriebsanstalt, 1987.

Gillquist, Peter E. *Making America Orthodox*. Brookline, Mass.: Holy Cross Orthodox Press, 1984.

The Lenten Triodion. Trans. Mother Mary & Archimandrite Kallistos Ware. London: Faber & Faber, 1984.

Litsas, Fotios K., ed. *A Companion to the Greek Orthodox Church*. New York: Greek Orthodox Diocese of North and South America, 1984.

Lossky, Vladimir. *The Vision of God*. Trans. Asheleigh Moorhouse. Leighton Buzzard, England: Faith Press, 1973.

_____. *In the Image and Likeness of God*. Ed. John H. Erickson. Crestwood, N.Y.: St. Vladimir's Seminary Press, 1974.

_____. *The Mystical Theology of the Eastern Church*. Crestwood, N.Y.: St. Vladimir's Seminary Press, 1976.

_____. *Orthodox Theology: An Introduction*. Trans. Ian and Ihita Kasarcodi-Watson. Crestwood, N.Y.: St. Vladimir's Seminary Press, 1978.

Louth, Andrew. *The Origins of the Christian Mystical Tradition: From Plato to Denys*. Oxford: Clarendon, 1981.

McGuckin, John Anthony. *The Transfiguration of Christ in Scripture and Tradition*. Studies in the Bible and Early Christianity 9. Lewiston, N.Y.: Edwin Mellen Press, 1986.

Meyendorff, John. *The Orthodox Church: Its Past and Its Role in the World Today*. Trans. John Chapin. New York: Pantheon, 1962.

_____. *Christ in Eastern Christian Thought*. Rev. ed. Crestwood, N.Y.: St. Vladimir's Seminary Press, 1975.

_____. *Byzantine Theology: Historical Trends and Doctrinal Themes*. Oxford: Mowbray, 1975.

_____. *Living Tradition: Orthodox Witness in the Contemporary World*. Crestwood, N.Y.: St. Vladimir's Seminary Press, 1978.

_____. *Catholicity and the Church*. Crestwood, N.Y.: St. Vladimir's Seminary Press, 1983.

_____. Introduction to *Gregory Palamas: The Triads*. Ed. John Meyendorff. Trans. Nicholas Gendle, 1–22. New York: Paulist, 1983.

Meyendorff, John, and Robert Tobias, eds. *Salvation in Christ: A Lutheran-Orthodox Dialogue*. Minneapolis: Augsburg Fortress, 1992.

Meyendorff, John et al. *The Primacy of Peter*. Leighton Buzzard, England: Faith Press, 1963.

Millennium of Christianity in Ukraine: A Symposium. St. Paul, Minn.: St. Paul University Press, 1987.

Nassif, Bradley. "Eastern Orthodoxy and Evangelicalism: The Status of an Emerging Global Dialogue." *Scottish Bulletin of Evangelical Theology* (spring 2000): 21–55.

O'Callaghan, Paul. *An Eastern Orthodox Response to Evangelical Claims*. Minneapolis: Light & Life Publishing, 1984.

Ouspensky, Leonid. *Theology of the Icon*. Vol. 1. Trans. Anthony Gythiel, with selections trans. by Elizabeth Meyendorff. Crestwood, N.Y.: St. Vladimir's Seminary Press, 1978.

————. *Theology of the Icon*. Vol. 2. Trans. Anthony Gythiel. Crestwood, N.Y.: St. Vladimir's Seminary Press, 1992.

Ouspensky, Leonid, and Vladimir Lossky. *The Meaning of Icons*. Rev. ed. Trans. G. E. H. Palmer and E. Kadloubovsky. Crestwood, N.Y.: St. Vladimir's Seminary Press, 1982.

Pelikan, Jaroslav. *The Christian Tradition: A History of the Development of Doctrine*. Vol. 2, *The Spirit of Eastern Christendom (600–1700)*. Chicago: University Press, 1974.

Sarafian, Krikor A. *The Armenian Apostolic Church: Her Ceremonies, Sacraments, Main Feasts, and Prominent Saints*. Fresno, Calif.: Sunday School Council of the Armenian Diocese of California, 1959.

Scanlin, Harold P. *The Old Testament Canon in the Orthodox Churches*. In *New Perspectives on Historical Theology: Essays in Memory of John Meyendorff*. Ed. Bradley Nassif, 300–312. Grand Rapids: Eerdmans, 1996.

Schmemann, Alexander. *The Historical Road of Eastern Orthodoxy*. Trans. Lydia W. Kesich. New York: Holt, Rinehart & Winston, 1963.

————. *Introduction to Liturgical Theology*. Trans. Asheleigh E. Moorhouse. Leighton Buzzard, England: The Faith Press, 1966.

————. *For the Life of the World: Sacraments and Orthodoxy*. Crestwood, N.Y.: St. Vladimir's Seminary Press, 1973.

————. *Of Water and the Spirit: A Liturgical Study of Baptism*. Crestwood, N.Y.: St. Vladimir's Seminary Press, 1974.

————. *Church, World, Mission: Reflections on Orthodoxy in the West*. Crestwood, N.Y.: St. Vladimir's Seminary Press, 1979.

————. *The Eucharist: Sacrament of the Kingdom*. Trans. Paul Kachur. Crestwood, N.Y.: St. Vladimir's Seminary Press, 1988.

Stavropoulos, Archimandrite Christophoros. *Partakers of Divine Nature*. Trans. Stanley Harakas. Minneapolis: Light & Life Publishing, 1976.

Torrance, Thomas. *Theology in Reconciliation: Essays towards Evangelical and Catholic Unity in East and West*. London: Geoffrey Chapman, 1975.

Ugolnik, Anthony. *The Illuminating Icon*. Grand Rapids: Eerdmans, 1989.

Ware, Kallistos. *The Orthodox Way*. Rev. ed. Crestwood, N.Y.: St. Vladimir's Seminary Press, 1995.

————. *The Orthodox Church*. Rev. ed. Hammondsworth, Middlesex, England: Penguin, 1997.

Zernov, Nicolas. *Moscow: The Third Rome*. New York: MacMillan, 1937.

————. *The Russians and Their Church*. New York: MacMillan, 1945.

————. *Eastern Christendom: A Study of the Origin and Development of the Eastern Orthodox Church*. London: Weidenfeld and Nicolson, 1961.

————. *The Russian Religious Renaissance of the Twentieth Century*. London: Darton, Longman & Todd, 1963.

Zizioulas, John D. *Being as Communion: Studies in Personhood and the Church*. Crestwood, N.Y.: St. Vladimir's Seminary Press, 1985.

Author Index

Subject Index